Katherine Bomer

Ela Area Public Library District
275 Mohawk Trail, Lake Zurich, IL 60047
(847) 438-3433
www.eapl.org

3124100874 158

AUG – – 2016

THE JOURNEY
IS EVERYTHING

*Teaching Essays That Students Want to Write
for People Who Want to Read Them*

HEINEMANN
Portsmouth, NH

Heinemann

361 Hanover Street

Portsmouth, NH 03801-3912

www.heinemann.com

Offices and agents throughout the world

© 2016 by Katherine Bomer

All rights reserved. No part of this book may be reproduced in any form or by any electronic or mechanical means, including information storage and retrieval systems, without permission in writing from the publisher, except by a reviewer, who may quote brief passages in a review.

"Dedicated to Teachers" is a trademark of Greenwood Publishing Group, Inc.

The author and publisher wish to thank those who have generously given permission to reprint borrowed material:

"Joyas Voladoras" by Brian Doyle, *American Scholar*, Autumn 2004. Copyright © Brian Doyle. Reprinted with permission from the author.

Acknowledgments for borrowed material continue on p. xiv.

Library of Congress Cataloging-in-Publication Data
Names: Bomer, Katherine, author.
Title: The journey is everything : teaching essays that students want to
    write for people who want to read them / Katherine Bomer.
Description: Portsmouth, NH : Heinemann, [2016] | Includes bibliographical
    references.
Identifiers: LCCN 2016008884 | ISBN 9780325061580
Subjects: LCSH: English language—Composition and exercises—Study and
    teaching. | Essay—Authorship.
Classification: LCC LB1576 .B515 2016 | DDC 808/.042071—dc23

LC record available at http://lccn.loc.gov/2016008884

Editor: Katie Wood Ray
Production: Vicki Kasabian
Cover and interior designs: Suzanne Heiser
Cover photograph: © Travellinglight/Getty Images
Typesetter: Kim Arney
Manufacturing: Steve Bernier

Printed in the United States of America on acid-free paper
20 19 18 17 16 PAH 1 2 3 4 5

To my mother-in-law, Joyce,
for all the lives she has lifted on her journey

CONTENTS

ACKNOWLEDGMENTS

When I was young, the song "Something Good" from *The Sound of Music* (the Julie Andrews version) touched my heart and made me weepy every time I sang and played it on the piano. The words still fit: I must have done something good to deserve the loving support I received while writing this book. To the circle of friends and colleagues who held me aloft on the long journey to finish this book, thank you.

My deepest gratitude goes to Randy Bomer, my life partner and also my wisest colleague. The brilliant thinking about essay he brought to his nonfiction study group at the Teachers College Reading and Writing Project two decades ago as well as the subsequent definitions of the genre in his own books absolutely anchor my book. Surely my book harbors sentences that fell trippingly from Randy's tongue on our daily walks, as he talked me through the knots of my work, but if so, he has generously invited me to steal them. He was my rock as I journeyed through crises of confidence, and he gave me the best advice for finishing: "Scowl it down." I thank him also for reminding me what matters, spiriting me away from my deadline to celebrate our anniversary on the pristine Caribbean beach where we married twenty years ago. Randy knows that when I sing "Something Good," I am singing it to him.

In his recent book *Minds Made for Stories*, Tom Newkirk honors three men who greatly influenced his thinking. Now I must acknowledge Tom's influence on my thinking. My daily writing routine involved at least one glad hour spent rereading his books. I am grateful for his estimable work in the world and for his kind assurance that I had enough and knew enough to write my own book about essay.

I thank Brian Doyle and Dagoberto Gilb for permission to print their gorgeous essays. Possibly, they could hear me scream when I read the emails that let me know they said yes. I am indebted to the authors of the essays gathered in

the back of this book, beautiful writers and friends, who accepted my invitation to think and see the world through a young person's eyes in an essay. These pieces are gifts to students, who will find inspiration in their words and shapes.

Thanks to the Heart of Texas Writing Project, directed by Randy Bomer, for sponsoring my essay study group with scary-smart Austin-area teachers. Ilza Garcia, Melissah Hertz, Deb Kelt, Stacia Long, Darla Ruggiero, Gusty Simpson, Suzie Smartt, Tracy Spruce, Katherine Watkins, Dorothy Meiburg Weller, and Patty Young met several times after school to grow ideas about essay, culminating on a Saturday morning, when they shared their classroom work in essay with an appreciative audience of 125 teachers on a Heart of Texas Writing Project conference day. *Muchisimas gracias* to Ilza Garcia, for inviting me to learn in her fourth-grade bilingual classroom as her students wrote essays. Special appreciation to my friend and HTWP codirector Deb Kelt, for her endless empathy and encouragement, for helping with tedious details, and for the sweet memory of weeping as we read bits of shattering writing out loud to each other from my stacks of essays.

Thank you to institutions and school districts that invited me to explore essay with teachers and students at various points in the past two decades, especially Lucy Calkins and the Teachers College Reading and Writing Project; Dr. Annette Seago and the Blue Springs, Missouri, Independent School District; and Tom Marshall and the Paramus, New Jersey, Summer Writing Institute. Teachers in my summer institute sections in Blue Springs and Paramus responded to a draft of the Introduction and helped me puzzle through assessment ideas for Chapter 9. But it was the honest, moving essays they wrote during those two weeks that gave me energy to finally finish this book. The biggest thank-you to my stellar friend Corrine Arens, instructional coach in Blue Springs, who showered me with inspiration and love to persevere.

To my generous friend and colleague Ellin Keene, who frequently checked in about how the writing was going. Ellin invited me, Debbie Miller, and Cris Tovani to the back patio of her gorgeous home one spring Saturday to talk about our work and offered me a chance to talk about this book in its skeletal stage. I thank all three for their perfect questions and suggestions.

Carl Anderson has been thinking with me about essay for two decades. He read an early version of Chapter 2 on a flight to Hong Kong, when he should have been sleeping, and he wrote a long, appreciative response. When writing got tough, I would reread that letter and think, "If Carl loves this chapter, perhaps I am on the right track."

For saying they couldn't wait to have this book in their hands, or for offering advice and cheerleading, I thank Kylene Beers, Deborah Cromer, Colleen Cruz, Mary Ehrenworth, Matt Glover, Gaby Layden, Kate Montgomery, Donna Santman, Amy Ludwig VanDerwater, Vicki Vinton, my bright and beautiful sister Pat Woods and niece Brianna Santillanes, and my best lifelong friends, Larry Deemer, Kris Kliemann, Tracie Storie, and Lynn Tveskov.

To Heinemann, for believing a book that pushes against the status quo is worth publishing for teachers, my sincere gratitude. Also to longtime friend, colleague, and now incredible editor Katie Wood Ray, whose compliments of my writing made me blush, and who remained patient throughout my bumpy process. Katie read drafts more closely than I could myself, always keeping teacher readers in mind with her suggestions to tighten and organize, making this a much better book. To Lauren Audet, Sarah Fournier, Suzanne Heiser (for her gorgeous cover and book design), Vicki Kasabian (for help above and beyond the book), and the production and marketing teams for ushering my work into the world. And to Margaret LaRaia, for filling my inbox with the coolest essays from her immense reading life, but mostly thank you for listening to my first words about essay and asking me to write those down.

I am grateful for Robert Atwan, series editor of The Best American Essays, for his commitment to collecting luminous writing since 1986. His vision of essay and curating of writers and guest editors provided the lifeblood for this book. When I read each year's collection, I am convinced there is something good in the world, in the voices I hold in my hands.

And finally, thank you to all teachers who are helping students' voices join that chorus.

Essay Lights Up the World

*I write entirely to find out what I'm thinking, what I'm looking at,
what I see and what it means. What I want and what I fear.*

—Joan Didion, "Why I Write"

*We should start without any fixed idea where we are going to spend the
night, or when we propose to come back; the journey is everything.*

—Virginia Woolf, "Montaigne"

n the electric, pulsating world around us, the essay lives a life of abandon, posing
questions, speaking truths, fulfilling a need humans have to know what other humans think and wonder so we can feel less alone. Essay lights up the Internet daily,
allowing us to reach across the globe to touch the minds and hearts of our fellow
human beings in ways unheard of before cyber technology. Essay explores topics
about everything in the galaxy, the living and the inanimate. This very moment, as I
attempt to live peaceably with my new rescue puppy and teach him manners for his
safety and our household's sanity, I reach out to Patricia McConnell's (2009) funny,
touching, and thought-provoking essays about canines, to follow her journeys of
thinking, and to know that even on the topic of how to build relationships with
dogs, there are gray areas and places of uncertainty.

Essay also finds a home in print and digital magazines and journals pertaining
to literature, history, music, art, pop culture, nature, medicine, psychology, sociology,
and science. Essay fuels photography and film, stand-up comedy, televised current
events, and political punditry. And essay appears on the cups and brown paper bags
at Chipotle Mexican Grill, inviting us to pause while ingesting the fresh, organic
ingredients in their burritos (I don't work for or own stock in Chipotle; I'm just a
fan of the food and the company's policies!), like the one I just read by Sheri Fink,

where she asks, "Whom would you chose? When, in the event of an unimaginable catastrophe, we had to ration medical care, whom should we save first?" (2014).

This profoundly deep question and Fink's lovely answer to it then cause us to drive home or walk back to our offices to search for more essays like this one at the website called Cultivating Thought Author Series (http://cultivatingthought .com), curated by novelist Jonathan Safran Foer. This website recently ran a contest for high school students to write essays, and the winning pieces were to be printed on cups and bags and included online, right along with work by Neil Gaiman, Toni Morrison, Amy Tan, and other famous writers. Wow. We can look to our burrito restaurants to cultivate thought these days. As Christy Wampole (2013) argued in a much-shared essay on the *New York Times Opinionator* blog, lately, it seems, we face the "essayification of everything"!

These are essays in the wild, unbounded by rules and regulations, and we know that creatures are happier and more fiercely beautiful in the wilderness than confined in a zoo, like Rilke's poor panther, who loses his vision of the world, grown weary from constantly passing by the "thousand bars" of his cage. Rather than conforming to the cage bars of any formula or template, these essays are driven by curiosity, passion, and the intricacies of thought.

In schools, however, the essay suffers. I am aware of the arguments for the efficacy of teaching what is called academic and argument writing. I've been hearing them for decades, ever since I first invited teachers to help their students write what Randy Bomer calls "journey of thought" essays (1995, 178). Over the years, I've led workshops and weeklong writing institutes where I've plied participants with some of the most moving, humorous, thoughtful pieces of literature ever published. We read essays, and we giggle, we weep, we find ourselves needing to talk about their content. We write our own short essays and laugh and cry all over again. And then people move back out into the world, eager to say *yes!* to essay writing with their students, only to send an email later, telling me their school administrations or their department chairs or their state testing formats won't allow them to stray from the five-paragraph formula.

In this era of high-stakes accountability, academic writing, which is indeed a rich and viable mode of writing, absolutely worth teaching students to do well, gets funneled down into the five-paragraph formula because it is easy to check for its requisite parts and assign a score. Tom Newkirk calls this "mechanized literacy," when to satisfy the human or computer scorers, "writing has to be bent out of recognition to be tested" (2009, 4). Peter Elbow argues that the five-paragraph formula is an "anti-perplexity machine" because there is no room for the untidiness of inquiry or complexity and therefore no energy in the writing (2012, 309).

The preponderance of formulaic writing, traditionally reserved for high school students, now finds its way down to kindergarten, where I've seen tiny children dutifully filling in worksheets with sentence starters such as "My favorite ice cream flavor is _____. One reason I love ice cream is that _____." Practicing this algorithm over and over, from kindergarten on, so the logic goes, will ensure that students' writing can achieve high scores on state tests, which require little more than a sterile standardization of human thought and composition. The rationale sounds at times like some geometrical shape that bends back on itself forever and ever, always ending up at the same point, at what Alfie Kohn calls (hysterically) "BGUTI," or "better get used to it," because kids need it for the next grade, for high school, for college, for career (2015, 42).

English professor Bruce Ballenger burned up the Internet in a lively blog entry titled "Let's End Thesis Tyranny" in *The Chronicle of Higher Education* (2013), where he calls the thesis a "thug and a bully" that stops his first-year college students' thinking dead in its tracks. He suggests that perhaps asking deep questions and writing to discover what they think might be a better way for his students to arrive at an essay. Dozens of responses to Ballenger's blog entry argued defensively for the need to maintain proper thesis-driven essays because, in essence, (1) no one wants (or has the time) to read what students wonder and think, (2) young people need to know this for their other academic work in middle school, high school, and college, and (3) this is the way we've always done it; it's how we all learned to write when we were in school.

To me, the arguments fail to convince that teaching kids, sometimes as early as kindergarten, to produce a one-sentence, conclusive thesis statement in answer to a question they aren't even asking and then to invent sufficient proof of that statement before they've had the opportunity to think and to question, to change their minds, to discover and surprise themselves, will ever help them learn to write well or find their own unique way of looking at the world or turning a phrase. When writing is taught as a formula, students fail to discover that their writing can truly *engage* readers. And they have little chance to fall in love with writing, to feel how fun it can be, and to see how writing can help them solve problems and figure things out. Teaching writing to a formula loses more writers than it wins.

But that's just my opinion.

And also my thesis statement (!), which I will support throughout this book (it will take more than five paragraphs). Along the way I will suggest helpful ways to teach students how to read and write essays, and, as a bonus, I've included a lovely set of essays composed by some phenomenal, well-known writers with young people in mind.

 ## Why Essay, Why Now?

Whole generations of adults fear writing because they grew up in schools thinking writing means sentence diagrams, penmanship, spelling, and proper placement of that darn thesis statement. Our students deserve better than this. They need essays to help them think in reflective, open-minded ways, to stir their emotions, teach them about life, and move them to want to change the world. And now more than ever, with the hyperattention paid to preparing students for college and careers, young people need practice in finding subjects of interest and passion to write about. They need lessons that show them how to think deeply about these topics and how to write about them in compelling ways.

My dream in this book is to *occupy essay*! I want to reboot the original name of it—*essais*: little attempts, experiments, trials—and bring essay writing back to its exploratory roots. I want to take the noun, *essay*, and convert it to the verb, *essaying*, as Paul Heilker suggests (1996, 180), to describe the trying out we do when we write. When I sit beside students in writing workshops and ask, "What are you working on in your writing?" I hope to hear something like one of my former fifth graders once said: "Well, I'm *essaying* how it's weird that all us kids are friends and work together in this class, but at lunch, we sit in little groups with our own . . . um . . . colors . . . races? . . . and stuff. And does that mean those are our real friends and not the ones in the class? And why do we do that?"

In this book, I'll ask you to occupy beautiful and brilliant essays, what Robert Atwan calls "the sparkling stuff" featured in his annual Best American Essays series, to create possible models for how to teach essay in ways that will let students discover what they think and want to say. Beginning in Chapter 1, you'll read closely two spectacular examples by Brian Doyle and Dagoberto Gilb just to see and hear and be moved, and to say, "Ah, this. This is it!" Chapter 2 defines explicitly what essay is and is not; then in Chapter 3, I use excerpts from published essays to name specific craft features you can show students. I also suggest how to help students read mentor texts to develop their own definitions of essay.

The chapters in Part 2 of the book will show you how to teach students to develop ideas into essays. We'll explore the writer's notebook as a place to generate, store, and experiment with material (Chapter 4) and then as a place to collect thinking and thickly texture the material to elaborate an essay idea (Chapter 5). Chapter 6 offers strategies for the move from notebooks to first drafts, and then Chapter 7 shows how to help students revise drafts and find a shape and structure without formulas.

As you consider how to teach your students to write essays, I invite you to write along with them because being a writer of your own essay will anchor your understandings and your knowledge of the content and process of writing. You can then teach from "what writers really do," a phrase I borrow from Dorothy Barnhouse and Vicki Vinton, authors of *What Readers Really Do* (2012), who argue so eloquently for teachers to look to our own reading experiences to know how to teach reading. Our authentic experiences "need to serve as our rudder as we navigate through curricula and standards, data and assessments" (46).

In Part 3 of the book, I show how practicing essay writing can indeed lead to powerful and well-written academic writing (Chapter 8), and I explore assessment that honors the essay's open-ended and organic essence (Chapter 9). Finally, in the Afterword, I cap off my argument and sound a clarion call for making time to write essay in schools.

Credit lines continued from p. ii:

"Pride" by Dagoberto Gilb from *Gritos: Essays*. Copyright © 2003 by Dagoberto Gilb. Published by Grove/Atlantic, Inc. Reprinted with permission from the author. "Pride" was first published in the exhibit catalog *It Ain't Braggin' If It's True* for the Bullock Texas State History Museum (2001).

Amy Ludwig VanDerwater's essay "Drop-Off Cats" copyright © 2016 by Amy Ludwig VanDerwater. Reprinted with permission from the author.

Vicki Vinton's essay "The Thing About Cats" copyright © 2016 by Vicki Vinton. Reprinted with permission from the author.

1

How to Read
an Essay Closely

*For me, reading the essays . . . was as satisfying
and invigorating as glimpsing a school of dolphins
rippling in and out of the water: a privilege.*

—Ariel Levy, *The Best American Essays 2015*

The key to teaching essay well is understanding deeply what essay is. We don't need to invent a definition; we only need to pay attention to what we see, hear, and feel as we read essays closely. We can notice for ourselves what essays stir up in the minds and hearts of readers and then make that seeing explicit, naming the features of essay we can use in our own writing or teach to students.

In this chapter, I invite you to go on a journey with me as we read two extraordinary essays and I demonstrate how reading closely leads to powerful curriculum. I will attempt to replicate what I do with adults and young people when we read and talk about essays together. I wish we could be in the same room, curled up on couches, with cups of coffee or tea, reading and having a grand conversation, but for now, we'll just have to pretend. As we journey, no doubt you will have your own responses and notice different features, so please write these in the margins of this book or in your writer's notebook. What we notice and name together will fill us with teaching ideas for the genre of essay, and the process we'll follow for reading like writers is something you can do with students in your classroom.

We'll begin with an essay by the very gifted Brian Doyle, one of my favorite essayists because he writes like a poet in prose. His compassionate voice, his gracious way of looking at the simplest, most human, frequently ignored or judged of subjects, and his lifting up of the lowliest in life take my breath away. Reading his work feels like a blessing. Though the essays are often about profound feelings like grief, loss, forgiveness, and redemption, they escape sentimentality and he bathes each topic in beauty. And as often as he makes me feel deeply, Doyle can also make me laugh out loud!

"Joyas Voladoras" (pronounced hoy-ahs voh-la-dor-rahs) is perhaps my favorite Brian Doyle essay. Doyle takes readers on a quietly staggering intellectual and emotional journey in the space of three typed pages. I have read it possibly fifty times, usually out loud, and my throat tightens and chokes out the words in the last paragraph—though I know good and well what is coming—every single time. I've read this essay with many groups of teachers, and I've read it to students as young as ten who are fascinated by the cool details about the hearts of hummingbirds and whales. I can't imagine a better place to start understanding the full potential of essay than with "Joyas Voladoras."

 ## Exploring the Craft of Essay

For maximum effect, I invite you to read this essay out loud first. Then, after you've dried your eyes and composed yourself, read it a second time with my comments next to it. Think of these comments as something like a good "Extra Features" section of a DVD, where you gain valuable insights about how the movie was made. When we train our eyes to see and think about how an essay is made, we uncover what will become powerful curriculum behind the genre. My comments are meant to show this kind of thinking in action.

Joyas Voladoras
by Brian Doyle

Consider the hummingbird for a long moment. A hummingbird's heart beats ten times a second. A hummingbird's heart is the size of a pencil eraser. A hummingbird's heart is a lot of the hummingbird. Joyas voladoras, *flying jewels*, the first white explorers in the Americas called them, and the white men had never seen such creatures, for hummingbirds came into the world only in the Americas, nowhere else in the universe, more than three hundred species of them whirring and zooming and nectaring in hummer time zones nine times removed from ours, their hearts hammering faster than we could clearly hear if we pressed our elephantine ears to their infinitesimal chests.

Each one visits a thousand flowers a day. They can dive at sixty miles an hour. They can fly backwards. They can fly more than five hundred miles without pausing to rest. But when they rest they come close to death: on frigid nights, or when they are starving, they retreat into torpor, their metabolic rate slowing to a fifteenth of their normal sleep rate, their hearts sludging nearly to a halt, barely beating, and if they are not soon warmed, if they do not soon find that which is sweet, their hearts grow cold, and they cease to be. Consider for a moment those hummingbirds who did not open their eyes again today, this very day, in the Americas: bearded helmetcrests and booted racket-tails, violet-tailed sylphs and violet-capped woodnymphs, crimson topazes and purple-crowned fairies, red-tailed comets and amethyst woodstars, rainbow-bearded thornbills and glittering-bellied emeralds, velvet-purple coronets and golden-bellied star-frontlets, fiery-tailed awlbills and Andean hillstars, spatuletails and pufflegs, each the most amazing thing you have never seen, each thunderous wild heart the size of an infant's fingernail, each mad heart silent, a brilliant music stilled.

Hummingbirds, like all flying birds but more so, have incredible enormous immense ferocious metabolisms. To drive those metabolisms they have racecar hearts that eat oxygen at an eye-popping rate. Their hearts are built of thinner, leaner fibers than ours. Their arteries are stiffer and more taut.

HOW TO READ AN ESSAY CLOSELY

They have more mitochondria in their heart muscles—anything to gulp more oxygen. Their hearts are stripped to the skin for the war against gravity and inertia, the mad search for food, the insane idea of flight. The price of their ambition is a life closer to death; they suffer more heart attacks and aneurysms and ruptures than any other living creature. It's expensive to fly. You burn out. You fry the machine. You melt the engine. Every creature on earth has approximately two billion heartbeats to spend in a lifetime. You can spend them slowly, like a tortoise, and live to be two hundred years old, or you can spend them fast, like a hummingbird, and live to be two years old.

The biggest heart in the world is inside the blue whale. It weighs more than seven tons. It's as big as a room. It is a room, with four chambers. A child could walk around it, head high, bending only to step through the valves. The valves are as big as the swinging doors in a saloon. This house of a heart drives a creature a hundred feet long. When this creature is born it is twenty feet long and weighs four tons. It is waaaaay bigger than your car. It drinks a hundred gallons of milk from its mama every day and gains two hundred pounds a day, and when it is seven or eight years old it endures an unimaginable puberty and then it essentially disappears from human ken, for next to nothing is known of the mating habits, travel patterns, diet, social life, language, social structure, diseases, spirituality, wars, stories, despairs, and arts of the blue whale. There are perhaps ten thousand blue whales in the world, living in every ocean on earth, and of the largest animal who ever lived we know nearly nothing. But we know this: the animals with the largest hearts in the world generally travel in pairs, and their penetrating moaning cries, their piercing yearning tongue, can be heard underwater for miles and miles.

Mammals and birds have hearts with four chambers. Reptiles and turtles have hearts with three chambers. Fish have hearts with two chambers. Insects and mollusks have hearts with one chamber. Worms have hearts with one chamber, although they may have as many as eleven single-chambered hearts. Unicellular bacteria have no hearts at all; but even they have fluid eternally in motion, washing from one side of the cell to the other, swirling and whirling. No living being is without interior liquid motion. We all churn inside.

So much held in a heart in a lifetime. So much held in a heart in a
day, an hour, a moment. We are utterly open with no one, in the end—not
mother and father, not wife or husband, not lover, not child, not friend. We
open windows to each but we live alone in the house of the heart. Perhaps
we must. Perhaps we could not bear to be so naked, for fear of a constantly
harrowed heart. When young we think there will come one person who will
savor and sustain us always; when we are older we know this is the dream
of a child, that all hearts finally are bruised and scarred, scored and torn,
repaired by time and will, patched by force of character, yet fragile and rickety
forevermore, no matter how ferocious the defense and how many bricks you
bring to the wall. You can brick up your heart as stout and tight and hard
and cold and impregnable as you possibly can and down it comes in an
instant, felled by a woman's second glance, a child's apple breath, the shatter
of glass in the road, the words I have something to tell you, a cat with a
broken spine dragging itself into the forest to die, the brush of your mother's
papery ancient hand in the thicket of your hair, the memory of your father's
voice early in the morning echoing from the kitchen where he is making
pancakes for his children.

Entering the World of This Essay

"Consider the hummingbird" lures me in instantly, not just because I love hummingbirds, but because it is such a polite and elegant invitation to enter the text.
The word *consider* reminds me of a favorite poem by Christopher Smart: "For I shall
consider my cat Jeoffry." *Consider* asks me to be curious about the hummingbird—
not to form judgments or find answers, but just to sweetly ponder for the "long
moment" that it takes to read this essay.

Next, Doyle gives me some amazing facts about the hummingbird's heart.
The first time I read that it "beats ten times a second," I had to tap my finger on the
table while I watched the second hand pass on my clock. I couldn't manage ten taps
per second until the third or fourth try. That's a rapidly beating heart. It's also a tiny
heart—the size of a pencil eraser, such an adorable, surprising comparison. I can't
help but wonder, "How long did it take Doyle to find that image? Did he have a

less precise comparison in his writer's notebook or his first draft?" And then comes a sentence written with beautiful simplicity, as if a child were explaining something technical on his own terms. Without a single reference to sophisticated measurement, I can see a heart that is "a lot" of the bird's body. The language is conversational and friendly and doesn't put me off.

So far, I am impressed, delighted, and comfortable with the three short statements of fact that each begin with the repeated phrase "A hummingbird's heart." Repetition creates rhythm. Rhythm is what the heart has, so the form matches content here.

Next comes a truly long sentence, pummeled with phrases and clauses, almost mimicking the relentless (until it is dying) racing of the hummingbird heart. This sentence does so much work. First, it connects back to the title, which had been mysterious until now, with a translation from the Spanish of a name that paints an image of these birds' extraordinary beauty—little flying rubies and sapphires and emeralds. Can you imagine seeing them, dozens and dozens of them, for the first time ever, deep in some Central or South American jungle? And they weren't merely flying around. In Doyle's description, they were doing fabulous actions: whirring and zooming and, wait . . . is *nectaring* a verb? Yes, it is, just one I've not heard before.

In another precise word choice, Doyle uses the muscular verb *hammering* to describe the action of the heart instead of the more common *beating*. Besides painting a clearer picture, the verb also creates a rhythm and pleases my ear because the number of syllables matches *hummingbird*, and because of the alliteration winding through these sentences: *hundred, heart, hammering, hummingbird*.

As far as I know, there is no such thing as "hummer time zones," but this wordplay works to nail the point that these teensy creatures have hearts that beat so rapidly, time itself is measured differently—"nine times removed from ours"—and the sound between the beats all but disappears. And how many drafts did Doyle go through before finding the surprising adjectives *infinitesimal* and *elephantine* to compare the size of the hummingbird's chest with the size of human ears? I can't imagine my ear "pressed" against its chest—surely I would crush it.

One paragraph into this text and I am utterly seduced by Doyle's voice. I want to go to the Internet and purchase everything he's ever written.

Reading Forward and Making Meaning

I could certainly linger at this level of detail with every word in this essay, but now I'm going to widen my lens just a bit. Let's look at the second paragraph, where my heart practically breaks thinking about the "sludging" hummingbird hearts when they are near death from freezing or starving. Like *nectaring*, this perfect noun-made-into-verb is enough to make me buy twenty of those red plastic feeders and boil vats of sugar water all day to keep their beating hearts alive.

When Doyle repeats his opening invitation, "Consider for a moment" the dying hummingbirds, it's almost as if he is cupping his fingers under my chin to make me turn my face to see what he's seeing. And then begins his paragraph-long list of specific kinds of hummingbirds with names so lovely and lyrical, they sound like poetry: "amethyst woodstars" and "glittering-bellied star frontlets." Doyle folds in facts like a waterfall, a cascade of amazement.

These strings of facts could sound like a science textbook, but lest I nod off as he demonstrates his vast species knowledge, Doyle pulls out another stunning image, comparing the size of "each thunderous wild heart" to an infant's fingernail. The first time I read that, I gasped. The image is visceral, specific, and it squeezes my heart. I'm starting to build a theory here that Doyle wants to squeeze my heart; he wants me to care about these little beings, to see their lives as connected to mine and to all living creatures, so he purposely compares their hearts to images that are precious to most humans.

Now that I care, Doyle can throw out some science facts in that third paragraph and I am open to reading them. In Doyle's hands, again, facts become poetry. First, he strings together four adjectives that all mean "big" to describe hummingbird metabolism, then he names those rapidly beating hearts "racecar hearts" (many kids' favorite part of the essay). And the series of three short clichés about machines using too much energy to the breaking point is nothing short of masterful.

Speaking of breaking, I am shocked to learn that hummers have heart attacks and aneurysms, and I'm increasingly suspicious that Doyle is writing about more than hummingbirds. This intriguing fact has me naturally thinking about humans now, people I've loved who have suffered heart attacks. Doyle has connected facts about hummingbirds to something I know and care about, and that human connection provides an emotional anchor in the midst of all the facts. And if I weren't already thinking of humans when he mentioned heart disease, he next connects all creatures on earth through one striking fact we have in common. He makes me think about how we all spend our own two billion heartbeats.

A quick word about repetition here: I count twenty-eight times the word *heart* is used. Sometimes it appears in one sentence after another, in quick succession. In school, most of were told not to repeat a word, to find a different word that means the same thing. Doyle probably got the same lesson in school, but I trust that he knows what he is doing here. There isn't another good word for *heart*, and the repetition of *heart* feels like the beating of a heart. The essay is ultimately about hearts, and not hummingbirds, as the title might lead you to believe. (Of course, those lovely Spanish words in the title, "flying jewels"—perhaps they are a metaphor for the heart as well?)

In the fourth paragraph, Doyle pulls out one of my favorite essay moves when he swings next door (to what would, in the five-paragraph formula, be considered off-topic) to the subject of blue whales and their hearts. A few more facts skillfully rendered in poetic imagery, like filigree, but why are we talking about blue whales now? So artful, isn't it, to park the largest creature on the planet right next to one of the tiniest, by comparing the size of their hearts? Then he reels me in closer still; he makes me care about these enormous, mysterious creatures that travel two by two, communicating with their moaning and piercing cries, and though we do not know for certain what whale cries mean, from our human sensibilities we might interpret them to be the emotional cries of their hearts.

I now suspect that this essay is not merely about the hummingbird, but about the physical and emotional properties of *all* hearts, and my suspicions are confirmed in the fifth paragraph when I get a rundown of the number of chambers in various creatures' hearts. Doyle has not written the word *human* yet, but suddenly, in the last two sentences of this paragraph, he scoops every living thing on earth into the first-person-plural *we*. I become one with all the world's creatures—even bacteria—because I am also a "living being" with liquid sloshing around in my cells. And then, "We all churn inside." Four little words, the final sentence of the paragraph. Many people I've shared this essay with have declared that if I had asked them to find Doyle's thesis statement, they would have underlined this tiny sentence, buried late in the essay. Oh yes, and somehow I know he is talking not just about blood or cell fluid, but about the emotional upheaval of hearts, and the astonishing ability to feel hope and fear, joy and sorrow.

Closing the Essay with Thinking That Lingers

In his sixth and final paragraph, Doyle opens all the stops to include the hearts of human beings—not the physical structure, which most of us know almost "by heart"—but the poignant truth of what it means to be alive and sentient. Every time I read this paragraph, especially if I am reading it out loud, my voice catches and my eyes burn and fill. For one thing, I am continually amazed by the lyricism of this paragraph: repetition, metaphor (especially "a child's apple breath"), vivid imagery (the cat with the broken spine), alliteration ("savor and sustain" and "scarred and scored"), the list that gathers to a crescendo, and the rhythmic power of opposing pairs ("mother and father," "wife or husband").

Finally, Doyle leaves the essay with one truly long sentence containing precise and exquisitely emotional scenarios, each capable of melting the heart of even the most stoic reader. The last image, of the father making pancakes for his children, made me sob the first time I read this essay. I have written about my own father making my breakfast on Saturday mornings as a picture book for children, as a short memoir for young people, and in a longer adult-version memoir. Writing about it has made me realize that the reason these mornings stand out so vibrantly (when I remember little about my childhood) is that for an hour or two, my father and I were able to be alone together before my mother woke and took all the energy and attention in the room. My father and I did not talk much on

At a Glance: Essay Features from "Joyas Voladoras"

- Uses poetic language.
- Mixes very long sentences with very short ones.
- Layers in different examples to elaborate a larger point.
- Includes scientific facts.
- Uses lists.
- Opens with an invitation.
- Closes by crushing our hearts.
- Surprises with language—nouns become verbs.
- Creates structure through six paragraphs of varying lengths.

those mornings because he was a silent, unexpressive man, but for a few moments I could be alone with my Daddy, and that was enough to help me feel special. So when I first read Doyle's essay and I reached that last line, after all the beauty and poetry that preceded it, I fell apart.

Doyle does not tell me how to feel about this moment, about the voice of the father "echoing from the kitchen," as he leaves all these tiny scenes open for readers to find their own responses. Whether he writes about buoyant babies or about sorrow and loss, Doyle writes about them with honesty and keen intelligence. He refuses to write sentimentally or cloyingly about emotions. What he tells us in that last paragraph is both true and rather hard to bear; that no matter what we do, whom we love and care for, we must at last live alone in our hearts, in some kind of deeply lonely chamber, and that no matter how much we try to defend ourselves against hurt, some tiny moment, like a child's sweet breath, reaches in to twist our hearts. The moment is ephemeral, so fast and furious, like a hummingbird's heartbeat.

 ## Six Steps to Reading an Essay Deeply, Closely, and Powerfully

Reading any essay closely—as I read Doyle's essay—involves a predictable set of steps that you'll use as you search for mentor texts and as you study those texts with your students. Let's look at an overview of those steps first, and then I'll invite you to try them out with a new essay.

Step 1: Read Out Loud

An essay changes when you read it out loud, so I always recommend reading it this way first—to yourself, with a group of colleagues, or to your students.

Step 2: Respond as a Reader

Next, respond (verbally or in your notebook) as a *reader*. What does this essay make you think about? What does it remind you of? What from your life makes you respond the way you do to these words?

Step 3: Reread

Read the essay again, this time silently, using a pen, a pencil, or colored highlighters to mark up the text. Circle favorite images, words, phrases, and sentences. In the margins, make notes about the craft you can name (see my examples from Doyle's essay).

Step 4: Read with a Lens

After a second pass, marking whatever you notice and wonder about the text, you may wish to quickly reread with some specific lenses to narrow your gaze. I suggest viewing through the following lenses to reveal the heart and soul of any essay:

- Voice: How would you describe the voice in the essay?
- Structure: How does the writer shape the essay? What are the different parts?
- Craft: How does the writer flesh out the thinking in the essay—anecdotes, dialogue, images, time?

Step 5: Talk

With a partner or small group, talk about the particular craft moves you noticed in the essay and theorize about why the author used them. You're not looking for right answers. You are reading like a writer, noticing the workmanship of words and structures that essayists use, much like brushstrokes or types of clay or textures of fabric. You are naming features of essay another writer might imitate.

Step 6: Record

Record the craft features you find in your writer's notebooks and on chart paper so that you and your students can revisit them—like a road map—when it is time to compose your own essays.

Before you try the steps of reading an essay closely with your students, I recommend you try them first with a partner or a group of friends or colleagues so you are comfortable with the process. The conversation you have will deepen and become multilayered with more perspectives included. Prepare to learn things from others' responses. Prepare to have your thinking changed. I once shared "Joyas Voladoras" with a teacher who did not like it at first because the form was so different from what she thinks of as essay. But as she tried to explain why, and as she heard the responses of her colleagues, she completely changed her mind, and now she adores the essay.

 ## Exploring the Craft of Essay: Your Turn

I am touched and honored to be able to include the lovely, powerful essay "Pride," by Dagoberto Gilb. I have read "Pride" to middle and high school students, and especially in places like San Antonio and Austin, Texas, someone always gasps or calls out, "My father calls me *mi'jo!*" because he can't believe I am saying something in Spanish, right out loud in his classroom, something that feels familiar and makes the listener think about his own family and experiences. For this reason and more, this essay is quite important to me. While Gilb squeezes my heart in similar ways, his craft in this piece feels more narrative, more edgy and divergent than Doyle's. But I don't want to take the pleasure of discovery away from you, so go ahead: try your own deep, close, and powerful reading of "Pride."

PRIDE
by Dagoberto Gilb

It's almost time to close at the northwest corner of Altura and Copia in El Paso. That means it is so dark that it is as restful as the deepest unre-membering sleep, dark as the empty space around this spinning planet, as a black star. Headlights that beam a little cross-eyed from a fatso American car are feeling around the asphalt road up the hill toward the Good Time Store, its yellow plastic smiley face bright like a sugary suck candy. The loose muffler holds only half the misfires, and, dry springs squeaking, the auto-mobile curves slowly into the establishment's lot, swerving to avoid the new self-serve gas pump island. Behind it, across the street, a Texas flag—out too late this and all the nights—pops and slaps in a summer wind that finally is cool.

A good man, gray on the edges, an assistant manager in a brown starched and ironed uniform, is washing the glass windows of the store, lit up by as many watts as Venus, with a roll of paper towels and the blue liquid from a spray bottle. Good night, m'ijo! he tells a young boy coming out after playing the video game, a Grande Guzzler the size of a wastebasket balanced in one hand, an open bag of Flaming Hot Cheetos, its red dye already smearing his mouth and the hand not carrying the weight of the soda, his white T-shirt, its short sleeves reaching halfway down his wrists, the whole XXL of it billowing and puffing in the outdoor gust.

A plump young woman steps out of that car. She's wearing a party dress, wide scoops out of the top, front, and back, its hemline way above the knees.

Did you get a water pump? the assistant manager asks her. Are you going to make it to Horizon City? He's still washing the glass of the storefront, his hand sweeping in small hard circles.

The young woman is patient and calm like a loving mother. I don't know yet, she tells him as she stops close to him, thinking. I guess I should make a call, she says, and her thick-soled shoes, the latest fashion, slap against her heels to one of the pay phones at the front of the store.

Pride is working a job like it's as important as art or war, is the happiness of a new high score on a video arcade game, of a pretty new black dress and shoes. Pride is the deaf and blind confidence of the good people who are too poor but don't notice.

A son is a long time sitting on the front porch where he played all those years with the squirmy dog who still licks his face, both puppies then, even before he played on the winning teams of Little League baseball and City League basketball. They sprint down the sidewalk and across streets, side by side, until they stop to rest on the park grass, where a red ant, or a spider, bites the son's calf. It swells, but he no longer thinks to complain to his mom about it—he's too old now—when he comes home. He gets ready, putting on the

HOW TO READ AN ESSAY CLOSELY

shirt and pants his mom would have ironed but he wanted to iron himself. He takes the ride with his best friend since first grade. The hundreds of moms and dads, abuelos y abuelitas, the tios and primos, baby brothers and older married sisters, all are at the Special Events Center for the son's high school graduation. His dad is a man bigger than most, and when he walks in his dress eel-skin boots down the cement stairs to get as close to the hardwood basketball-court floor and ceremony to see—m'ijo!—he feels an embarrassing sob bursting from his eyes and mouth. He holds it back, and with his hands, hides the tears that do escape, wipes them with his fingers, because the chavalitos in his aisle are playing and laughing and they are so small and he is so big next to them. And when his son walks to the stage to get his high school diploma and his dad wants to scream his name, he hears how many others, from the floor in caps and gowns and from around the arena, are already screaming it—could be any name, it could be any son's or daughter's: Alex! Vanessa! Carlos! Veronica! Ricky! Tony! Estella! Isa!—and sees his boy waving back to all of them.

Pride hears gritty dirt blowing against an agave whose stiff fertile stalk, so tall, will not bend—the love of land, rugged like the people who live on it. Pride sees the sunlight on the Franklin Mountains in the first light of morning and listens to a neighbor's gallo—the love of culture and history. Pride smells a sweet, musky drizzle of rain and eats huevos con chile in corn tortillas heated on a cast-iron pan—the love of heritage.

Pride is the fearless reaction to disrespect and disregard. It is knowing the future will prove that wrong.

Seeing the beauty: look out there from a height of the mountain and on the north and south side of the Rio Grande, to the far away and close, the so many miles more of fuzz on the wide horizon, knowing how many years the people have passed and have stayed, the ancestors, the ones who have medaled, limped back on crutches or died or were heroes from wars in the Pacific or Europe or Korea or Vietnam or the Persian Gulf, the ones who have raised the fist and dared to defy, the ones who wash the clothes and cook and serve the meals, who stitch the factory shoes and the factory slacks, who assemble and sort, the ones who laugh and the ones who weep, the ones who care, the ones who want more, the ones who try, the ones who love, those ones with shameless courage and hardened wisdom, and the old ones still so alive, holding their grandchildren, and the young ones in their glowing prime, strong and gorgeous, holding each other, the ones who will be born from them. The desert land is rock-dry and ungreen. It is brown. Brown like the skin is brown. Beautiful brown.

Make a List of Essay Features from "Pride"

- _____
- _____
- _____
- _____
- _____

HOW TO READ AN ESSAY CLOSELY

2

RECLAIMING ESSAY

*I do not sit down at my desk to put into verse
something that is already clear in my mind.
If it were clear in my mind, I should have no
incentive or need to write about it, for I am an
explorer. . . . We do not write in order to be
understood, we write in order to understand.*

—C. Day-Lewis, *The Poetic Image*

the engine of the essay—doubt and the unknown

—Charles D'Ambrosio, *Loitering*

Now that you have had the chance to read and think about two fine
examples of contemporary essay, you can see that the kind of writing I am after in this book looks and sounds remarkably different
from the formulas we are used to seeing in school settings. I hope
you found powerful, passionate ideas and craft features inside the pieces by Doyle
and Gilb, and I hope you trust that we can help our students write just as brilliantly
when we open our minds to the possibilities for this intriguing and lovely form.

In this chapter, I explore the wide world of essay, and I argue for why I think
it is an important genre to teach. My thesis statement is ridiculously simple, though
it will likely take this entire book to argue it convincingly: I wish we would not call
things essays that are not essays. Literary analyses, summaries, critiques, reviews, editorials, research papers, this book—which is both argument and how-to—and most
especially test writing are all fine forms of writing, but they are not essay. Any kind

of paper that *requires* a thesis statement and supporting paragraphs is not an essay, as far as the stance of this book is concerned.

Oh, I can hear voices arguing already! Smart, expert voices that might be quick to jump on such an outrageous, possibly unwarranted claim as the one in the previous paragraph, and they may be correct to do so. But I ask you to bear with me as I spin out my thinking, and as I offer, across this book, alternative definitions of essay, demonstrate with excerpts from dozens of published essays, provide some entertaining exercises to help young people compose the non-thesis-driven essay, and justify why I think an essay unit of study is valuable. I'm not suggesting we banish those other types of writing from school or from the world, for those are viable, purposeful forms. I only wish we would call them more precisely by their names—literary criticism, reports, feature articles, arguments, advice columns—and not essays. And I believe that studying essays has a place in our writing curricula because essay teaches kids many important lessons about writing and reading. Perhaps my thesis statement would be better stated this way: essay, the kind I consider in this book, is a comprehensive and fully engaging form for teaching young people how to write well, period.

 ## Taking Back the Word *Essay*

The word *essay* often follows an adjective. Joseph Epstein, Carl H. Klaus, Philip Lopate, Dinty W. Moore, and others call it the "personal essay." Across the centuries, the word *essay* has been modified with the words *moral, philosophical, political, familiar, occasional, narrative, satirical,* and—my favorite—*true.* Robert Atwan, in one of his twenty-eight introductions to his annual Best American Essays series, called it the "lyric essay." If I had my way, there would be only one word: *essay.* It would not need a qualifier in front of it, and it would describe *only* the kind of writing I am arguing for in this book: prose pieces that are personal, lyrical, literary, descriptive, reflective, narrative, expository, philosophical, political, spiritual . . . all of the above.

Essays do not act in the world as informational texts (though there can be a truckload of fascinating facts in them, as we saw in Doyle's "Joyas Voladoras"). They do not intend to teach or to preach (though we often learn things and decide to be-come better people from essays, as I did when I read Gilb's "Pride") or to be classed as argument (though I think some element of argument exists in the DNA of every kind of writing). Essays do contain a powerful point of view, and you would not accuse the writer of being obtuse or wishy-washy about her stance on the subject; however, the tone, language, and structure might be humble, halting, open-ended.

An essay does not offer to help us install window shades; it does not claim to know the three major causes of the Civil War, and it does not try to win a debate for or against the death penalty. Instead, an essay gives its author the space, time, and freedom to think about and make sense of things, take a journey of discovery, and speak her mind, without boundaries besides those imposed by the writer herself (and perhaps by the rules of polite society, but not always). And most importantly, an essayist can absolutely use what Lynn Z. Bloom calls "the vertical pronoun," the "I" (2008, 88).

Many essays qualify as literature, Atwan says, and they "emerge from the same creative urgency as do short stories and poems" (2007, viii). To me, an essay is most like a poem in tone. Like poems, essays might focus on something minuscule and, with luminous language, render it enormous; or they might find something con-sidered ordinary and demonstrate how extraordinary it is. Essays stun me the way poems do, inviting me to consider an aspect of the world that I did not know about or to look with fresh eyes at something I thought I already knew.

The modern essay has changed outfits over the years, fluctuating with trends and fashions in the reading and publishing arenas. Essays might find themselves tucked in under a larger genre umbrella called "creative nonfiction" or "literary nonfiction," which includes feature articles, memoir, and so-called new journalism. There were also years, depending on what appeared in journals and magazines, and depending on the tastes of that year's guest editor, that the Best American Essays series might have been more aptly titled Best American Minimemoirs because so many of the samples were driven by personal narrative. Don't get me wrong—I am keen on memoir; I wrote a book about how to write it! But if I were ever invited to edit an essay anthology, my selection would include expository pieces that explain and have ideas as the central propelling force. Memory and bits of narrative would absolutely be woven in, so powerful for texture and illustration, but the craft of story would not overwhelm the overarching point of the essay, for as Virginia Woolf says, "the art of writing has for backbone some fierce attachment to an idea" (1984a, 221).

I agree with Woolf and, to a degree, with Cristina Nehring (2003, 2007), who has written scathing attacks on the contemporary essay for containing too much "littleness" and for being about mundane topics (fishing, childhood memories, and pieces about suffering major illnesses seem particularly to offend her), incapable of stirring ire, fear, or interest in readers, and that's why collections of essays languish in basements or on nightstands, unread and, finally, thrown out (2007). Instead, Nehring wishes essayists would abandon "this cult of personal detail, this hermetic attention to the self," to be more like the work of Montaigne, the essay's creator, who stated that he was writing about himself but also "undertaking a study, the subject of which is man" (in Nehring 2003, 80). Essays, Nehring argues, should use their author's personal experience "as a wedge to pry open the door to general insight" (81). Essays should have as their subject a concern for everyone and everything in the world. They should offer "Big Ideas with Vast Application" (81).

Charles D'Ambrosio offers one of the most exquisite descriptions of essay I have come across. He reminisces about precisely where (what the sky looked like!) and when he read his first essay—M. F. K. Fisher's celebratory works about food—and fell in love with this kind of writing. D'Ambrosio writes that Fisher's prose, "taught me how to pay attention, and it was the essay, as a form, that was the container, the thing that caught and held the words like holy water, offering the gift of awareness, the simple courtesy of acknowledgement, even to a life as ordinary as mine" (2014a, 14).

That is it, I think. The essay pays attention, and its words, "like holy water," awaken readers to worlds both ordinary and extraordinary, where we can find ourselves and also learn about lives and worlds far different from our own.

 ## The Active Stance of Essay

Essay explores. The constantly curious essayist circles around questions, emotions, objects, memories, events, and ideas, using the tentative language of thinking, of trying on an idea: *maybe*; *perhaps*; *on the other hand*; *I wonder*; *it seems to me*; and, shockingly, *I don't know*. And though essays have lovely, aesthetically satisfying endings, they may not resolve in final, concluding paragraphs. Instead, they might open to new ideas and new inquiries.

Essay questions. Let me quote D'Ambrosio (2014a) again here because his language is ambrosial (like his name). He says that he discovered in his early reading that the personal essay "left its questions on the page, there for everyone to see; it was a forum for self-doubt, for an attempt whose outcome wasn't assured" (15). This quality of self-doubt, of a "flawed man revealing his flaws, the outspoken woman simply *saying*" (14), led D'Ambrosio to lean in his own writing toward a stance of longing and not knowing, the polar opposite of most writing, speaking, and punditing in the world today, in what he calls the "insane clarity of public discourse" (17).

Essay travels. The experience of reading essay can feel like we are on a long car ride, sometimes a bumpy one, of the author's thinking. We are offered an idea or set of ideas to pursue, perhaps with some narrative pieces to make it human and meaningful, or some facts or quotes to substantiate it, and we find ourselves accepting this request to go along for the ride with this fun, fascinating travel companion. Sometimes, we disagree with what the writer is saying, and we argue in the margins of the text with our pen (or talk out loud to the computer screen). Other times we exclaim, and give virtual high fives, thrilled to find a like-minded thinker. We are privy to an essayist's divergent thoughts and unanswered questions because often the writer narrates, right there on the page, that she just now thought of something or is changing her mind. Annie Dillard, writing about Loren Eisely's iconic and exceedingly beautiful essay "The Star Thrower," notes that it reads as if Eisely has "lived through . . . [his life experiences and scientific knowledge] . . . *in the space of the essay*," and arrived at "an altered and compassionate vision" (1988, xv).

Essay lingers. The writer caresses an idea, turns it over and over, sometimes for many pages, examining all its nooks and crannies, uncovering hidden, even taboo, truths.

Essay reveals. When I read courageous authors, willing to say what no one else will, I walk around with their ideas and images haunting me, sometimes for weeks, or years. The most frequent response I hear from teachers and students after reading the beautiful essays I bring as mentor texts matches what Desiree Madrid, a fourth-grade teacher in San Antonio, Texas, said, with a sigh, as she finished Doyle's "Joyas Voladoras": "I never thought of it like that before." Exactly. Desiree's statement could almost be the title of an essay collection, as a matter of fact. We read great essays, and we see the world in a brand-new way.

Essay exposes the mind of the writer, her thoughts, feelings, experiences, and passions. It's almost as if the point of the essay is to watch an author actively thinking. As Christy Wampole (2013) asserts, "The essayist is interested in thinking about himself thinking about things." The trick to elevating essay from diary jottings about this and that, or the private ramblings of a mad and inquisitive mind, is harnessing the very qualities of great writing that would apply to any type of public text, carefully composed with readers in mind.

Essay arouses. When I shared an early draft of the table of contents for this book with my friend Ellin Keene, she said, with a perfectly grave face, "I love essays because they're short. Novels are too long, too heavy to carry!" I was not sure how to respond to that pronouncement from this brilliant person who changed the way the world teaches reading. "I'm kidding!" she laughed. "Really, essays fill a strong need for me as a reader to be surprised. And pissed off. I do really like to be pissed off."

No one who knows Ellin Keene would think of her as a person who likes to pick fights. What she wants, as do most powerful readers, is to have her mind activated, to get an intellectual fix, and she can find that sustenance inside a good essay about a controversial topic, with a strong, no-holds-barred stance and voice.

As readers of essay, we sign up to "saturate ourselves" in the author's mind, as Philip Lopate (1994, 45) says about the experience of reading Montaigne's essays. We care deeply what the essayist thinks, and we don't care where we go or how we get there. We say, "Hey, if bits of narrative and dialogue help express the idea, use them. If metaphor paints the best picture, then compare this to that, as you desire. If numbers and facts provide the most mind-bending examples, then google away. If humor and jokes best reveal the writer's heart and mind, then go for it—make us laugh. If a heart-wrenching story best demonstrates the point, then oh yes, make us sob." And if you want to make Ellin Keene happy, take a surprising angle on a topic, or make her angry with your revelations about injustices in the world!

An essay has room for everything.

Perhaps, then, a definition of essay begins to take shape: a nonfiction prose piece, whose author unveils a central idea(s) about the world and its occupants and

Five Foundational Features of Essay

1. A distinctive, first-person voice. Essayists develop a voice so particular it is like a fingerprint: lyrical, political, curmudgeonly, riotously funny.
2. Honesty. The way to create a distinctive first-person voice is simply to tell the truth.
3. Centrality of idea(s). The essay traffics in ideas, in asking questions, explaining and thinking about things, and in a desire for readers to become equally enthralled with these ideas.
4. Multiple voices. Essayists reach for and reflect on things they read, hear, and see.
5. Organic, yet logical, structure. Essay structures develop along a line of thinking that belongs to each particular text.

invites—with bold, sometimes lyrical exposition and an interesting kaleidoscope of facts, observations, memories, anecdotes, and quotes from others—readers to watch him or her think about that idea for a few pages, without needing to win an argument or necessarily reach a conclusion.

Or, if I were forced to tweet a 140-character definition of essay that I want to promote in this book, I might try this:

> Essays explore, explain, express. But *que sais-je?* What do *I* know? Read
> *mountains* of them (Montaignian in-joke) & let's talk! #seemynewbook

 ## The Essay as Writing to Think

It occurs to me now that the feature I most want to restore to composing essays in school settings is writing to think. Let me demonstrate what I mean by the phrase *writing to think*, the sound of that on the page, with a short, essay-ish entry from my writer's notebook:

> What does a "day" mean? How has a day that counts as valid, that feels good at the end of it, come to be defined by work hours and specifically how much work is accomplished inside those hours, rather than the usual definition of hours of

daylight or the 24-hour standard imposed on the world by clocks and commerce and Greenwich mean time?

Why do I feel that a day is wasted if I do not tick major accomplishments off my to-do list? No, it's worse than that; I feel panicked. My heart races. I am irritable and impossible to appease. At the end of a day, if I have not fulfilled my purely imagined requirement to move mountains and rearrange the planets, all before dinner, I feel heartsick and worthless.

Instead, what if a "day" meant pulling some weeds, reading a few chapters of a great memoir, feeding hummingbirds and finding out what type they are in my book about Southwestern hummers, walking into the dusty hills as the setting sun turns them purple, listening to some Patti Griffin while Randy cooks another delicious dinner, giggling with my beloved mother-in-law as we sip our glasses of wine. Why can't that count as a day, and a rich one at that, full of blessings?

What will it take to make me wake up to the radiant world I actually inhabit and not one I concoct in the worst, most harried parts of my brain?

So that is one example of writing to think. Now, what makes me say this bit of meandering soul-searching sounds essay-ish? Here's a list of some ways my notebook entry already leans toward essay:

- The structure is primarily expository. Though it is personal and relates events from memory, it is not a narrative of my day. There is no story to tell, no action or denouement, no "first this happened, then that."

- There are no announced transitions, such as "Another reason is" or "In conclusion," no discrete beginning, middle, and end, no topic sentences, no arranging of strongest to weakest points of argument.

- The entry begins and ends in questions but never answers those questions.

- The entry takes on a philosophical subject about a state of being. It is not informative or argumentative, and it does not report in a journalistic manner. It is not a procedural, how-to piece, and at least in this early, notebook-entry stage, it requires no research other than experience, observation, and memories.

- I change my mind, or uncover a deeper truth, right there in the act of writing: "No, it's worse than that."

- Essentially, this is writing to discover, and perhaps writing to think my way to a better self, and nothing more or less than that.

If I decided I wanted to revise and elaborate on this entry for an essay draft, I could try any number of essay moves. For example, I might

- find out the history of the twenty-four-hour day;

- relate other people's experiences with time wasted and time fulfilled;

- read to find out if the push to get things done has become more pronounced in U.S. culture, as I suspect it indeed *has*;

- layer in some memories of what time felt like when I was a little girl—how it seemed to last forever, when I was doing essentially nothing at all—which might lead me to quote from a book about this topic called *Why Life Speeds Up as You Get Older: How Memory Shapes Our Past*, by Douwe Draaisma (2004);

- explore more through the perspective of my mother-in-law, whose experience of time has changed forever (and changed my husband's and my idea of time, as well) after suffering a massive stroke and losing completely her ability to speak, read, write, and use her right arm or leg;

- write (in true essay fashion) into places and ideas I can't even imagine right now because that's the nature of writing to think: I must write a great deal more about this idea to discover what I don't yet realize I know, think, or wonder about this idea.

When we think with ink on the page or with fingers on keys rather than with ideas bouncing around inside our heads, we are able to look back at that thinking and argue with, question, add onto, and layer it, and finally, share that thinking with readers around the world and across time. Surprisingly, against prevailing logic, this freedom to think without forcing ideas into templates can actually produce better writing from students. It helps young people write flexibly, fluently, and with emboldened voices, qualities they can translate into any assigned writing task in school or in life. Surely there are types of expository writing, like formal arguments, history papers, and science reports that follow more scripted paths, but excelling at those forms grows out of students' fluency with and confidence in knowing how to generate ideas, question, and reflect.

Besides the practical benefits of students learning to compose powerful writing for school and career requirements, I am also arguing for the inherent gifts of this exploratory type of writing to help students find their writing voices for life. Instead of struggling to conform their thoughts into strict, rule-bound structures before they have a chance to write to find out what they think or want to say, young people can learn to put pen to paper or fingers to keyboard and follow trails of thinking to surprising places, to stretch an idea out across pages of unbroken prose, to discover hidden irritations, unexpected ironies and spots of humor, or bottomless joys and sorrows.

The Value of Writing to Think and Discover

1. Writing to think and discover is how writers work toward more formal or academic projects.
2. Writing to think and discover can feel electric and generative because, as Donald Murray says, you find out what you didn't know you knew (in Newkirk and Miller 2009, 162).
3. The act of writing requires different kinds of thinking: "classification, synthesis, analysis, transformation, and organization, to name just a few" (Graves and Stuart 1985, 113). The more time our students spend on writing, the stronger they will become as *thinkers* in all academic disciplines.
4. Many young people write to express, think, and discover outside of school. If we let them do this in our classrooms, perhaps they will be more excited to write in school.
5. Essay writing is a time-honored genre, with contemporary, digital ancestors called *blogs, websites,* and *wikis.*

Essay—the wondering, discovering, thinking-on-the-page kind—is full of potential because it does not try to fit into what poet A. R. Ammons (1965) calls "boxes of preconceived possibility" first, but rather, it pours life and thought and feeling onto the page, and the writer begins to notice an organization emerging that matches the content of this one particular essay and not a different essay. True essay structures feel surprising and fluid. Flip through a book of contemporary essays—you will be amazed at the variety of shapes, many experimental in nature.

 ## The Birth of the Essay: Montaigne and *Les Essais*

When Michel de Montaigne retired from public service at thirty-eight to his tower of the Chateau de Montaigne in the French countryside around 1571, he decided to spend most of his time reading and writing. From his essays it seems he wrote to stave off a depression he felt creeping in—perhaps from becoming less necessary to the world; perhaps from a fear of death; perhaps from the ongoing grief he felt after the deaths, all within a short time, of a daughter, a brother, his father, and especially his best friend at thirty-two, Etienne de la Boetie, the man Montaigne wrote about loving, spiritually and emotionally.

Montaigne did not write for publication, at least not at first, but entirely for himself, writing seemingly whatever entered his mind the moment he put quill pen to paper. He wanted to think on the page about people, ideas, and the world as he experienced it, and to weigh that against his voracious reading of classical philosophy. He was not afraid to explore his own vulnerable and personal self: his illnesses (particularly the tortured bouts with kidney stones), his daily work and leisure schedules, his memories, his near-death experience. But his personal life was merely the springboard to larger philosophical, political, spiritual, and humanitarian ideas. Anything and everything became *essais*-worthy, including a moment when Montaigne's cat batted a paw at his feather pen, which allowed Montaigne to do what he loved best, to wonder about another perspective or reality, this time the cat's. "When I play with my cat," he wrote, "who knows if I am not a pastime to her more than she is to me?" I love that part. How many times do my own cats walked across my keyboard as I write, causing all sorts of chaos to erupt on my computer screen?

Though earlier essay-like forms existed in biblical texts, in Greek and Roman philosophical texts, and in letters (Heilker 1996, 14–15), the kind of writing Montaigne was doing—personal, observational, exploratory, and divergent—was not available as a named genre of writing. Whether he intended to push against the prevailing forms of writing or not, Montaigne seemed to find joy in sitting and ruminating. Not only inside his head, for the mind wanders, changes direction, gets hungry, and wonders what's for lunch. The mind with a pen, however, has things to say, then adds something onto that, and fairly soon, spins a vast web—thousands of words connected to one another, which one can reread, add to, omit, and rearrange. The result didn't merely blur the boundaries of genre; Montaigne actively pursued a new form of writing that did not fit into existing categories—drama, poetry, philosophy, speech, and ledger keeping.

Montaigne claimed to be merely *essaying*, which in French means *trying*—note the liveliness of that verb, the forward motion, as well as the exploratory, unresolved nature—*trying out* some thinking on the page. The essence of this kind of writing coils inside the name he gave it: *essais* (little attempts, or trials). Much of his writing sounds to my ears as contemporary as a blog. Montaigne writes, "The world always looks straight ahead; as for me, I turn my gaze inward, I fix it there and keep it busy. Everyone looks in front of him; as for me, I look inside of me; I have no business but with myself; I continually observe myself, I take stock of myself, I taste myself" (2003, xvii).

But mixed in with these intimate "tastes" of himself are quotes from classical literature, snippets of political intrigue, reflections on philosophy . . . you know, complicated, ambitious things! Here is a sampling from the table of contents of his essay collection:

Of Cannibals

Of the Custom of Wearing Clothes

Of Drunkenness

Of Thumbs

Of the Affection of Fathers for Their Children

Of Repentance

That to Study Philosophy Is to Learn to Die

It's almost as if Montaigne gave himself a daily prompt that began, "On the topic of _____," and began writing from there. One day perhaps he shut a heavy wooden door on his thumb or something, and that got him thinking on the simple topic of thumbs. Another day he was doing some light reading of Cicero, and it occurred to him: *You know, I think this guy has an interesting point. Maybe he means that "all the wisdom and reasoning in the world boils down finally to this point: to teach us not to be afraid to die"* (2003, 67). *Well, let me think about that for several thousand more words, and throw in some quotes from Horace and Lucretius. And what I finally wonder is this: "Why do you fear your last day? . . . All days travel toward death, the last one reaches it"* (81). Montaigne's mind was so fluid, his writing so fluent, and his knowledge from books so vast, that he could write circles around any topic in the universe, and he knew he could consider anything, even a body part, and compose such engaging ideas about it that we are still reading and imitating his work today.

One of Montaigne's most intriguing ideas was his overarching belief that humans are not able to reach certainty. His mantras, if you will, were "I don't know" and "*Que sais-je?*" ("What do I know?"). He said of his own writing style: "I cannot keep my subject still. It goes along befuddled and staggering, with a natural drunkenness" (2003, 740). I love the essay form as much as I love poetry, and I think these genres have something in common: tentativeness. The meandering nature of essay fits my personality; the questioning, skeptical quality of essay suits me because I feel most declarations and absolute statements instantly warrant a "Really?" and "But what about . . . ?" and "From another perspective, it might be completely different."

I am also liberated by the freedom of Montaigne's writing to contradict itself. As all of creation is in a constant state of change, so goes an essay, which mirrors its author's mental, emotional, even physical states in flux. Essay is not an argument or a thesis-and-support form after all, which tends to move like a speeding train toward a predetermined destination. Essay is allowed to change its mind as its author changes hers, perhaps inside the very act of writing. Montaigne said of himself: "I look at myself in different ways. All contradictions may be found in me by some twist and in some fashion. Bashful, insolent; chaste, lascivious; talkative, taciturn" (2003, xxiii).

The essay is also built to include multiple questions and points of view. Montaigne welcomed opposing opinions, believing that variety is part of nature, so why fight it? He apparently loved conversations more than life itself, and the art of great conversation includes examining all sides of an issue.

I talked about Montaigne recently with Tom Newkirk, who has written voluminously about essay. We are both in the Montaigne fan club, if you will. When Tom told me that he and his wife visited the room in the tower in France where Montaigne read and wrote, surrounded by his thousand-book private library, I got shivers imagining myself standing there and craning my neck to read the quotes by famous classical philosophers that are carved into the ceiling beams. (This sounds like pretty nerdy fun, I admit, but Tom did mention that there were lovely vineyards with wine tastings on the way to the tower.) Tom pointed out that Montaigne's essay writing was utterly generative. "He would write and keep writing and never stop, never run out of things to say, 'as long as there are ink and paper in the world,' as Montaigne himself wrote," Tom said. "And the act of reading essays is also generative. The having of ideas never needs to stop."

Montaigne's published essays were hugely popular in his own time, and they influenced writers all over the world—including, in the English-speaking parts, Francis Bacon and Shakespeare. The essay ultimately became a canonical genre, practiced by the most famous authors T. S. Eliot, Emerson, Thoreau, Virginia Woolf, E. B. White, and James Baldwin, as well as modern writers such as Annie Dillard, Joan Didion, Joseph Epstein, Edward Hoagland, Philip Lopate, Barry Lopez, John McPhee, and Gay Talese.

Their essays, these legacies of Montaigne, haunt with the questions they ask, the bold topics they explore, the boundaries they push, and their radient writing. Like poetry, language from essays can become part of our personal lexicon, as it has for me, when James Wood describes the particular kind of grief we suffer when a parent dies of Alzheimer's disease as "grief in stages—or *terraced grief*" (italics mine; 2014, 199). That phrase fits like a knife stab of truth. Reading brilliant essays is similar to the experience of listening to shows on NPR, like *This American Life,* where you don't care what the topic is because you know you will be intrigued; you will probably laugh; and you might even have to pull the car to the side of the road to

For a brilliantly organized and engaging Montaigne biography, I recommend *How to Live; or, A Life of Montaigne in One Question and Twenty Attempts at an Answer,* by Sarah Bakewell (2011).

cry for a few minutes. The best essays can make you angry or make you pledge to live differently, now that you have this new perspective the author has given to you.

But here's the thing: not one of Montaigne's essays or a single piece by a published essayist ever since fits into the templates popular on the Internet and in school settings for at least a century—the five-paragraph form; the inverted pyramid; the "hamburger"; or the red, green, and yellow (like a traffic light) color-coded paragraph.

 ## Problems with Standardized Essay Forms

How the essay transformed from Montaigne's expansive mental explorations, reminiscences, and frank observations in the 1570s to its current form in schools is a long, tedious story belonging to curricular systems, evaluation, and standardization, and not to the authentic world of writing and writers. In many schools, students write "essays" using blocky, step-by-step formulas developed to help young, unpracticed writers wrestle their material into an organized structure teachers can easily evaluate. Most students are bored out of their minds with this formulaic approach, and their writing loses energy, humor, and soul. Students are bored because they are not writing for themselves, which is a fundamental requirement for people who make writing their life's work. Writers write what they want, the way they want to write it. In school, kids write for a grade or test score—to pass through and get out.

Young people are assigned formulas for their analyses of poems and books, or to prove their understanding and retention of content, such as the causes of a certain war or the parts of a cell, and their writing has a get-this-over-quickly quality to it from the very start. And when we teachers are handed, in the final sentence of the first paragraph, the entire what, how, and why of the piece, why read on? The formula leaves no room for us to be seduced by astonishing topics or invited to climb inside the quirky, lively thinking of our students. Novelist Zoe Heller, in her bitter complaint about the "graceless formula" assigned to her daughter to use for her book report, compares this to "wearing a too small, too stiff bridesmaid's dress: it's a joyless exercise, and the results are never pretty" (2014).

Formulaic essay writing is like a gigantic Stop sign for thinking and learning because students' minds are focused on the formula and not on what they think and want to say. This does not lead to quality writing, where, as Tom Romano points out, "something must take place of far more significance than the learning of patterns and formulas. Young writers must cut loose. They must write frequently in high-speed chases after meaning, adventures that will take various routes, each different from the previous one" (1987, 6). Also, as Donald Bartholomae argues, because of the "tyranny of the thesis," the act of writing to support this bossy, single sentence causes writing to "close a subject down rather than to open it up, to put an end to discourse rather than to open up a project" (in Newkirk 1986a, 149). I don't believe anyone's definition of a quality education would include closing down subjects and ending discourse.

Some teachers fear abandoning standardized formulas, believing they provide a helpful scaffold to teach students how to organize their content appropriately, like clear maps, from beginning to end. However, I fear that the prescribed structures have nothing to do with helping kids write better and everything to do with control. I worry that the true reason for their popularity is that writing by number is easier to teach and easier to grade: A robust thesis statement in correct position? Check. Topic sentences lined up like toy soldiers at the head of each of three body paragraphs? Check. We hardly need to glance at what the writing actually says or means, as long as the template is filled in correctly.

The sad truth is that we hate reading these papers because they are bland and repetitive, written in that hollow voice from nowhere. Sometimes they do not even make sense; again, that's because kids are paying more attention to putting the puzzle together than to what they are meaning to say. They haven't had enough chances to discover what they think and feel, what intrigues or enrages them; they haven't found the sound of their particular writing voice. "We have an enclosure but no wild animals to be controlled," writes Tom Newkirk (2005, 19).

New Metaphors for Essay Structures

The structure of the true essay flows from its own organic logic, which is determined by the content itself and also by how the writer wants to affect readers: bring us to our knees; make us laugh out loud; reveal the true underbelly, slowly but surely. Helping students understand structure in this way is critical, and it's also more challenging than simple graphics of hamburgers or inverted pyramids can convey. Metaphors, however, can still be useful for helping students visualize more organic structures.

If we compare essays to other types of art, for instance, we might imagine they are like Impressionism and abstract art. We might compare essays to the evolving colors and designs swirling inside a kaleidoscope; or to a collage, with its multiple images and textures chosen to illustrate one concept or theme; or to the different sizes, patterns, and colors uniting in a mosaic. In essay, the multiple voices and perspectives on the central topic or idea render that collage or mosaic effect. Timothy Dansdill has had success teaching a college course on essay writing with a practice he calls the "pastiche effect," another art metaphor (2005, 103).

The problem even with those colorful, multifaceted, less fenced-in metaphors is that they still present the essay as a visual frozen in time, when actually, the experience of reading a great essay is more like traveling *through* time. Tom Newkirk says, "We are propelled from paragraph to paragraph or we come to a standstill [if the writing is dull], moving on only out of a sense of duty. Writers build this momentum not by withholding or transforming the mental processes of exploration but by revealing them and allowing the reader to participate in them" (2005, 48).

Essayists, in other words, almost write the story of their thinking, even though the essay is more expository than narrative, so that there is a kind of constant opening up to a new thought or feeling in the text. Paul Heilker terms this aspect of essay "chrono-logic," where thoughts are "associatively flowing from one into another into another" (1996, 66).

Perhaps an image for the continuous opening of thinking can be found in photographs of the extraordinary mud-brick ruins of Native American communal living found in Chaco Canyon, New Mexico. From certain vantage points, you can stand in one room and see a door opening into another room that has a door opening into more rooms, as far as the eye can see. (You can find beautiful shots of what I'm describing on the Internet.) This is the effect of the essays I love to read: they do not close down thinking, do not conclude arguments, but rather open up to new thinking, new possibilities, new perspectives on the world. You want to keep reading them, from beginning to end, and then you want to keep thinking about them and talking about them, long after you turn away from the final paragraph.

We might create metaphors for essay that kids can hear, perhaps comparing it to the improvisation of jazz music. A jazz composition has a central melodic line or theme, then individual musicians riff on that, staying inside a boundary and also careening away. Similarly, essay circles around a central idea, riffing on it with stories, questions, observations, and next-door topics, but ultimately cohering around the core idea. Or perhaps essay is like hip-hop, which often remixes, or makes a mash-up from other songs and sounds, as essay mixes in stories and quotes from other sources. The benefit of music as a metaphor for essay is that music *does* move through time, from beginning to end. Maybe essay is a symphony orchestra and chorus, with multiple instruments and voices, which are like the varied voices that essays often include.

What Are Contemporary Essays About?

Just as Montaigne wrote about everything from cannibals to repentance, so do today's writers: open any collection of contemporary essays and you'll see a world of possible topics represented in the titles. For example, notice the range in these few titles from *The Best American Essays 2001*:

"Mail," Anne Fadiman
"The Work of Mourning," Francine de Plessix Gray
"India's American Imports," Adam Hochschild
"On Being Breathless," Bert O. States

Early in a study, consider looking at tables of contents from essay collections so your students discover that essays are about anything and everything: sports, science, philosophy, art, war, race, gender, music, psychology, illness and disease, literature, television, animals.

Sometimes, essays sound almost noisy to me, as if I am at a cocktail party and I'm standing close to my friend, trying to hear an intimate bit of story, but then someone pulls up beside us with a big hug and hello for each of us, and in the background music pulses, and the doorbell rings, and a group cheers because the life of the party just walked in. It's all fun and fantastically interesting. Paul Heilker offers a magnificent term (via Mikhail Bahktin) for this multiplicity of voices: *polyglossia* (1996, 55). Share that word in your classroom—kids will love it!

Where Essays Live in the World

In the United States, in high school and college English literature anthologies, we have our renowned essay heroes, the British and American lineage from Monsieur Montaigne: Addison and Steele, William Hazlitt, Jonathan Swift, Samuel Johnson, Frederick Douglass, Ogden Nash, Flannery O'Connor, George Orwell. Globally, we find Montaigne's lineage unfolding across time and in every language: Baudelaire, Jorge Luis Borges, Italo Calvino, Albert Camus, Umberto Eco, Carlos Fuentes, Boris Pasternak, Rousseau, Albert Schweitzer, Junichiro Tanizaki.

For serious admirers of essay, there are hundreds more contemporary, global names, including Chinua Achebe, Sherman Alexie, Wendell Berry, J. M. Coetzee, Gretel Ehrlich, William Gass, Dagoberto Gilb, Stephen Jay Gould, Christopher Hitchens, bell hooks, June Jordan, Barbara Kingsolver, John McPhee, Bharati Mukherjee, Cynthia Ozick, Adrienne Rich, Marilynne Robinson, Richard Rodriquez, Edward Said, Scott Russell Sanders, David Sedaris, Susan Sontag, David Foster Wallace, Terry Tempest Williams.

My tastes lean toward the lyrical, as poetry has been my literary home since I was a little girl, the edgy and quirky, and I also crave to read about social justice issues, so any essayist whose prose makes lyrical leaps or who breaks rules and boundaries, or who casts a critical lens on the world becomes a mentor for me. I'm smitten with dozens of contemporary writers, among them Charles D'Ambrosio, Ta-Nehisi Coates, Roxane Gay, Leslie Jamison, Lisa See, Zadie Smith, John Jeremiah Sullivan, and Sarah Vowell, all of whom write essays that are brilliant, brave, often dark, humorous, and wildly inventive.

In print, we can find essays in magazines and journals, and in collections by single or multiple authors. A wonderful source, because it includes diverse voices, topics, and styles, is the Best American Essays series, edited by Robert Atwan since 1986, in which an annual collection from literary journals and magazines—what Atwan calls, in his foreword to every edition, "essays of literary achievement that show an awareness of craft and forcefulness of thought"—is chosen by a guest editor, someone who also writes essays and has probably been included in past years.

Another resource for contemporary essays is the annual PEN/Diamonstein-Spielvogel Award for the Art of the Essay; winning essays are posted on PEN's website. The website states that the award "aims to preserve the dignity and esteem that the essay form imparts to literature. Here we feature selected essays from this year's finalists, whose wide-ranging topics and often dramatic differences in style, tone, approach, and subject matter are a testament to the creativity inherent in the essay form" (www.pen.org/2015-diamonstein-spielvogel-award-feature). As with all the resources I mention, please be sure to read the essays before using them in class to make sure they are appropriate for your students.

Many essayists have found an audience on the Internet in the past two decades, in blogs, on websites, and in e-zines, and because of the accessibility of the digital environment around the world, I would venture to guess they have tons of readers. Technology also affords exciting multimodal writing projects where authors include elements such as photos, graphics, sound, and video that enhance the experience for readers.

For young people in classrooms around the United States, the chances of doing any kind of writing that feels exploratory, expressive, and evocative seem rather rare. Mostly, students are busy producing arguments and persuasions, reading responses, and other carefully calculated products not of their own choice or design. Writing to think—to be *inside the writing* instead of always at the end of it, as Randy Bomer says—appears to be out of reach for students. My hope is that together, as we work to understand the incredible potential of essay, this will change. Not only will writing to think feel within reach, but it will feel necessary.

Benefits of Essay Writing

The essay teaches students the following:

- how to grow and elaborate ideas using thoughts, quotes, questions, facts, stories, observations, numbers and statistics, and multiple angles or perspectives on a topic
- that writing does not always have to resolve or reach a conclusion to be meaningful and provocative
- that they should care about what they write
- complexity and depth, both in reading and in writing texts.

3

Naming Craft in Essay

The great thing about dead or remote masters is that they can't refuse you as an apprentice. You can learn whatever you want from them. They left their lesson plans in their work.

—Austin Kleon, *Steal Like an Artist*

Everything I know about essay I learned from reading. I've read a mountain of essays, beginning with E. B. White's glittering "Once More to the Lake" in high school, and I've read books *about* essay (sometimes referred to as creative or literary nonfiction), and finally, of course, I have practiced writing essays of my own. This is rich preparation, though I learn something new every time I read an essay. To build a vision of what essay looks and sounds like, we can all—writers, teachers, and students alike—immerse ourselves in published essays for inspiration and guidance, as if they are maps to pots of gold, and we can notice and name features to imitate in our own writing.

Spend time with the Best American Essays anthologies, and you will notice that the selections can bend and spill a bit into other genres—pieces we might call memoir, journalism, feature article, even, in the case of one collection, almost a script, consisting entirely of dialogue between two people. Most frequently, the essays fit the bill for the purposes of this book: meditations on ideas and pieces of writing-to-think, frequently arising from authors' questions, emotions, memories, events, and observations. If you feel you are unfamiliar with this genre, begin with a collection of contemporary writers whose topics and voices will feel modern and relevant. Dip into several volumes, and I promise you will find a favorite writer, one whose style or story appeals to you, who can become your guide and mentor. You will also find whole essays or excerpts to use as models for your students.

 ## Reading Teaches Students How to Write

I think the major characteristic that connects writers across time and geography is that they love to read, and by reading, they learn to write. Some of what writers learn happens almost magically, by osmosis, if you will. We could call this *loose imitation*. When I work with young people, I can often predict how much they read or are read to, sometimes even *what* they are reading, by looking at their writing. In my book *Hidden Gems* (2010), I tell the story of an eighth-grade boy whose archaic language and overwrought sentences were nearly indecipherable (frustrating for his teacher, who recognized their beauty but was concerned about the numerous grammatical errors). After reading pages of mazelike sentences in his notebook, the first thing I had to ask him was, "What are you reading?"

"The Bible," he answered instantly, and I almost said, "Bingo!" because I felt I could recognize the influence, at least of the King James Version.

Writers mimic the topics, voices, structures, and cadences of the writers they love to read, as if by magic, but they also intentionally deconstruct texts they admire in order to practice writing like that. We could call this *close imitation*. Austin Kleon made an engaging, inspiring little book called *Steal Like an Artist* (2012), about how artists and creators of all kinds steal in order to produce. By "steal," he means study and emulate your heroes, whomever they may be. Close imitation requires focused reading and rereading, attending to craft features a writer might wish to imitate. This intimate relationship between a mentor author and an emerging writer feels monumental. When we immerse ourselves in the voices and artistry of our favorite writers, their works become our teachers. Or, as Kerri Ward, a high school teacher in Philadelphia, says, "it's like finding a friend."

When I began working at the Teachers College Reading and Writing Project in the 1980s, I discovered that Lucy Calkins and my colleagues, several of whom were also published novelists and poets, recognized that close imitation was critical to learning how to write well. We believed that if teachers could bring this practice into their classrooms, it would help those who might not be as familiar with certain genres or qualities of writing develop content knowledge about writing.

And so, in our professional development in New York City classrooms, we included time and routines for teachers and students to study the kind of writing they were about to make, who composes it and how, and where it can be found in the world. We called this portion of a unit of study *immersion*, a concept inspired by Brian Cambourne's theory of language learning (1988), and we called the stories, poems, articles, and essays we gathered for students to read during this time *mentor texts* because they function, indeed, as teachers of writing. In her book *Study Driven* (2006), Katie Wood Ray uses a perfect phrase, "writing under the influence," to describe what it feels like to immerse ourselves in model texts, taking on the styles of our favorite writers. I cling to the practice of immersion when I work with teachers and students in classrooms across the country because I learned how to write under the influence of my favorite writers, and so did all my friends who are writers, and I know that time spent closely reading will directly and indirectly lift the quality of students' writing.

Immersion might take from two to five days of students reading and talking with peers about a number of published texts similar to those they are about to make. As I explained in Chapter 1, with the first read, you'll simply linger in the text for what it says, for what it makes you think and wonder, and for how it makes you feel. On subsequent readings, you'll zoom in to analyze language, voice, tone, and structure in order to name specific features of the genre. You can closely read two or three shared texts (sometimes called *touchstone texts*) during minilessons with the whole class to build an understanding of the genre. Then, have students continue this work in partnerships or small groups with other examples. In all these configurations, you and your students will notice and name the features of a given text, construct your knowledge of what this kind of writing looks and sounds like, and develop lists that you will use to inform your own writing.

The good news is that for most kinds of writing we want students to try—narrative, expository, poetry, drama—there are countless possibilities we might collect and read, with more being written and published every day. These texts become our partner teachers, and in fact, whenever I am stumped about how to teach something in writing, I say, "Let's see how so-and-so [insert author's name] did it!"

Choosing Texts for Immersion

There are fabulous lists of mentor texts for most kinds of writing available in professional books and on blogs and websites about writing workshop and teaching writing (e.g., K. Bomer, R. Bomer, Calkins, Kittle, Marchetti and O'Dell, Ray, Burkins and Yaris, the *Two Writing Teachers* blog); however, I think it is important to find personal favorites as well. If you have not yet collected your own bookshelf or basket of best-loved mentor texts for teaching writing, you may appreciate having some guidelines for choosing before you click the Purchase button on your favorite bookseller's web page. I have a few simple criteria for choosing mentor texts for teaching writing, no matter the age group.

First, mentor texts should be *relevant* to the students I am teaching. Relevance includes having topics and situations that kids care about and experience, as well as looking and sounding contemporary. Poe's "The Raven" is a fine poem to read and know, but not one that young people should have to imitate. Next, mentor texts should be *diverse* in as many ways as possible and represent the students I teach. Diversity includes language, topic, perspective, style, structure, age, gender, race, and ethnicity of characters and authors. Mentor texts should be *accessible*; kids should be able to read them, or if they can't, I need to provide a structure (audio file, class read-aloud) to make the text available to all. Finally, the texts I teach from in minilessons should be *beloved* texts so that I know them well and my enthusiasm will carry over to my students. The larger collection of mentor texts that students read on their own or with partners should also include texts students love or discover (even if I'm not so fond of them) so they can choose their own writing heroes to emulate.

 ## Naming Craft in Essay

Susan Orlean (2005) describes essay as perhaps the "most intimate of reading experiences." The essay invites readers to "eavesdrop as the writer works through a thought or excavates a memory. . . . It's as if, for those few thousand words, we are invited deep inside someone's mind" (xvii). By following the six steps to reading essays deeply, powerfully, and closely during the immersion phase of study, you and your students will climb deep inside the thinking and the craft of the authors you admire as you notice, name, and record the features of essays.

You might begin by just admiring flat-out gorgeous writing, for instance, the rhythm, repetition, and metaphor in these sentences from Daniel Orozco's essay about California earthquakes, "Shakers":

> Inside aquariums in dentist offices and Chinese restaurants and third-grade classrooms, fish huddle in the corners of their tanks, still as photos of huddled fish. Inside houses built on the alluvial soils of the Sacramento Delta, cockroaches swarm from behind walls, pouring like cornflakes out of kitchen cabinetry and rising in tides from beneath sinks and tubs and shower stalls. (2007, 159)

With the essays you share, invite students to find a place that is luscious to their ears and read it out loud. They might also wish to copy the words into their notebooks for repeated study.

Beyond luscious language, however, you'll also want to highlight specific essay features so students can imitate them in their own writing. To prepare for that teaching, let's look closely at some of the most common features of essay craft in essays written for adults. These same features are found in essays written for audiences of all ages; the content may be more or less adult, but the crafting stays the same. You may not use all you come to know about essay through this exploration, and certainly, some of the example texts I provide here would not be appropriate for your students, but it is always comforting to know your teaching well is deep and won't run dry in minilessons and conferences. For your reading pleasure, I chose examples from some extraordinary essays and organized them by specific features you might wish to teach, perhaps demonstrating with the age-appropriate essays collected in the back of this book. Here, where it worked to do so, I italicized the words and phrases that illustrate those features.

Shaping and Structuring

Structure is one of the first and probably most radically different (from what we're used to in schools) features to notice in a pile of essays because of the wide variety. Some tell stories, while others are expository, reportage, or even lean toward argument. Some essays are written like letters, such as Barbara Kingsolver's two extraordinary essays "Letter to My Mother" and "Letter to a Daughter at Thirteen" (2002). Martin Luther King Jr.'s critical "Letter from Birmingham Jail" (1963) has all the features of essay, and in his book *Between the World and Me* (2015), Ta-Nehisi Coates begins, like a letter, with one word, "Son," then continues addressing his son by name (Samori) or by "you" in this book-length essay/memoir.

Some essays have dramatic visual features, like numbered, lettered, or subtitled sections. Occasionally, we find diagrams and sketches. Some are quite short; others go on for pages. Not one has five paragraphs!

When working with students, you might find it helpful to outline the structure of some of the essays you study together. As an example, here's an outline of "Joyas Voladoras," by Brian Doyle, which you read in Chapter 1.

- It has six paragraphs.

- It begins with facts about hummingbird hearts and ends with scenes of human emotion, the moments that both fill and stop our hearts.

- It moves from hummingbird hearts to whale hearts, then back to hummingbirds again, then finally to all hearts.

In addition to describing structure in words, you might find it helpful to use a diagram or sketch to show students different ways to think about how the shape of an essay works. For example, see Figure 3.1 (on the next page) for six quick experiments I did with sketching the structure, balance of content, and even a possible theme (shape 6) of Doyle's essay. There is not one correct way to visualize structures; the purpose of this activity is simply to become aware of the diversity of essay shapes. Students often come up with much more lively, inventive drawings to represent the

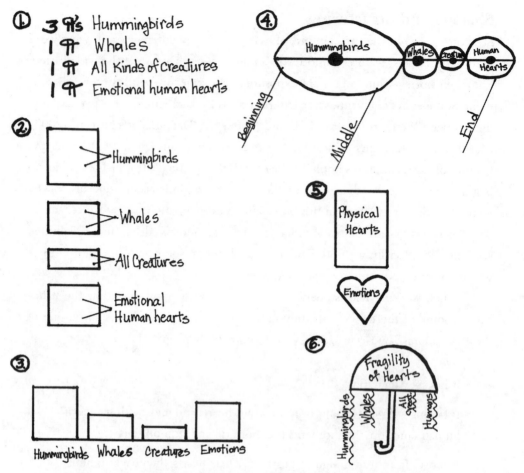

Figure 3.1 Six Visual Sketches of the Shape of an Essay

structures of their mentor essays. Later, as they are drafting and revising their own essays, they can draw and play with numerous possible structures.

For more practice, you could make a quick outline and a visual sketch for the structure of "Pride," by Dagoberto Gilb (which you also read in Chapter 1).

Weaving

"Everything in the world is woven," a wise weaver told me in the Medina in Rabat, Morocco. His name was Said, and he made gorgeous, finely woven bedspreads, drapes, scarves, and wall hangings. He wanted to point out the slightly different textures of threads from silk, wool, cotton, and other plant fibers, some shiny and smooth, others a bit fluffy, some even rough. But he quickly moved from talking about fabrics to other woven things, like the way he and I were trying to understand each other by weaving what phrases we knew from Arabic, French, and English.

Brenda Miller (2001) writes about the first day of the college course she teaches on "writing the lyric essay," when she sets a loaf of challah bread in the center of the table. Challah is the special bread eaten during the Jewish Sabbath meal and is made by braiding strands of dough to form a loaf. Miller uses this metaphor to make her own fascinating and beautifully shaped, braided essay, including numbered and titled sections on topics like her attempts to make challah; French braids in hair; a story of writing her first personal essay; Joseph Cornell's art boxes containing found objects that seem to belong together; even a recipe for challah!

Whether woven textile or braided bread, the point is that the essay can weave multiple strands of thought, one word (like *braid*), stories, and events into one gorgeous whole cloth. As you explore the idea of shape and structure, remember that ultimately what binds an essay together is a concept or big idea, or a metaphor.

Naming Thinking

A hallmark feature of essay is that writers think on the page before an audience, and that thinking sounds as if it is happening in real time. Rather than the preordained, conclusive thesis statement followed by paragraphs of proof, the essay conveys the voice of a writer in the *process of thinking through* ideas. Language that accompanies thinking is tentative and vulnerable—"I'm not certain of this . . ." and "I am struggling with the idea that. . . ." What a privilege to read this, when so much of what we hear and read these days demands a harsh, bloviating, or argumentative voice. Instead, the effect in essay is open and inviting, as if we are "in cahoots with the writer, like we are on the same side," as one teacher described it. Often, essays are written in present tense, and even use second person, as if the author is literally thinking out loud, and talking directly to us. Notice how conversational the naming of thinking (in italics) makes these excerpts:

Before we go any further, let's acknowledge that the questions of whether and how different kinds of animals feel pain, *and of whether and why* it might be justifiable to inflict pain on them in order to eat them, turn out to be extremely complex and difficult. (2005, 262)

 —DAVID FOSTER WALLACE, "CONSIDER THE LOBSTER"

Which brings me, after some rumination, back to my Visible Cow. (2005, xvii)

 —SUSAN ORLEAN, INTRODUCTION TO *THE BEST AMERICAN ESSAYS 2005*

Judaism is nothing if not down to earth in its approach, and sets more store by behavior than by belief. *It's either a weakness in me or a strength—I haven't decided—that I still haven't figured out* where I stand on so consequential a matter as the quality of my Jewish life. But if I should happen to die before I've made up my mind, I'm counting on my family to give me an Orthodox burial. (2001, 192)

 —DAPHNE MERKIN, "TROUBLE IN THE TRIBE"

Revising Thinking

In addition to naming thinking, writers change their minds and revise their thinking in an essay (sometimes midsentence), alerting us to this fact with language that says something like, "No, that's not what I meant," or "As soon as I wrote those last words, I knew I was wrong about that." This flip-flopping, if you will, creates an even more immediate experience for the reader, for the writer seems so defenseless, committing to print that she thought one thing, but now, having teased it out for a few pages, she thinks something else.

Peter Elbow claims that "the best hook for an essay is a piece of genuine uncertainty" (2012, 309). Readers feel a kinship with an author who expresses uncertainty. We are human. We are in this together, and we feel propelled to keep reading to find out what the author might finally decide. Notice the change of mind inside the following examples. Here again, I have put the changes of mind in italics:

The obvious advantage of brick as a building material is that it's already burned, which accounts for its presence in Chicago after the fire of 1871. Brick transformed the city, ushering in an era of industrial greatness, *completing—no, not completing, but extending—extending a process that* began with a mysterious extinction, a vast unimagined loss. (2014c, 148)

—CHARLES D'AMBROSIO, "WINNING"

Belief is easy. I believe in God, I never stopped, but to keep faith is another endeavor entirely. *It may be* that I am too exasperated with God, or too exasperated with religion to manage it. I have confused the two so thoroughly that I cannot separate them. *Or it may be* that they ought not to be separated at all. *It may be* that God and His flawed and paradoxical church are, in the end, God. *I wonder sometimes if* these doubts aren't acts of faith, if faith isn't also in the questions. *But then I think, surely that can't be right. Surely.* (2014)

—AYANA MATHIS, "WHAT WILL HAPPEN TO ALL THAT BEAUTY?"

Here are the opening words of Richard Rodriguez's essay "In the Brown Study":

Or, as a brown man, I think. But do we really think that color colors thought? (2005, 119)

Next, Rodriguez questions and argues across the entire essay against the idea that race, or the color of one's skin, creates one's thoughts, voice, or a body of literature. Then, he changes his mind, in the final sentence of his essay:

I think I probably do. (Have brown thoughts.) (2005, 131)

Revealing Truth

Often in essays, writers seem to peel back layers to reveal a deeper, more honest, often painful, or embarrassing truth. It's as if they are speaking to someone, a therapist, say, or a pastor, or at least an extremely close friend, and are coming to realize the truth in the act of writing it, exposing the underbelly of a statement. The effect, again, is to create intimacy with the reader, but also, it helps us trust writers who let us see this raw thought and emotion.

> People say it's because parents *love* [Kingsolver's emphasis] their kids so much that they want to tell them how to live. *But I'm afraid that's only half love, and the other half selfishness* [my emphasis here]. Kids who turn out like their parents kind of validate their world. That was my first real lesson as a mother—realizing that you could be different from me, and it wouldn't make me less of a person. (2002a, 149)
> —Barbara Kingsolver, "Letter to a Daughter at Thirteen"

> Before anyone ever cared where I would play basketball, I was a kid from Northeast Ohio. It's where I walked. It's where I ran. It's where I cried. It's where I bled. It holds a special place in my heart. People there have seen me grow up. I sometimes feel like I'm their son. . . . I want to give them hope when I can. I want to inspire them when I can. *My relationship with Northeast Ohio is bigger than basketball. I didn't realize that four years ago. I do now.* (2014)
> —Lebron James, "I'm Coming Home"

Weaving in Voices of Others

Since Montaigne, essayists have pulled in other voices from literature, philosophy, religion, history, science—everywhere, really—quoting others so it almost seems as if they're having a conversation with them on the page. These writers engage with other voices not out of formulaic obligation (e.g., "include three quotes from other sources, properly footnoted"), but rather, out of passion. Sometimes you feel the essayist has a love affair going with another (even long-dead) writer, and sometimes it feels more like a heated argument or a bone to pick. When done well, quoting other texts allows multiple voices to gather around an idea and put in their two cents.

> Put in a slightly different way, *it was Charlie Chaplin, I think, who said that life up close is a tragedy, but from a distance it's a comedy.* (2014b, 259)
> —Charles D'Ambrosio, "Salinger and Sobs"

"If you're black, you were born in jail," Malcolm [X] said. And I felt the truth of this in the blocks I had to avoid, in the times of day when I must not be caught walking home from school, in my lack of control over my body. (2015, 36)

> —Ta-Nehisi Coates, *Between the World and Me*

Weaving in Facts, Statistics, and References

Similar to the way they include quotations, essayists often include facts, statistics, or references to elaborate their ideas. Specific information is like another voice that joins the chorus, sometimes adding a lovely sound, sometimes a bold, authoritarian one, always the power of many voices. Because these facts and references are so integral to the overall sound and meaning of the essay, writers choose carefully, using only fantastic and meaningful facts that elaborate and advance the ideas.

The rich, then, should give. But how much should they give? *Gates may have given away nearly $30 billion, but that still leaves him sitting at the top of the* Forbes *list of the richest Americans, with $53 billion. His 66,000-square-foot high-tech lakeside estate near Seattle is reportedly worth more than $100 million. Property taxes are about $1 million. . . .* Has Bill Gates done enough? More pointedly, you might ask: If he really believes that all lives have equal value, what is he doing living in such an expensive house . . . ? (2007, 274)

> —Peter Singer, "What Should a Billionaire Give— and What Should You?"

The obstinacy of my kidney stones, especially in the penis, has sometimes cast me into long retentions of urine, for three, even four days, and so far forward into death that it would have been madness to hope, or even to wish, to avoid it, in view of the cruel attacks that this condition brings. *Oh what a grand master in the art of torture was that good Emperor [Tiberius] who had his criminals' penises tied so they would die from not being able to piss!* (2003, 771)

> —Montaigne, "Of Diversion"

Using Lists

Lists are self-explanatory, but I will say that the effect of a little list inside an essay is one of surprise and relaxation—a breath of fresh air. As you read this very book about teaching essay, notice how relieved your eyes and mind are to find a dense idea summarized nicely in a little list.

> I searched my nightstand for my list of things to do that day. Immediately I checked off "get up" and proceeded to read through the rest of my tasks:
>
> - Pick up socks at dry cleaners.
> - Measure dental floss to determine how much is left on the roll.
> - Mail ketchup rebate form.
> - Special-order James Lipton bobblehead.
> - Buy more paper to write lists on. (2004a, 51)
>
> —ELLEN DEGENERES, "MAKING YOUR LIFE COUNT
> (AND OTHER FUN THINGS TO DO WITH YOUR TIME!)"

In his deeply moving essay about death and loss, and what it means to be alive, called "In the Bone Garden of Desire," Charles Bowden (2001) includes one recipe for salsa and another for risotto, little lists that are tributes to the loved ones he is mourning.

 ## Naming Craft in General

The following excerpts are examples of more general stylistic moves, ones you see in most well-written texts. I include them here because I think some readers might find them radical suggestions for essay writing, especially if essay has always meant the more rule-bound, familiar school form. Again, I point out each feature in italics.

Sentence Length Variety

When a very short sentence follows a long one, it draws attention and is emphasized by its contrasting length.

> In contrast to India, where at least fourteen languages co-exist as legitimate Indian languages, in contrast to Nicaragua, where all citizens

are legally entitled to formal school instruction in their regional or tribal languages, compulsory education in America compels accommodation to exclusively white forms of "English." *White English, in America, is "Standard English."* (2003, 158)

—June Jordan, "Nobody Mean More to Me than You
and the Future Life of Willie Jordan"

Shocking Image or Metaphor

Sometimes essayists shock readers with images so sharp they jolt.

> We [mothers of daughters] love you *like an alcoholic loves gin*—it makes our teeth hurt, it's the first thing we think about before we open our eyes in the morning—and like that, we take little swigs when nobody's looking. (2002a, 145)
>
> —Barbara Kingsolver, "Letter to a Daughter at Thirteen"

Extended Image or Metaphor

In "Dust," Mary Oliver (2001, 218) shapes her poetic essay in three numbered sections, all circling the metaphorical meaning of dust. She writes of her loved one, who could not let a single thing, not even an empty envelope, go, gathering around her objects long past usefulness, literally disintegrating to dust. Oliver writes of the cycle of seasons at the ocean, with its constantly varying colors and birds. She writes of the cruelty and sadness of loss, particularly of her beloved dogs. Oliver does not include the biblical quote "for dust thou art, and unto dust shalt thou return," but that deep truth lingers beneath the lists of things, seasons, people, and animals that cease to be.

Humor

Comedians sometimes craft essays, and you expect to find humor in them, of course. But humor is a device used in all kinds of essays, sometimes even serious ones, where it can be delightfully unexpected.

> Sometimes, when I'm trying to get dressed, I find myself just staring at my clothes for an hour. I have not a clue as to what I should put

on. It is so hard to decide what to wear. And it got me thinking: *That's why prison wouldn't be so bad.* (2004b, 15)

— ELLEN DEGENERES, "THAT'S WHY PRISON WOULDN'T BE SO BAD"

Smith sees that I'm awake and tells me that help is on the way. He speaks calmly, even cheerily. His look, as he sits on the rock with his cane across his lap, is one of pleasant commiseration: *Ain't the two of us just had the shittiest luck?* it says. He and Bullet had left the campground where they were staying, he later tells an investigator, because he wanted "some of those Marzes-bars they have up to the store." *When I hear this detail some weeks later, it occurs to me that I have nearly been killed by a character out of one of my own novels. It's almost funny.* (2001, 122)

— STEPHEN KING, "ON IMPACT"

Repetition

We usually think of repetition as a feature of poetry, but it's not uncommon to find essayists repeating words, phrases, even whole sentences for effect.

Was it a thing a nonbeloved child could figure out—could replicate? How long would it take? This was an emergency. I was *wrong*, in my *wrongness* I was alienating them, and either I was doing things *wrong* or I was imbued with *wrongness*, irretrievably *wrong*, a *wrong* self, and that could not be changed, and it could not be borne. Therefore it must be the case that I was doing things *wrong*, and if I was doing things *wrong*, then it was only a matter of beginning to do things right, and I could do that, I would, I had to, it was life or death to be loved by them, so I would do things beautifully, beginning now. (2014, 164)

— ELIZABETH TALLENT, "LITTLE X"

Specific Detail

Including specific detail is a hallmark of all good writing and is one way writers convey a sense of care for their topics. In an essay you might find numbers, statistics, times, dates, and the names of people, streets, signs, restaurants, food, toys, perfume; details add texture to the prose.

> And yet the *Las Vegas* wedding business seems to appeal to precisely that impulse. *"Sincere and Dignified Since 1954,"* one wedding chapel advertises. There are *nineteen* such wedding chapels in Las Vegas, intensely competitive, each offering better, faster, and by implication, more sincere services than the next: *Our Photos Best Anywhere, Your Wedding on a Phonograph Record, Candlelight with Your Ceremony. . . .* All of these services, like most others in Las Vegas . . . are offered *twenty-four hours a day, seven days a week*, presumably on the premise that marriage, like craps, is a game to be played when the table seems hot. (1981, 91)
>
> —Joan Didion, "Marrying Absurd"

Lively Language

Sometimes essayists do a little rockin' and rollin' with their language, using the kind of colloquialisms or slang some of our English teachers might have circled in red (and I'm not even talking about the body parts referenced in the first example!).

> Penis or vagina? I couldn't possibly tell you it wasn't to be discussed, or didn't matter. It matters, *boy howdy,* does it ever. (2002a, 159)
>
> —Barbara Kingsolver, "Letter to a Daughter at Thirteen"

> And you can thank the *wanking* eighties, if you wish, and digital sequencers, too, for proving to everyone that technologically "perfect" rock—like "free" jazz—*sucks rockets*. Because order *sucks.* (1997, 101)
>
> —Dave Hickey, "The Delicacy of Rock-and-Roll"

"Talk" Language

As they explore ideas, essayists sometimes use dialect or a mix of different languages for effect, essentially capturing the sound of talk on paper.

> *It ain't about gangs here. You know what?* I'm tired of hearing about *cholos.* It's about *quinceaneras* and weddings and birthday parties. . . . It's about Little League diamonds, Ponder Park, where my boy hit a grand slam last night and struck out ten. "*Echela al guante, m'ijo, al guante! . . .* Don't swing at the piñatas! *. . . Se van los elotes, calientitos, se van los elotes!*" *Okay,* so that last one was about the man who sells the corn getting ready to leave. (2003a, 71)
>
> —Dagoberto Gilb, "Living al Chuco"

 ## Hearing Voice in Essay

If someone were to ask me what adjective describes the most popular or dominant voice across multitudes of essays, I would have to say *audacious*—as in bravely honest, sometimes embarrassingly so—though *skeptical* would come in as a close second. The voice of essay can range from sentimental to sappy to angry to newscaster. As you and your students immerse yourselves in model essays, be sure to talk about the quality of voice in each one. To begin thinking about how to *name* voice, consider the following examples, where I've italicized the language I believe gives the voice a particular quality.

Skeptical

> I should love <u>Orange Is the New Black</u> for the same reason I should (but do not) love <u>Red Tails</u> or <u>The Butler</u> or <u>42</u>. Here is popular culture about people who look like me. *That's all I should need, right?* Time and again, people of color are supposed to be grateful for scraps from the table. There's this strange implication that we should enjoy certain movies or television shows simply because they exist. (2014d, 250)
>
> —Roxanne Gay, "When Less Is More"

Sarcastic

Anyone new to the experience of owning a lawn, as I am, soon figures out that *there is more at stake here than a patch of grass.* A lawn immediately establishes a certain relationship with one's neighbors and, by extension, the larger American landscape. Mowing the lawn, I realized the first time I gazed into my neighbor's yard and imagined him gazing back into mine, *is a civic responsibility.* . . . Lawns, *I am convinced*, are a symptom of, and metaphor for, our skewed relationship to the land. (1990, 220)

— MICHAEL POLLAN, "WHY MOW? THE CASE AGAINST LAWNS"

Understated

Help is on the way [King's emphasis], I think, and *that's probably good* [my emphasis] because I've been in a hell of an accident. (2001, 122)

— STEPHEN KING, "ON IMPACT"

No-Holds-Barred

Some people claim never to have been bored. *They lie.* One cannot be human without at some time or other having known boredom. Even animals know boredom, we are told, though they are *deprived of the ability to complain directly* about it. (2012, 102)

— JOSEPH EPSTEIN, "DUH, BOR-ING"

Friendly and Intimate

Sometimes the voice is friendly, even in the midst of dense, difficult, or more formal material.

I may seem to have wandered from my original subject. What has personal holiness to do with politics and economics? Everything, from the liberal Protestant point of view. (2007)

— MARILYNNE ROBINSON, "ONWARD, CHRISTIAN LIBERALS"

Crafting Seductive Beginnings

We already know to teach our students that their opening paragraphs need to hook the reader and entice her to continue reading. Unfortunately, some of the strategies for how to do that have become a bit clichéd (e.g., sound effect, dialogue, a question), compared with the rich variety that exists in published texts. Beginnings are important, and that's just as true for essay as for any other kind of writing, so as you immerse students in model essays, pay close attention to how the writers invite you in. Look for ways to describe the *effect* an opening has on a reader. Here, I've called beginnings *seductive*, but in case that's too risqué for kids, you might also use words like *inviting, alluring,* or even *can't put the essay down now* beginnings.

Often, essayists begin with surprise, tension, or the presentation of an unusual idea or point of view. "The lead is a promise to readers that they and the writer will discover something . . . that will make them view the world differently than they have in the past," writes Donald Murray (1996, 58). In the examples of first lines that follow, notice how several of the writers use style features mentioned earlier: repetition, shocking images and language, short, declarative sentences for effect, and humor. You'll also see features usually associated with poetry, like rhythm and alliteration. Notice how the intense honesty of these sentences—even to the point of embarrassment—excites and intrigues. And of course, if the leads are truly seductive, you'll wish you had the rest of the essays in front of you right now, just to find out what happens.

> During menopause, a woman can feel like the only way she can continue to exist for ten more seconds inside her crawling, burning skin is to walk screaming into the sea—grandly, epically, and terrifyingly, like a fifteen-foot-tall Greek tragic figure wearing a giant, pop-eyed wooden mask. Or she may remain in the kitchen and begin hurling objects at her family: telephones, coffee cups, plates. (2012, 218)
> —Sandra Tsing Loh, "The Bitch Is Back"

> I am failing as a woman. I am failing as a feminist. To freely accept the feminist label would not be fair to good feminists. If I am, indeed, a feminist, I am a rather bad one. (2014a, 314)
> —Roxane Gay, "Bad Feminist: Take Two"

There are many kinds of prayer. There is a kind of prayer that's like breathing. There is a kind of prayer that's like talking to your best friend all day long. There is a kind of prayer in the face of beauty that lifts your hands up because it would be harder to keep them down. (2014, 22)

> —Kristin Dombek, "Letter from Williamsburg"

In an earlier time, a lynch mob would display the body of its victim with impunity, often gathering around it for a group photograph. These images, and the bodies they represented, were the icons of white supremacy. Circulated in newspapers, the pictures displayed the power of the white mob and the powerlessness of the black community. After the highly publicized lynching of Claude Neal in 1934, photographers took hundreds of shots of his mutilated body and sold them for fifty cents each. (2001, 261)

> —Ashraf Rushdy, "Exquisite Corpse"

Let me tell you about what I have never been allowed to be. Beautiful and female. (2005, 93)

> —Dorothy Allison, "Two or Three Things I Know for Sure"

 ## Crafting Haunting Endings

Just as with beginnings, the ways writers leave an essay are as almost as varied as the number of essays you can find. Most of us were taught in school that the final paragraph should reiterate the thesis statement and tie the whole essay up, nice and tidy. Compare that advice with the closings of essays in any Best American Essays collection. Not one of them sounds like a repeated thesis statement; not one sounds preachy. Instead, they leave us alone to smile; weep; shout out loud, "No!" or "Are you kidding me?"; reread the whole essay; share with our best friends; and sometimes hear the words echo in our minds and hearts forever. Essays often end with new thinking, or new questions, having the effect of opening up possibilities for further exploring rather than shutting ideas down or wrapping them up.

The endings of essays can resound like the clarion chords of a pipe organ, with short, staccato sentences and no room to argue—this is how it is. In Chapter 1, you saw Dagoberto Gilb end "Pride" this way: "The desert land is rock-dry and ungreen. It is brown. Brown like the skin is brown. Beautiful brown" (2003b, 246).

Or the last lines of an essay can sound like tinkling glass, soft, like fog gently lifting off the tip of a mountain. Richard Seltzer's essay "A Mask in the Face of Death" (1988), about the devastation of the AIDS epidemic in Haiti, ends like a tragic whisper. Seltzer's final paragraph celebrates the famous, colorful, exuberant murals of Bible stories in the Cathédral of Sainte Trinité and then says: "Perhaps one day the plague will be rendered in poetry, music, painting, but not now. Not now" (219).

I've noticed essayists often end with a rush of short sentences (sometimes even one-word sentences), repeating words, phrases, or questions, giving the effect of ocean waves crashing against a rock cliff, or a snowball effect, gathering and ac- cumulating images and emotions to reach a climactic final line, as in this piece by photojournalist Camilo José Vergara, who photographed the Twin Towers in New York City as they were being constructed in 1970 and then across decades until 9/11. When the World Trade Center's Twin Towers were under construction, Vergara says, he would never have imagined living longer than those buildings:

> Early on, I resented them and all that I thought they stood for. Even-
> tually, I grew to see them as great human creations—such simple
> buildings that could turn into upright fields of amber in late after-
> noons in winter, and reflect passing clouds in the summer sky.
>
> Now, I miss them. (2011)
> —"The Looming Towers"

I call the endings haunting here to draw attention to the utter importance of closings. Students and I have also named them using phrases such as whispered, cry-out-to-the-world, stop-your-heart, and leave-'em-wanting-more endings. The endings that follow contain elements of poetry and craft, just as beginnings do.

I want to remember the expectant soldier as a person with a name, but I have come to accept that I cannot. I remember instead the triage room. I recall the general who placed his hand on a young man. And I see the drifting once again—the fading of a soldier back into the womb from which he was born into life. I see him loved. He is a soldier. Wounded. Triaged. Expectant. (2013, 131)

—Jon Kerstetter, "Triage"

Hector prances along the street Buster skulked, greeting neighbors and strangers and men in hats and toddlers in snowsuits. He loves everyone, and everyone loves him. I often think of Buster, and it breaks my heart. People say, "You did everything you could." But did we? What about phenobarbital, even though every vet recommended against it? What about the autism suit? We should have moved to the country or sent him to the man in San Diego who leads a pack of dogs through the hills. What *about* the pet psychic? Then Hector pounces on an empty forty-ounce Budweiser can, almost as big as he is, and carries it home proudly. He kisses babies like a politician. He comes in peace. (2005, 104)

—Cathleen Schine, "Dog Trouble"

And though the debate she sparked about Asian American life has been of questionable value, we will need more people with the same kind of defiance, willing to push themselves into the spotlight and to make some noise, to beat people up, to seduce women, to make mistakes, to become entrepreneurs, to stop doggedly pursuing official paper emblems attesting to their worthiness, to stop thinking those scraps of paper will secure anyone's happiness, and to dare to be interesting. (2012, 295)

—Wesley Yang, "Paper Tigers"

NAMING CRAFT IN ESSAY

What Writers Learn from Reading Essays

- There is a wide diversity in essay topics.
- Essays circle around an idea, object, text, or person.
- Essays most often use the first person and present tense, creating a conversational tone.
- Each has its own distinctive voice (snarky, poetic, emotional, pensive, elegant, whiny).
- They contain a multiplicity of voices and perspectives.
- They use quotations from multiple texts and overheard utterances.
- Essays ask questions that may or may not be answered in the text.
- They have a logical, organic structure determined by content, not a formula.
- They experiment with language (multilingual, casual, formal, imagistic).
- They have striking beginnings and endings.
- They often include narrative elements (dialogue, setting, action).
- Essays often incorporate forms of evidence, including observations, quotes, anecdotes, and facts.

Since Eva went off to college, I find it hard not to think of our home as a chrysalis from which the butterfly has flown. I miss my daughter. The rug bristles with the absence of her dancing feet. The windows glint with the history of her looking. Water rings on the sills recall where her teacup should be. The air lacks a sweet buzz.

Unlike a butterfly, a daughter blessedly returns now and again, as Eva comes home soon for summer vacation. Ruth and I have been preparing the house to receive her. Before leaving in August, Eva bet me that I would not have finished remodeling the sun porch by the time of her return in May. I stole hours to work on it all autumn and winter. Now I must go and put on the last coat of varnish, so that, when she enters, the room will shine. (1993, 35)

—Scott Russell Sanders, "House and Home"

Finding Essays for the Classroom

As I explained earlier in the chapter, the content of an essay may be more or less adult, but the crafting features writers use are the same (though they be more or less complex). As you prepare for reading immersion, you'll need to consider the age and maturity of your students and select essays with them in mind. Finding appropriate mentor essays for younger students or less experienced writers has been, in fact, the greatest challenge I've met in teaching essay. To address that challenge, I reached out to some of my favorite writer friends—people you no doubt know and love—for what excites me most about this whole project: at the end of this book, you will find a set of eleven original essays written with young readers in mind.

Essays Written for Adults

Besides the bonus gift set of essays, let me offer a few additional ideas for finding mentor texts for your students. First, as you begin to read essays more widely, you will see that many of those written for adults are perfectly appropriate for young people. And if the topic is appropriate but the text seems too long, consider using just an excerpt.

The two essays included in Chapter 1, for example, have been used successfully with students in eighth through twelfth grades (in fact, they've blown students' minds). In "Joyas Voladoras," Kerri Ward's tenth graders in San Antonio, Texas, took note of "racecar hearts," the spelling of "waaaay," the "piercing, yearning tongue," and the fact that the first paragraph is one loooooong sentence. They were struck by how Doyle plays with the idea of hearts, both physical and emotional. Finally, one young man made all the observing teachers in the room tear up when he noted, in a hushed voice, "I love that last sentence, the way it names one thing after another, and another. It's heartbreaking."

Oh yes, it is.

Picture Books

For students who may find the complexity of some essays too challenging, consider using picture books (and occasionally excerpts from short stories and novels) that sound expository, like journey-of-thinking essays. You can type up a picture book text so it looks like a regular essay and make copies for students to read like writers. Here are a few excerpts from books I've used with young students (see the Appendix for more). As you read them, notice the essayistic quality they each have in common:

From *The Way to Start a Day*
by Byrd Baylor (1978)

High on a mesa edge in Arizona they were holding a baby toward the sun. They were speaking the child's new name so the sun would hear and know that child. It had to be a sunrise. And it had to be that first sudden moment. That's when all the power of life is in the sky.

From *Matilda* (opening paragraphs)
by Roald Dahl (1988)

It's a funny thing about mothers and fathers. Even when their own child is the most disgusting little blister you could ever imagine, they still think that he or she is wonderful.

Some parents go further. They become so blinded by adoration they manage to convince themselves their child has qualities of genius.

Well, there is nothing very wrong with all this. It's the way of the world. It is only when the parents begin telling *us* about the brilliance of their own revolting offspring, that we start shouting, "Bring us a basin! We're going to be sick!"

From *I Have the Right to Be a Child*
by Alain Serres (2012)

I have the right to all these rights just because I am a child, especially if I live in one of the 193 states in the world that have agreed to . . . The Rights of the Child. When will all children everywhere really have their rights respected? Tomorrow? The day after tomorrow? In twenty years?

FROM *APPALACHIA: THE VOICES OF SLEEPING BIRDS*
by Cynthia Rylant (1991)

There will be a lot of singing in that church and maybe some crying for joy and after the service people will linger in the yard, talking, till the women say it's time to eat, and they will go home and sit around a table spread with potatoes and beans and meat and good hot coffee or sweet iced tea and they will eat until they can eat no more except for the piece of lemon pound cake they saved some room for.

FROM *A QUIET PLACE*
by Douglas Wood (2002)

You could look by the sea on a beach in the early morning fog. Your footprints are the first of the day. The waves are roaring, and the gulls are crying, but it doesn't seem noisy. And you can just be an explorer discovering a lost continent. The beach could be your quiet place. But if the beach is not your cup of tea . . .

Magazines and E-zines for Children

Occasionally, short essays appear in magazines for young people. As a resource, magazines are a bit tricky because most of the content in children's magazines falls into categories I would call feature articles, advice columns, how-tos, and other types of informational text. Also, magazines can feel ancient to many kids, so I prefer online sources, blogs, literary journals, and e-zines, for essays for young people. The Appendix includes a list of digital resources.

Public Radio

Very often, the pieces read aloud by different contributors on public radio are essays and are quite accessible. If you hear a good essay possibility on your drive home, look it up on the station's website; you can almost always find the written text online. Some teachers have used pieces from NPR's *This I Believe* series, which I adore, but which can sound formulaic if all students respond to "This I believe" as a kind of writing prompt. I've seen lesson plans on the Internet that turn the idea of this essay into a step-by-step formula, thereby reducing any possibility for original, organic structures. Since some students do find inspiration in these emotional, spiritual-sounding pieces, you might consider including just a few examples you like and that fit your criteria in your pile of mentor texts.

As you and your students pay close attention to meanings, craft details, and structures during reading immersion, you'll be fulfilling the recommendations of state and national standards currently in circulation around the country. The difference is, of course, that you will be reading as *writers*, knowing that soon enough, you'll be writing essays that look and sound something like the essays you're discussing. Moving from reading to writing is the subject of the next part of this book.

4

LIVING LIKE
AN ESSAYIST

Art is an act of total attention.

—Dorothea Lange, photographer

*The material is the world itself, which,
so far, keeps on keeping on.*

—Annie Dillard, *Best American Essays 1988*

Try to be one of the people on whom nothing is lost.

—Henry James

ow that your students have spent several days poring over mentor texts, noticing the features, voices, and variety of structures in
published essays, they are ready to become essayists themselves. If
your mentor texts contained evocative, relatable, and contemporary
examples, I can bet that many of your students are brimming over with ideas. Spending time reading before writing often has that effect: it inspires writers to want to
respond—to send their own voices into the world. Perhaps you had students write
words or phrases in their writer's notebooks to remind them of their ideas, or you
left five minutes at the end of your writing time for kids to work on a list of ideas
in their notebooks.

But now, it is officially time to begin generating ideas for essays. Your students
will spend the next several days trying out ideas for essays, creating lists, paragraphs,

sketches, mind maps, and full-page entries. They will learn habits of mind and ways of living in the world like essayists. You can begin by asking students to think about what they love, what haunts them, what they want to make better about the world, and what pulls their attention like a bee to a flower, for those are the sources of great essay writing.

 ## Habits of Mind and Living

If I had to describe the type of person who prefers to write essays, I might offer adjectives like *curious, pensive, amused, critical, passionate,* and *open-minded.* While these descriptors easily fit writers and artists of all kinds, as well as millions of people who do not write down their musings, they feel particularly apt for someone who wants to think on the page in an essay.

There is currently a cool ad campaign for bringing awareness and funding support to public libraries, which are at risk of extinction. The website shows gorgeous photographic portraits of people, famous and not, with captions that say things like "I geek worms" and "I geek hip-hop." The formerly bullying noun *geek* has morphed into a positive verb for people who are living life to the fullest! The ad copy asks, "What do you geek? Everyone has something they are passionate about— something they geek. Maybe you geek football or hip-hop. Maybe you are passionate about organic gardening, classic movies, or volunteering. Or maybe you just geek the weather" (http://geekthelibrary.org). The ad proposes that public libraries are the source for any and all information a person could ever want, and they are especially crucial for the millions of Americans who do not have other ways to access resources. "For many," the copy states, "the library is not a luxury, it is a necessity."

When I first saw the display in one of my favorite writing spots, my local public library, I grabbed a few brochures to share, and I also had the idea that, yes, this word could describe an essayist—someone who *geeks* things. If some of my favorite essayists had their faces on this website, the taglines might read, "I geek the unseen and bizarre" and "I geek social justice." *Geeking,* I decided, is a habit of looking at the world, being addicted to it, and wanting to share this passion with others through essay. But first, there must come a habit of recording and reflecting as the writer reads, watches, listens, and lives in the world. All your efforts in this phase of an essay study are meant to help students geek the topics and ideas that matter to them. And the perfect place for note taking, thinking, and geeking is a writer's notebook.

The Writer's Notebook: A Storage Room, Workbench, and Think Tank

Donald Murray describes writing as a process of "prevision, vision, and revision" (2009a, 141), and he suggests that in classrooms, we have spent so much time on the revision, or what a piece of writing is supposed to be in the end, that we have lost the initial discovery work that many writers claim is critical and that may be, in fact, the main reason they write. If we spend more time on *prevision*, then "students will have a greater opportunity . . . to discover an area they want to explore and more time to explore it" (141).

Essayists—in fact, writers of all genres—do much of this prevision work in their heads. Many speak of trancelike moods, when they are doing something else, say, chopping vegetables or vacuuming out the car, and all the while they are composing inside their minds. Writers speak of hearing voices and of creating sentences—even paragraphs—as they go about their daily business. During the revision process, this mind work can be even more intense because now they have pages of a manuscript that need reworking, so the internal dialogue ramps up to a fevered pitch.

Experienced writers can do much of this work inside their heads because over time they have discovered a process that works. And they write in their minds for practical purposes: they have jobs to perform, people and homes to care for, and they simply cannot sit in front of computers twenty-four hours a day. Our students, on the other hand, have less experience with this process. They have trouble developing ideas as mind work because the process is too abstract. In our classrooms, we can create experiences that enable kids to literally see and touch the process of idea generating as it unfolds before them. The writer's notebook works supremely well for this—a tangible version of a mind that contemplates, sparks connections, remembers, and changes course.

Many writers keep a notebook as a catchall place to list, practice, comment, question, observe, and argue—basically, to think on the page, or "speak on the page," as Peter Elbow has come to describe what is necessary to find one's way to meaning (2012, 139). A notebook is a place to put down a word, any word, and keep writing from there, without direction, *Expecting the Unexpected*, as Donald Murray aptly titled one of his books (1989). The writer uses the pages for herself for capturing ideas, thinking and planning, even for purposes of living a better life. What fills those pages may or may not appear in a story, poem, article, or novel. Much of it can look dashed-off and chaotic. But for writers, this thinking space feels like freedom from rules, conventions, and especially critique or evaluation—a necessary latitude for the act of creating and composing.

For any kind of writing, but especially for nonfiction genres, the notebook is also the perfect tool for gathering material, which is the crucial *step one* in the process of creating, according to James Webb Young, who in 1940 published his famous advice to young people wanting to make it big in the advertising world (this was pre–*Mad Men*!). Young claimed that ideas are merely new combinations of old ideas, and that in order to increase our capacity for idea making (or really, to produce anything, even a car), we must go through a process or technique. The technique begins with the gathering of "raw material." Young thinks that inexperienced artists ignore this critical first step because it's not the fun and sexy (my word) part of the process. "The time that ought to be spent in material gathering is spent in wool gathering," Young writes. "Instead of working systematically at the job of gathering raw material we sit around hoping for inspiration to strike us" (1940, 14).

For writers, gathering raw material requires being open to anything and everything in the world: the colors, sounds, smells, yearnings, and irritations that strike them as they move through their days. This material might include responses to the obsessive reading most writers do, general facts, or thinking, planning, and research toward a specific project. In a notebook, it looks like lists, outlines, sketches, single-sentence paragraphs, or long chunks of uninterrupted text. Gathering material is process-oriented, not product-driven, and it's a step of the writing life and process that cannot be left behind.

Today, writers can choose to type into digital notebooks on their computers and tablets, but the substance looks similar (if perhaps easier to read!) to that in the handwritten versions. In classrooms, we can make decisions, based on accessibility and manageability of paper notebooks versus laptops or tablets, but we need to provide our students with some kind of space to write to think. I hope you will consider asking students to find themselves a fabulous notebook or providing one for them, if your students aren't already using one. I prefer the seriousness and durability of a hardback notebook: the good old marbleized composition notebook works well, and now it comes in dozens of cover designs and colors.

In the immersion phase of an essay study, students can use their notebooks as a place to respond, record favorite authors and quotes, and note the features of essay. As students move closer to writing their own essays, however, their notebooks will take on new significance as they become engaged in the content that will eventually develop into essays. In notebooks, students will list, think about, and try out multiple topics and ideas for their essays. Many call this the generating part of the writing process, though the word *generating* implies that the mind is empty, the notebook is empty, and now it's time to invent ideas. However, if we invite students to live their lives as essayists, they won't be generating so much as *capturing* the fountain of thoughts that flows all day and even in dreams at night. They'll need our help to make that transformation from coming up with an idea "because it's school and I have

A Brief Note About Moving from Notebooks to Essays

With its features of free-flowing, multifaceted text, notebook writing lends itself magnificently to essay writing. Often, kids' notebook writing has a richer voice than the text of their drafts, when they are paying more attention to form and language conventions than meaning. The safety net of notebook writing tends to give students courage to open their hearts and minds to the page. And, as Ken Macrorie notes, "when a person is bearing down hard as he can to tell truths, great things happen. His sentences pick up rhythms. He slides in to a style that fits his subject. One true, telling detail leads to another" (in Romano 1987, 13).

To be clear, essays have been taken through the process of drafting, multiple revisions, and edits; they are more formal, focused, and attendant to the needs and expectations of external readers. But since the sound of thinking on the page can be similar in notebooks and in published essays, I have found that for students, the transition from notebook to essay draft is easier than moving to other genres, simply because the tone and timbre of the writing are similar.

to write this essay thing" to living like essayists who *must* write down the flow of life before it escapes the mind and memory. As teachers we can reinforce this notion when we

- write often in our own notebooks and share them with students;

- guard thinking spaces for students by giving them enough class time to work in their notebooks and not feel continually rushed toward final products; and

- place the notebooks center stage, use them throughout the process, refer to them often, and ask students to share from what they've written with partners, small groups, or the whole class.

The Contents of an Essayist's Notebook

A sensible way to help students transition from the days spent reading published essays to filling notebooks with their own material is to invite them to think about what they would find if they looked inside the notebook of an essayist. What does someone who writes essays *need* in a notebook? Your students will have recently read a great collection of essays, so the timing is right to have them think about this question.

You might begin by imagining the kinds of notebook work writers of different genres are likely to do. Consider the authors your students know and love, and then think together about what you might find inside their writer's notebooks. Ask, for example, "What kind of entries might Gary Soto have had in his writer's notebook as he worked on his short story collection *Baseball in April*?" Perhaps he had memories of his childhood, character sketches, plot possibilities, maps of streets in Fresno, California. Or you might ask, "How do you think Naomi Shihab Nye walks through her neighborhood as a poet? What does she pay attention to?" Perhaps she stops to capture sounds, bits of beauty, or snippets of conversation. You're not looking for correct answers to these questions, of course, for you actually have no idea what was in Soto's notebook, or if he even *had* a notebook! The point of these questions is to help frame a discussion about how different writers move through the world, what they pay attention to, and where they can record their ideas and observations to use again and again.

In contrast to poetry and fiction, you might ask these same questions about familiar nonfiction writers like David Macaulay, Vaunda Micheaux Nelson, Andrea Davis Pinkney, or Eric Schlosser (choose from writers your students know). The responses will be different because a nonfiction writer needs different material from what a short story writer or a poet needs. Students will likely imagine that nonfiction writers need more research-based writing, facts from primary sources, interviews, and close observations of the physical world.

The kind of writing authors plan to do impacts how they live in the world, what they pay attention to, and what material they gather in their notebooks. You can follow this line of thinking right back to the essays you've been reading. What might these essayists have had in their notebooks? Students can generate lists of the kinds of entries they imagine they might find and refer to specific places in an essay that made them think of a particular kind of notebook entry. For his extensive list of facts about hummingbirds in "Joyas Voladoras," for instance, Brian Doyle surely kept a notebook beside him as he scoured reference books or the Internet for facts. Perhaps he observed hummers at feeders outside his writing space.

For his essay "Pride," it seems as if Gilb sat on a bench in front of a convenience store and observed people working, people filling cars with gas, and families buying things. Perhaps he listened and scribbled down the dialogue he overheard. Maybe he put the word *pride* in the center of a web and made connections to that word coming out like wheel spokes: *love, hard work, family, land, high school graduation, pretty dress*. Being specific in guessing about the notebook work of mentor authors will go a long way toward helping students imagine how randomly collected ideas grow into powerful essays.

You don't want to leave a conversation like this without helping students imagine what difference it can make for them as writers of essays. Ask your students how they might move through the day differently in order to record it. How might they *look* differently, at their own lives and memories, and at the natural world spinning around them, and invite the world to give up its riches? Invite kids to live open to possibilities, to pay total attention, even when they are not sitting at desks. Let's consider this invitation as we move forward and explore habits of mind, thinking tools, and activities students can use to generate essay ideas in their writer's notebooks.

Upcycled Material from the Writer's Notebook

In the quest for a sustainable earth, a movement is afoot to upcycle products and objects. Beyond recycling, which uses a great deal of energy and creates its own kinds of waste, upcycling imagines new uses for an object, like planting flowers in a cast-off bathtub, for instance. Upcycling is a useful idea for writers as well. Writers can upcycle old material and never feel empty of ideas. If your students have already been keeping writer's notebooks or something similar, consider having them look back through previous entries, even ones that lean more toward fiction or poetry, to find ideas that point toward essay; in other words, look for entries that sound like thinking, observing, and questioning the world. I think this concept is particularly important for young and unpracticed writers, who often believe that every piece of writing must be new and shiny, so you might consider offering upcycling as a first move toward finding ideas for essays.

Almost any memory, emotion, or observation might lend itself to essay-worthy thinking, but students may not realize this at first. You will likely need to demonstrate how to look at an old notebook entry and consider it as essay material. Skim through your own notebook and put sticky notes on places where you think you could upcycle the material into essay. Then you'll want to choose one of the entries you've marked and try writing to think about it so it leans toward essay. Finally, as you share both the original entry and the new writing with your students, talk about the qualities of essay students see in your new thinking about the topic. To help you imagine this process, here's an example from my own teaching.

In a demonstration lesson with a group of seventh graders, I showed some of my writing from several notebooks about the Rio Grande Gorge, near Taos, New Mexico. I've been in love with this place since I was a little girl, growing up in New Mexico, and I write about it often. I shared some lines from a poem draft: "Black basalt boulders / dark ships riding foam of sage and wheatgrass." I also read some nonfiction bits about the geology and the flora and fauna of the place, and even tried a bit of a short story about a white-water rafting trip. I explained how as I reread these old notebook entries, it got me thinking about the fact that President Obama had recently created a new national monument of the gorge, and this gave me an idea for a potential essay. I showed students some new writing-to-think about the gorge so they could see what this kind of writing looks like, long before it gets drafted, revised, and edited:

As he enters the "twilight" of his two terms in office, it seems that President Obama pulls surprises left and right! Well, they're surprises to me anyway, which might just mean I haven't been reading the news enough. The president has created the Rio del Norte National Monument in my favorite place: Taos, New Mexico. As a national monument, the Rio Grande River Gorge will be forever protected by federal laws. No apartment buildings along its rim, no vacation mansions, no strip malls. This gives me hope for the future of this land I love. I wonder why as a nation we have to make laws to protect our most important, magnificent natural places, when just down the road from the gorge there is Taos Pueblo, where native people have been living continuously for, I think, over one thousand years? I mean they don't need a federal law to tell them not to hurt or destroy their home! I have read that there are internal rules, or not really rules, but more like ancient ways of thinking that govern what people can and cannot do to their land. Is that different from or similar to federal laws? What is a law anyway? What makes a person, an individual person, follow or respect a law and another person break that law? And are there people living in the pueblo who do not follow whatever internal rules the group has made? What happens if they don't follow the rules?

As we talked about the new, upcycled entry I'd written, students considered the qualities that made it sound essay-like already:

- There are parts where I seem doubtful of the facts. I reminded students that this is just some thinking in my notebook. If I decided to make an essay out of it, I could research the facts to get them right, or I could even decide to write phrases like "I don't know" and "I have heard" in the final draft.

- The writing takes a turn away from its main topic—from the gorge to the history of Native Americans living in the area, to wondering what laws mean. This is what essays do: one idea begets another idea.

- I ask questions and don't answer them. Yes! That's what makes it sound *essayistic*. I may never know the answers; I just feel the need to ask the questions.

Interestingly, in this particular discussion, one student noted that the way I moved from talking about the Rio Grande River Gorge to laws and politics reminded him of an essay we read by Barbara Kingsolver about the Grand Canyon, "Saying Grace." Well, that makes sense, since Kingsolver is one of my favorite essayists and a mentor to my writing.

After you have demonstrated for your students how an existing entry can lead to an idea for an essay, they will be ready to search through their notebooks for essay-worthy material. Since they've only seen the one idea, however, you might consider showing them a list of other essays you could make from the entries you marked with sticky notes when you reread your notebook. Here's a list I made from different entries in one of my old notebooks:

- Do animals have emotions anything like human emotions?

- Hospitals do not feel like places to heal and get well.

- Stores play music in the background to make people feel good about shopping and want to buy things. Hmm . . . maybe we could play music in the halls of schools and in our classrooms for similar reasons.

- Why do people love games? (I do not.)

- Sometimes I find it hard to teach college students when I remind myself that they might carry guns in their backpacks. Legally.

Young people notice, and you might as well, the sometimes cranky nature of my essay topics. Indeed, I think that places of irritation, anger, and dissatisfaction can make terrific subjects because they have a lot of heat for writers. After all, once we claim we love chocolate ice cream and give a reason why, there just isn't much more of interest to say!

If you have worked with students on writing essays in the past, you might also share lists of ideas they've made when they searched through their notebooks for ideas to upcycle. Here's a short list of essay ideas my former fourth- and fifth-grade students found from rereading their notebooks:

- Hatred is stronger than love. (From an earlier memoir entry about a difficult family relationship)

- How can women leave their own children in other countries to take care of children in the United States? (From an entry about the student's after-school caretaker)

- When I watch just one TV show at a time I think I am missing out on everything else. I wish I had three TVs next to each other like circus rings. (From an entry about going to the circus on Saturday night)

- No one else has a runaway mother. I can't talk to anyone. Everyone else has a mother. (From a poem in a student's notebook)

If you decide to include upcycling as early notebook work in your essay study, ask students to reread their notebooks and begin a list called "Essay Ideas" on a clean page. They won't begin working on their ideas just yet; the point is to look for the upcycling potential in their own material and continue adding to this list over time.

Essay Eyeglasses: A New Way to View the World

One of my favorite quotes for writing comes from the poet and magnificent writing teacher William Stafford. He says, "When I began to try to write things, I felt this richness. One thing would lead to another; the world would give and give" (1986, 25). The idea that the world gives and gives feels so true to me as a writer. Living like an essayist means being ready for subjects and ideas to appear, expecting the world to keep giving as long as a writer keeps looking and listening. I often describe this to students as a concrete act, like putting on "essay eyeglasses" or having "essay eyes and ears" to be ever alert to writing possibilities. When I've got my essay eyeglasses on, suddenly everything becomes an essay-worthy idea. I take a long walk or move through an airport or lie on my couch watching birds at the feeder outside my study window, and whole sentences that sing essay float into my mind.

Another magnificent writing teacher, Dorothea Brande, advises to "turn yourself into a stranger in your own streets" of a neighborhood or town. She suggests seeing the streets as if in a "strange town or a strange country when you first enter it," and to "tell yourself that for fifteen minutes you will notice and tell yourself about every single thing that your eyes rest on" (1934, 115).

Many writers describe travel to new places as the supreme idea-generating or research-gathering activity. When we travel, we are hyperalert to experiences, no longer sleepwalking through our usual routines, our minds on myriad gripes and worries, and we take joy in the visceral wealth immediately in front of us. While most young people do not have control over their ability to travel, we can help them see that any movement—from one classroom to the next, or to the cafeteria; from this neighborhood or city; from this store or that place of worship—can be seen as an adventure to record in our notebooks, if we use our essay eyeglasses and essay ears to find it. True, it might mean turning off the electronic devices for a bit and turning on curiosity and appreciation for the ways people talk, dress, and move, or the features of buildings, or the sounds and smells in the air.

The fact is, writers of every genre get some of their best ideas when they are away from their desks, and your students will too. I help students see potential in the world by showing them what essay-worthy ideas look and sound like to a writer, and for this I often use my own notebook writing. Here are some examples of thoughts and observations I jotted down in my notebook over the last week. As you read them, notice how they are leaning toward essay already, and how they obviously occurred to me in the course of ordinary days.

Adults never stop staring in the direction the bus, train, or subway comes when they are waiting impatiently, even though they should know by now, shouldn't they, that staring angrily in the direction doesn't make the train come any faster?

When people are annoyed and impatient, they always have ideas about how things could be better managed. So far, the couple behind me waiting for coffee has come up with six ways this shop could reorganize to avoid long lines. Ex: "They should have 2 lines—1 for regular coffee and 1 for the special drinks. Like, why should I have to wait so long just for a Venti Blonde?"

Sometimes I think life is simply a loose thread of chance circumstances and luck. When I wonder how did this particular person get where she is and that person did not, the answer seems to be sheer luck—good or bad. Born in this country, not that country. Born to this family, not a different family; in this body and skin, not that body. Turned down this street instead of the usual street. Took the place of someone who got sick, etc. Most people would argue with me about this, tell me how hard so-and-so worked to get what she has, what sacrifices, but if you break it down, step by step, year by year, if you trace precisely what someone gets or someone else loses, even though she is very good and works so hard, it looks like luckity luck, luck, the good and the bad kind. Nothing just or right about it.

Why do people hate grackles [a type of blackbird] so much? What makes some birds, like bald eagles, hummingbirds, and parrots, the darlings of the bird world, and others like grackles and pigeons just get trash talk about them?

· 75 ·

These are simply little observations, questions, and thoughts about the world that I may or may not decide to explore in a longer piece. Feel free to share these with your students as models, or better yet, write your own similar "things I think about and observe as I stand in the grocery checkout line, or mow my lawn, or sit on the highway in rush-hour traffic." Once students have taken their notebooks home, looked at the world through essay eyeglasses, and written down what strikes them, you can share their entries and grow everyone's understanding of what it means to find essay ideas all around them.

 ## Tools and Activities for Generating Essay Topics and Ideas

The concept of writing-to-think—sometimes called *freewriting*—will be abstract for many students, just as it is for many adults who do not keep a daily writing practice and who perhaps composed analyses and reports in school with little or no prewriting, sometimes the night before the papers were due. (Remember?) You will need to teach students the power of freewriting to strengthen the quality of their prose. In the following sections I offer several activities for doing this kind of writing in notebooks, as well as some examples you can share with your students. But first, to set the stage for those activities, let's think about the nature of freewriting itself.

Peter Elbow, whose book *Writing with Power* (1981) taught me about the practice of freewriting when I was studying writing in college, has recently grown his thinking in a fascinating tome called *Vernacular Eloquence* (2012). Elbow pushes on the freewriting idea even more to find its similarities with oral speech, and to consider it "speaking onto the page" (311). I love this idea for kids of all ages who, for whatever reasons, find talking so much easier than writing. It makes sense: people learn to talk in infancy and they do it all day (sometimes even in sleep!). Elbow assures us that writing is different from speaking, ultimately, as it is more formal, fixed, and text-based, but in the process of generating ideas, talking out their writing can help students *hear* their thoughts in order to write them down. In fact, as Elbow argues eloquently throughout his book, kids' oral language can be much more clear and sensible than their literate text. Writing makes many people, adults included, overreach, obfuscate, and turn perfectly reasonable words into ugly, multisyllabic verbiage as they attempt to write like school.

Now, before the teacher in you has heart palpitations over the idea of students writing like they talk, filling pages with "I dunnos" and "OMGs," remember this is notebook writing and therefore is predraft writing. Also, I have found that most young writers understand that when a thought leaves their brain and travels through the pen to paper or keyboard to screen, it sounds differently than when they are talking with a friend on the bus. Perhaps it is the result of years of reading literate texts or just because it's school, but most kids do not purposely produce unconventional text. And even if their freewriting needs significant editing before the final draft, the payoff for that extra work is that students elaborate more when they become as comfortable thinking on paper as they are thinking out loud.

Freewriting is useful for developing ideas in any genre, but it's particularly helpful with essay because the freewriting itself almost sounds like some published essays. If your students have limited experience in writing to think on paper, you will need to demonstrate the process of freewriting and name the intentions behind it as you do.

Ken Macrorie, the college composition professor who invented freewriting, invites students to follow these four easy steps (I have taken the liberty to number them):

1. For twelve minutes, write as fast as you can whatever comes to mind.

2. Don't worry about spelling, punctuation, or grammar.

3. Don't stop. If at any point, you can't think of what to write, look in front of you—at the wall, window, ceiling, whatever—and start describing what you see.

4. Say to yourself, "What goes down here is going to be truth of some kind, nothing phony, nothing designed to make me look good." (1984, 6)

I am a huge fan of step four, and I worry that without it, we risk pages of half-hearted drivel. Telling truths does not mean letting it all hang out, Jerry Springer–style; it simply asks for a willingness to lift the fog of half-truths and make an attempt to say what we truly think and feel. Macrorie says it's easier for him sometimes if he closes his eyes while he writes and says to himself, "Nothing but truths," opening his eyes only when he comes to the end of a sentence. "It's frightening to let truth take over, but remember—the great advantage of writing . . . is that when you've put the words down, you can edit them, censor them, or throw them out before showing them to anyone else—if you feel the need" (1984, 33).

Topics Students Frequently Essay About

The following is a sampling of subjects that students often write about (when they can choose their own topics!).

Concrete Objects and Concepts		
music	games	social media
divorce	friends	death
sports	family	money
adoption	the future	makeup
jobs	pets	movies
popularity	food	illness
toys/electronics	science	race
dating	identity	neighborhood
gender	cars	freedom (and restraint)

These are topics that students love to think, write, and grow big ideas about. Any one of these could also be sliced thinner; for instance, *sports* might be narrowed to *soccer* or might adopt a stance like *who has or does not have access to soccer training*.

Emotions		
desire	disgust	anger
pleasure	avoidance	pain
grief	loneliness	worry
boredom	fear	jealousy

These are emotions that students choose to grow ideas about, using specific events, observations, and personal stories to flesh out the concept or idea of a particular strong feeling.

Freewriting in Short Bursts

With all the work you've done so far reading essays and thinking about how essayists keep notebooks, some of your students will have found and settled on topics, and they may indeed write about those ideas. Other students will have several topics in mind and may be struggling to settle on just one. A few others, despite your fabulous minilessons, your encouragement, and the help of peers, will claim they still don't know what to write about. But to push the thinking of all your students, keep asking for more.

I purposefully call these exercises "try-its" (my own version of Montaigne's *essais*) because I do ask all students to try them for five to ten minutes of writing time. Sometimes I spread them over days, one try-it per day. Other times I might offer three or four during a single forty-minute period to jump-start students' thinking. After time is up for each try-it, I tell students they can continue with that bit of writing if it feels fruitful, or they can find another topic to think and write about for the rest of the writing time (usually another fifteen or twenty minutes). I suggest that you write in your notebook along with your students for the first few minutes because you will then have examples of what this work looks like to share with individuals in writing conferences or with your whole class in minilessons.

Make a list

1. Begin by making a long list of words, phrases, and topics you know or wonder about: special people, memories, places, books, movies, TV shows, games, music, animals, sports, art, food, clothing. (Variations or extensions on lists: things that make you angry; things that make you sad; things that need to change; things you wish you had said or not said; things other people have said to you; things you will never, ever write about!)

2. Circle, star, or underline favorite items from your list.

3. Choose one of your circled items and talk to a partner about it for five minutes.

4. Now write about that same item for ten minutes.

(Adapted from Newkirk 1986b, 55)

Make a visual list

Thinking and generating ideas do not always need to be done with words; they can be visual. Students might make sketch lists of places, objects, animals, games. Or they might take photographs of their favorite places, home, bedroom, family members, friends, and special objects. They can print and paste them into their notebooks (old school) or post them on a Facebook or Instagram account, as Stacey Shubitz at the *Two Writing Teachers* blog suggests, in her 2013 post titled "Instagram Can Help Treat Writers' Block," as a visual guide to things that matter to them and that will inspire them to write to think.

Create a mind map

1. Put one topic from your list into a circle. Think of more ideas about that topic and put those in circles, with lines connecting them to the main topic. The connecting circles can branch out into smaller, baby circles, for as long as you can think and make connections.

2. If you don't like circles, try a tree, with the main topic in the trunk, connecting ideas in the branches, and subtopics in leaves attached to the branches. Or create a time line of an item from your list, if it lends itself to a chronology.

3. Now, take one of the ideas, large or small, from your visual map and free-write about it for ten minutes. Then take another idea and do the same.

Write a two-minute blast

I know I said that try-its last five to ten minutes, but this is a variation I call the *two-minute blast*. The *total* will still be ten minutes, but there will be four or five different attacks on the writing. The point here is to see what you can push out in the shortest time, almost without thinking. This works well, for instance, to give little stabs at five different ideas for a topic, or five different titles, or five different beginnings to a piece. I've used it with older students and adults as a way to unearth truths. Let me demonstrate that particular twist so you can see how it works.

1. Begin with a statement that seems obvious, unarguable.

> I love my cat

2. For the next two minutes, don't stop—write as much as possible about why.

> His fur is thick, luxurious, soft as a Gund teddy bear. His fur is lush, charcoal gray, my favorite color. He sleeps with me, curled inside the bend of my legs when I sleep on my side. He is attached to me, and when I come home from a long trip, I pick him up and hold him against my chest, his paws around my neck, like a baby. He is the baby I will never have.

You see how I'm already getting to something deeper, and it's only the first stab?

3. For another two minutes, say what bothers you about your original statement. Dig for deeper truths. Perhaps argue with the original statement.

> My cat is a pain in the you-know-what. He has insistent hungers—for food, warmth, attention—which he announces with loud bellows. He tries to escape out every open door or slightly cracked window. I spend a small fortune on pet-sitting when Randy and I travel. I feed him grain-free wet food to keep his urinary tract healthy because I want this cat to live forever. He must live forever. I cannot stand the idea of him dying. I will leave town when he is close to death because I refuse to put myself through that. I've been through that grief before with Jazz (my beloved soul-mate cat), and that's why I know I don't want to do it again. Why does a cat matter so much? I've been like this since I was 6 years old, when my pets filled that cavernous ache for love. If the death of my pets (dogs too) is so hard for me, how will I ever stand the illness and death of the human beings I love?

See what happens? Indeed, I am practiced and fairly fearless at writing to truth, and I can get there quickly. My unpracticed students do not go there so easily, and some of them never feel brave enough to write from the heart about what is meaningful and significant to them. As teachers, we have to show our students our own writing toward truth so they feel invited to try.

Ask twenty questions

Kids love to make lists and they usually love to ask questions, so this try-it can be quite liberating for some. Do this one with your students, modeling a wide variety of questions about how things are made or how they work, about emotions, science concepts, or moments from history. Write the questions, about anything and everything, without expectation of answers right now. In this generating phase, the questions are meant simply to stimulate topics and ideas.

Eliciting *twenty* questions might be hard for some kids to accomplish, and some questions might venture into wacky land, but the idea is to push past the boundaries of thinking. I've had students ask the deepest questions, about what happens after we die, and about what God looks like, and I've had students ask things like, "How much does Mickey Mouse actually weigh?" In fact, a question like that last one could lead a good essayist into interesting territory, and I might refer this student to a fun essay by John Updike called "The Mystery of Mickey" (1992).

Create a T-chart

I don't know when I first heard about T-charts, or double-column notebook entries, or who invented this remarkable thinking tool, but as soon as I learned about it, I taught my students how to do it and invited them to use T-charts all day long, in every subject area.

On the left side, you can put any fact, quote, problem, observation, concept, sketch—any object to be looked at and to reflect upon. On the right side, you can ask questions, argue, define, make a connection, interpret, or comment on the item to the left in some way. It makes thinking and reflecting concrete, and the visual T-chart helps many people.

Freewriting in Longer Stretches

While listing and writing in little ten-minute jots can help jump-start most minds and weave safety nets for apprehensive writers, ultimately, students will need to write for longer periods, building stamina and confidence in their ability to write *more* about one thing, to sustain an idea across multiple pages in an essay. Besides the fluency this practice can build, writing for an extended period of time is also the only way for a young writer to discover "how little he knows of what he thought he knew; how much he knows that he didn't know he knew" (Murray 1982, 6).

Words beget words, and when we commit them to paper, we can reread them, perhaps out loud, hearing them in our eyes and ears, letting the way they knock into each other make mental sparks fly. Murray says a writer "sees language evolving and working on his page," and this is his tool. He uses language to "lead him to understanding" (1982, 9). Murray compares this tool of language to a painter's tool of color. "The painter doesn't paint colors he has seen, he uses color on the canvas to see" (9). And so, the more words on the page, the more writers will be led to find what it is they want to say, and what they mean.

The following list of try-its with examples lend themselves to longer patches of writing. I call these "begin here" try-its because the point of each one is to begin somewhere and keep writing. Since these exercises come dangerously close to writing prompts (which can set up dependency), you'll want to use them sparingly. Offer them as a series of invitations, not as assignments, and encourage students to write and follow the thinking wherever it leads.

Begin with an intriguing quote or fact

> I read that 75% of water use in New Mexico goes to irrigation.
>
> I want to understand why we think we can have acres and acres of perfect, green grass for golf courses in the middle of the desert, while farmers worry about watering their crops and feeding their animals, and people worry about reaching the end of their drinking water supplies. Well, maybe "irrigation" also includes the many crops grown in New Mexico—corn, fruit trees, chilies—that we export that help farmers make a living and that actually put food in people's bellies. But still, I would like to know what percentage of water goes to creating green grass in a place that is mostly rock and desert

Begin with an interesting question

Why do some bird species mate for life and not others?

Birds share so many characteristics—wings, feathers, beaks, beady eyes—yet some, like whooping cranes and black vultures, choose mates and stay with them for life, while others have multiple bird partners. Only a few mammals are monogamous. I can't name offhand more than the otter and the beaver. So naturally, I wonder about how humans fit into this behavioral pattern. Are we like birds, similar in most ways, but some of us prefer to stay long-married, while others cannot be content with only one partner?

Begin with a hot spot

A hot spot is something that makes you frustrated, fearful, angry, or overwhelmed with joy.

Lovely fragrances frustrate me because, like happiness, I can't hang on to them.

I remember pain, and I can "re-smell" horrible odors (like skunk) without hardly trying. But happiness and delicious fragrances elude me. I try to hold onto them, which only gets ugly. While working and sightseeing in Rabat, Morocco, I felt overwhelmed by the fragrances of mint, citrus, wood, flowers. I think my hosts may have worried about me, as I was continually sucking in the smell of every amazing meal, every flower in my path, burying my nose in, trying to drown in the scent, then coming away with a frown on my face because I can't take it with me. I wonder if noxious odors have some chemical that makes them "stick," and if so, why can't the scent of spearmint also "stick"?

Begin with a claim

The grander and more unsubstantiated the claim, the better! Use words like *everyone*, *no one*, *always*, *never*, *certainly*, and *for sure*.

Certainly, everyone will eventually live on other planets in the galaxy.

Earth will not be able to sustain all living things, especially at the rate we are paving over and polluting it. We already build into the sky: in New York City, companies own what is called the "air space" above the already skyscraping buildings. We already build over water: Palm Islands, Dubai, has expanded tremendously in size, on top of rocks and sand reclaimed from the ocean. We already build homes up the sides of steep mountains and construct roads, train tracks, tunnels, and military bases inside of mountains. At some point, we will cover every livable inch of the earth, water, and sky, so we will have to look beyond to our neighboring planets to sustain life.

Begin with an observation

This time, smaller is better. Zoom in on something to lead your thinking.

I'm looking at some boards cut from different kinds of wood, and I'm noticing that pine has round knots every few inches, like polka dots; oak has few knots, but many wavy swirls, like sand on the beach when the ocean wave recedes.

What makes wood patterns so different? These are some things I predict may cause this, without having any facts to back me up: amount of water available; average temperatures; soil conditions; altitude. Wow, I am really making stuff up now! But I love looking at these differences in wood grain. It reminds me of human skin of different ages and colors, and different life experiences. Such high stakes in the history of this world for different colors of skin.

Begin with something ordinary

Something right in front of your nose will do—your pen, a T-shirt, the screen saver on your computer or phone. Write like an authority on it, teach about it, or just think about it.

The flowers of these basil plants are edible and actually taste exactly like the leaves of the herb.

For some reason, it's not customary to eat herb flowers. Gardeners often advise deflowering herbs, to make the plants bushier or to avoid reseeding. I am guilty of not cutting the flowers, especially of basil and oregano, because I love the beautiful, fragrant lavender and white flowers, and so do the bees, and I love bees. Bees need all the help they can get these days, since something we are doing or not doing is killing them by the millions. So if you grow herbs, you can let them flower, and use the flowers along with leaves in cooking. I think of eating herb flowers like eating skins of fruit and potatoes—that's where all the vitamins are.

Begin with a story

Write a story you've heard or a story about something that happened to someone you know, what it means, or why it is important to you.

Begin with a memory

Write about why that memory stands out in your mind, or why it is important to you.

Each day during class, give your students a chance to meet with partners or small writing groups to share the ideas they are generating so far. Teach students to be open to what I call "me too" feelings, to being reminded by someone else's writing of something they can now add to their ever-expanding list of possibilities. If you require some kind of writing for home-work, kids can continue from their in-class writing, choose another option from the lists of try-its, or create their own way of think-ing on the page.

As you explore multiple open-ended, writing-to-think invitations, some students will be tempted to choose a topic right away and begin drafting essays in their notebooks. Don't let them! Insist that these beginning days be spent exploring a wide variety of topics. Trying out different topics will help

Habits of Thinking Inside Writing Notebooks

- risk taking
- pondering
- ruminating
- musing
- exploring curiosity
- unleashing tenacity
- considering
- wondering
- questioning
- speculating
- talking back
- hypothesizing
- arguing
- revealing honesty
- observing

build fluency for young writers, and it will convince them that they have a world of things to write about if they learn to relax, think, notice, and dig ever deeper in their hearts and minds. Also, a lovely aspect of notebook work is that nothing is wasted: often, we can bump seemingly disparate topics up next to each other, adding depth and layers to our focus topic.

5

GROWING TOPICS
INTO IDEAS

*Rarely does the essay set out, hiking boots
afoot and compass in hand; instead it meanders.
Instead of reaching conclusions, the essay
ruminates and wonders. Rather than being
right or informative, it is thoughtful.*

—Samuel F. Pickering Jr.

*Ideas engage; they pique; they rattle; they move
the furniture around in the reader's head. That
is why they are so valuable and so dangerous.*

—Christina Nehring, "Our Essays, Ourselves:
In Defense of the Big Idea"

The first time I visited Ilza Garcia's fourth-grade bilingual class, in Austin, Texas, her students were deeply immersed in reading and talking about essays, building a vision of what the essay can do, and already bursting with ideas for the drafts they would soon be making. I sat in the circle with them and listened as one after another of the students talked about what they had written in their notebooks the night before. Amanda wrote that she felt a "storm of strong emotions" when her beloved *abuela* moved back to Mexico, and that she missed her every single day. Jaime wrote about visiting a relative in the hospital, where in the waiting room he saw a man in "old clothes" who told Jaime he lived in a tunnel.

Maria said, "Me and Vivian are doing the same thing, about people who have no food, clothing, no place to live. We have everything we need, and they don't. I saw someone homeless in the parking lot at the Stop and Go, and it was the snow day."

Estrella wrote about how cancer affects people, and she drew from her experience of losing her best friend. "My friend died at eight of cancer in her heart."

"Oh, that's a big one," a little boy chimed in.

Estrella continued, "She had to go to the hospital to get something like water to go through her whole body to feel better. But she didn't, and the last thing she ever said to me was, 'I love you.'"

"Ahh . . . ," the whole class sighed sympathetically in response.

Ilza spoke up then. "I'm noticing we're all getting ideas from things that happen to us and our friends and families and neighbors. Can we make connections from what we're writing to the larger world, to big ideas? Like Amanda is really writing about separation, and Maria and Vivian are writing about poverty."

That question led to connections with the reading the class had done about segregation; about people hiding Jewish children in their attics from the Nazis; about Native American code talkers in World War II and how no one ever heard of them, and somehow those connections led to a recent flood in Austin that had devastated several neighborhoods. The kids told stories about their friends and relatives who were stuck on roofs, and how they had to move away because their houses fell down, and how they lost their cats and dogs. Finally, Amanda, who began the circle share with her "storm of strong emotions" about missing her *abuela*, said, "We all chose topics to make you cry. I need some happy!"

When I visited Ilza's classroom the second time, her students were developing their ideas in their notebooks, about deep, thoughtful topics—poverty and loss and the inequalities that existed all around them. One tiny girl was writing about an organization called BACA—Bikers Against Child Abuse—that offers to protect children who have been sexually abused. She looked up at me with the most sincere concern in her eyes. "I'm really worried about those kids," she said.

I conferred with Damian, who was writing about how his *primo* (cousin) did not take good care of his *sobrina* (niece). "I am her uncle," he told me. "*Mi primo*, he goes to parties and smokes, and sometimes he has to go to jail. You know, he is a model for my little *sobrina. El dicho* . . . a saying in Spanish, '*Como la ves, tú serás.*' It means what she sees in front of her eyes, that's what she will be. I want her to see something better. I won't be like that [my cousin] when I grow up."

After each visit to this vibrant, caring classroom, this oasis in a national ocean of mandates, standards, testing data, and teacher bashing, I actually became weepy. I was moved by the gravity of the work the kids were doing, and by their intensely sweet and respectful listening to each other and empathizing with one another. I admired how clearly Ilza named the students' brilliance, how she helped them make connections with social studies and science topics, and her rich language instruction, moving so readily and generously between Spanish and English.

Through a powerful combination of reading immersion and notebook work to explore possibilities, Ilza's students settled on a variety of critical ideas for their own essays. When asked what frustrated or angered them, what they cared deeply about, this group of fourth graders found meaningful ideas that would not appear on the most clever list of scripted prompts. The students found ideas they wanted to linger with and develop, hoping to write essays that might change minds and make the world a better place. This selecting and growing work is the crucial next phase in the move toward essay.

 ## Finding Topics for Essay

After generating pages of possible topics and ideas for essays, your students will now decide on one of them as the direction for their writing. This is an important decision that students must make for themselves. From decades of working on my own writing, and teaching writing to thousands of teachers, university students, and children in grades pre-K to 12, I have come to believe that choosing the best subject to write about is the secret for writing well and for enjoying the work of an extensive project. But how does a writer find that best subject?

Ken Macrorie says that asking what topic one should write about is the wrong question. Instead, writers should ask, "What's choosing me? What do I need to know? . . . What keeps nagging me?" (1984, 71). We all have desires, annoyances, rants, and needs, and if we can learn to be brave and honest about committing them to paper, we will have the answer to "What's choosing me?" Making quality essays takes time and a lot of thinking, writing, and rewriting. It makes sense that if writers don't care about, even obsess over, their topic, the process becomes strained and boring. Some writers will just give up, not feeling a need to carry on if the work is no longer satisfying.

Topic choice is a bedrock principle of the writing process movement and writing workshop pedagogy, and the early researchers and practitioners (Calkins, Elbow, Graves, Macrorie, Murray) understood the power of choice for learning how to write well because they were writers themselves. Most often, they enjoyed ownership of their topics and projects. Although occasions exist for assigned writing tasks—college papers, job applications, certain journalistic duties—most professional writers have the privilege of working in their preferred genres on topics they feel passionate about. By choosing subjects they care about, in drafts that are not dripping in red ink all over the spelling and grammar errors (K. Bomer 2010), and by having time to reread and revise, writers are able to find and develop distinctive voices.

Teachers can help less experienced writers discover what they care about by providing a few days to briefly explore multiple subjects through generating activities such as the ones I described in Chapter 4. After this exploratory work, many students will know, as all writers come to know, the topics that feel most generative, the topics that are choosing them. For a few writers, though, the prospect of settling on just *one* topic for a final piece can feel like standing in front of forty varieties of cereal in the grocery store aisle: overwhelming and frustrating. Talking through the top contenders in conferences and peer discussions can help writers focus. I offer this advice to students who have a hard time settling on a topic:

- Don't worry about the topics you *don't* choose this time around; those ideas are safely stored in your notebook for future essays.

- We have about two more weeks to work on this essay before the deadline. Are some of your topics too big? Do they require more research than you can accomplish over the next two weeks?

- Choose your favorite three topics. Talk each one over with me (or with your writing group). As you talk, you will probably begin to feel more heat around one over the others.

- Choose your favorite three topics. Quickly, write a one-page entry in your notebook about *each* of them, and see which one begins to feel more exciting to you.

Moving from Topics to Ideas

You may have noticed that I use the words *topic*, *idea*, and *subject* almost interchangeably. In truth, writers approach their essays in different ways. Some might lean toward a topic or subject—the fashion and makeup industries; nontraditional families; race relations—then begin to develop ideas about that topic. Other writers start from an idea—*males seem more willing to crack jokes, criticize, and be skeptical in their Facebook responses than females*—and then they investigate and write longer about that idea. Ultimately, you will want to move all your students toward more idea-based essays, but at this point in the study when students simply need to get going, they can choose either a topic (subject) or an idea as a diving platform to get into some deeper writing.

Once students have a direction in mind and you begin moving them from topics to ideas, it's important to note that the word *topic* often labels an informational text. Video games, for example, is a topic, and young writers will likely have trouble moving from writing *all about* video games (popular titles, playing levels, degree of violence involved) to *having ideas* about video games (*video games prepare kids for dealing with loss and the rocky road of life*) without some intentional teaching about the nature of ideas. An idea is deeper and more layered. An idea takes some fleshing out, circling around, and looking at opposing sides to consider every angle. *Video games portray women and girls in sexist ways and that influences the kids who play them*, for example, is an idea. *Playing video games appears isolating and lonely, but gaming has actually allowed people to connect across global social networks* is another idea.

All the notebook work students will do to grow their thinking (described later in this chapter) is meant to help them find compelling ideas to explore in their essays, ideas they simply can't ignore. A good idea should prick a writer, like the spikey edge of a clothing label on the back of the neck. Once students find ideas worth exploring, you'll teach them to push forward by asking, "Why?" "What else about that?" "Why does this haunt me so?" An idea has the sound of something true, a revelation, a parting of the waters. Listen to the sound of this young woman coming to a revelation about her eating disorder: "[I realized that it was] an invading lie about what I had to do in order to feel better, be special, fit in. It was not my true self speaking, so it lost much of its power when I let who I really was step forward. The lie can be very strong if you feed it, but it remains only a lie" (Schleiff 2007, 36).

As students develop their thinking in a particular direction, you'll need to talk with them about the difference between the topic of an essay and the idea of an essay. To clarify and demonstrate that difference, let's look at a few of the wonderful mentor essays included at the end of the book. I constructed a T-chart to show the contrast between topics and ideas. You might create a similar chart with your students using whatever essays you read during immersion. Show students what you mean with one example and then let them work with partners or in small groups to think about the ideas and fill in the chart for the rest of the essays. They may come up with possibilities you hadn't even imagined.

Essay Title and Topic	Idea
"What I Want to Be," by Randy Bomer • what the author wanted to be when he was little	What we become is not the job we do, but rather who we *are* in that job, what qualities of self-identity we bring to our work.
"We Are What We Eat," by Katie Wood Ray • well-cooked green beans, the way the author's mother makes them, versus barely cooked, fancy green beans in expensive restaurants	We have an acquired taste for foods that were prepared by someone who loved and cared for us, and we pass that taste on (and the feeling of being loved that the food reminds us of) across families and time.
"Drop-Off Cats," by Amy Ludwig VanDerwater • adopting, nursing, and paying vet bills for a stray cat that was left on the porch	Taking care of vulnerable creatures, including accepting the costs of time and money, teaches us how to feel compassion and how to care for the world and its inhabitants.
"The Thing About Cats," by Vicki Vinton • all about cats, plus the memory from the author's childhood of wanting a neighbor's cat	Cats choose the objects of their affection, which might make us feel more specifically chosen than a dog's generous affection for pretty much anyone.

Once students have found a direction for their essays, it's tempting to leave their writer's notebooks and begin drafting too quickly, especially when they are excited about their ideas and eager to move forward. But writers need time to elaborate and develop content, to layer and texture with stories, quotes, memories, and facts, not because essayists need to win arguments, and not because they need evidence, as in a court of law, but because they need to make an audience *want* to read their essays. Students need time to find the details that will make readers care about their ideas, and they can find those words by doing some focused collecting and layering work in notebooks.

Making Time for Elaborating Ideas

My fearless essay study group of Austin teachers and I learned how crucial the layering and developing work is to achieving quality essays. In all phases of their essay studies, the grade 4 through 11 teachers brought student writing to our meetings so we could study it together. During the generating phase, students were brimming over with ideas, often with serious social and critical leanings, and always with a sense of passion and mission. The message of this work was loud and clear: give students relatable, evocative, amusing, and authentic essays to read, invite them to consider the things that make their hearts pound, then stand back as they flood the pages of their notebooks. We felt quite proud and successful as teachers of essay at this point.

Weeks later, as we read over the finished essays, we discovered a gap between students' brilliant notebook explorations and the quality of their final drafts. Even after revisions, many drafts did not reflect the quality we'd hoped for. We came to a similar aha realization: along with studying mentor texts, and talking with partners and groups to find fabulous topics, what students needed most was more time and attention paid to collecting and gathering—elaborating, essentially—around an idea. Apparently, many students were more familiar and comfortable with being given a prompt and composing on-the-spot essays all structured the same way. Even though they had chosen their own topics and were excited to write about them, many students struggled to flesh out ideas and grow the middles of their essays once they'd constructed snappy leads.

With reflection, we realized we had pushed students too quickly from note-books to drafts and not given them enough time to collect around their ideas and layer them with thinking. To help bridge this gap in the process, I offer the following suggestions for how students can linger with their topics and ideas, finding additional pathways to explore that will enrich and enliven the drafts they will soon make for readers.

 ## Collecting and Layering

All nonfiction writers, including essayists, have a repertoire of strategies to achieve their richly elaborated texts. They read extensively, looking for other voices to push their thinking, to argue with, or to recruit as support for their own stance. They research to find supporting facts. They craft metaphors and look for anecdotes that will illustrate their ideas. They remember. They interview experts and look at photographs and artifacts. They go to museums. They travel to places they are writing about to get firsthand experiences. They live life. Then they collect all that wealth of data and layer it onto their topics, growing their ideas.

We can teach students how to practice simplified versions of this elaboration work so their essays feel more textured and take more adventurous turns of thought. This work requires staying in the writer's notebook for several more days, talking about their ideas with peers, and inviting students to try some different approaches to their essay ideas that may or may not produce fruit for the eventual drafts, but that will loosen the skinny texts that students often produce and "layer them up," as an artist friend, Charles Hancock, calls the texturing he adds to his artwork.

What follows is a menu of specific tools and activities students can use to collect information and layer their thinking before they begin drafting their essays. A few of these activities might be suitable as ten-minute try-its for every writer in the class to experience, but generally, students should choose the methods that fit their specific topics and ideas: not every activity works for every essay. Trying out a humorous voice may seem completely out of place for someone who is writing about witnessing a terrible car accident, for example. On the other hand, exploring a move like weaving in the voices of others with quotes might prove helpful for any essay topic. You also can choose which of these tools you think would benefit your students' writing the most (and of course, you should add any strategies you have already found successful for teaching essay in the past). You can demonstrate any of these activities in minilessons using your own notebook work or examples from mentor texts, and you can also offer them to individual writers in conferences.

Find Significance in Chosen Topics

Young and unpracticed writers can have difficulty elaborating their topics because they have not yet found what makes the topics meaningful to them. To help students reflect on what is significant, you might ask questions in writing conferences such as "Why this topic?" or "What are you yearning to say to readers?" When students answer questions like this, follow up with "Say more about that." You can also provide a little list of reflective questions for students to respond to in their writer's notebooks. This material may or may not find its way into the finished essays, but writing to think about these questions helps students realize why they care about their topics (or, if they can't answer the questions, it helps them figure out they need to change their topics).

- Where have you seen or heard something like this in your life?

- What memories do you have of this?

- What stories do other people (two or three) tell about this?

- Why did you choose this topic?

- What are you wishing to say to your readers about this topic?

- What is important to know about your topic?

Look from Different Angles

You can teach the concept of a big idea in essay by showing students how to look at something from a particular angle. To introduce this idea, it works well to project a painting on a wall (you can find thousands of images on the Internet). Begin by imagining with students possible angles you might focus on in the painting: color, shape, light, shadows, patterns, texture, what is prominent and what recedes, a single object or person in the painting, and so on. Have students choose one of these angles and write what they notice for two minutes with that focus, then choose a different angle and write for two more minutes. Have students share this writing in small groups to see how varied the writing is (because of the different angles) even though everyone is looking at the same painting.

Next, show students how writers can also look at a topic from different angles. *Friendship*, for example, can be thought about from many different angles. Do the same work with this topic that you did with the painting. First imagine the different angles or points of view you might consider, then either think aloud or actually demonstrate a short bit of writing that might come from different attacks. I tried doing this in my writer's notebook:

ANGLE: FRIENDS IN TV SHOWS, MOVIES, SONGS, VIDEO GAMES

Being "just friends" with a boy has always been so hard. When I was in high school, I loved the song "You've Got a Friend" (written by Carole King, made famous by James Taylor) but it felt more like a love song than a friend song. I had a hard time finding books, poems, songs that described my friendship with Larry. "You've Got a Friend" came the closest, but I worried that if I gave it to him, he would think I was trying to say I was romantically in love with him.

ANGLE: OTHER PEOPLE'S FRIENDS (SIBLINGS, COUSINS, PARENTS)

My father did not have one single friend, male or female, the entire time I knew him—52 years. Why? What did he gain or lose by not having that kind of companionship?

ANGLE: GENDER, CLASS, OR RACE AND FRIENDSHIP

If I asked five males to describe what a "best friend" is, what would they say? How would it be similar to/different from what females say? The Lego company created "Legos for girls" built on a friendship platform because apparently their market research shows that what attracts girls and makes them want to buy things is social relationships, particularly between girls.

ANGLE: HISTORY OF THE CONCEPT OF FRIENDSHIP

Does the word <u>friend</u> or the concept of friendship appear in the original text of the Bible? What is an early appearance of the word in literature, and was it anything like our modern concept of friendship?

Finally, ask students to think of at least three possible angles on their chosen essay topic and to try writing from each one in short bursts. Students can work together on this, especially at first. The goal of this practice is to become flexible and fluid at seeing a topic or an idea from different angles or perspectives, an essential skill when working on more formal persuasions, argument, and analytical texts.

Examine with Critical Lenses

Closely related to angle is the concept of *lens*, another metaphorical term that describes a way of seeing. Though critical literacy is a modern formulation, Montaigne had a passion for exploring perspectives different from his own, in order to deeply understand the world. Critical lenses refer to systemic uses and abuses of power and privilege by one group over more vulnerable groups in images, texts, or world events. For an extensive discussion of critical lenses and how to teach them to young people, see *For a Better World: Reading and Writing for Social Action*, by Randy and Katherine Bomer (2001).

You might invite students to consider their topics through critical lenses such as race, gender, class, or power. They will need to see examples, of course, to know exactly what this means. Several of my favorite essayists consistently question and critique the actions of groups with power and privilege, and tell the stories and keep in mind vulnerable groups (people of color, women and children, the poor, the fragile ecosystems): Ta-Nehisi Coates, Roxane Gay, Dagoberto Gilb, Barbara Kingsolver, Marilynne Robinson, and Touré.

In a minilesson or a conference, show students either a whole essay or an excerpt where the critical lens is clear. Here's a good example from Roxane Gay, who writes passionately, bitingly, yet often with delicious doses of humor about the ways in which our culture continues to treat women and African Americans unjustly, with violence, with disrespect, and by silencing voices. Notice how clear that lens is in this excerpt from her essay about the novel and movie *The Help:*

> I think of myself as progressive and open-minded, but I have biases, and in reading and watching *The Help,* I have become painfully aware of just how biased I can be. My real problem is that *The Help* is written by a white woman. The screenplay is written by a white man. The movie is directed by that same white man. I know it's wrong but I think, *How dare they?*
>
> ...Kathryn Stockett tries to write black women, but she doesn't try hard enough. Her depictions of race are almost fetishistic unless they are downright insulting. At one point in the book, Aibileen compares her skin color to that of a cockroach, you know, the most hated insect you can think of. Aibileen says, staring at a cockroach, "He big, inch, inch an a half. He black. Blacker than me." That's simply bad writing, but it's an even worse way of writing difference. If white writers can't do better than to compare a cockroach to black skin, perhaps they should leave the writing of difference in more capable hands. (2014b, 217)

Examining topics through critical lenses has the potential to lead students to some of their biggest ideas. If this work makes sense for your students, immerse them in examples like Gay's and let them take this thinking as far as it can lead them.

Explore in Different Genres and Disciplines

Many writers take interesting spins around their ideas by thinking in multiple perspectives, as scientists, musicians, or artists, or even by trying bits of poetry or fictional passages in their essays. Invite students to do quick try-its about their ideas in different genres (poetry, fiction, op-ed, travel writing) or disciplines (anthropologist, biologist, sports enthusiast) to loosen things up, to help circle around a topic or idea from different vantage points of expertise, offering surprising, rich material.

To give you an example, let's return to a topic I did some writing-to-think about in Chapter 4, the Rio Grande del Norte National Monument in Taos, New

Mexico, site of an enormous gorge, at the base of which flows the Rio Grande River. Watch how it changes my thinking and ideas to consider this one place from different disciplines and genres.

If I were to write about the gorge through the sensibilities of a geologist, I might describe the scraping of the earth's plates against each other that created an eight-hundred-foot chasm in the surface of the earth twenty-nine million years ago. I could mention the volcanic basalt rock that rises in terraces up the canyon walls. As a fly-fisher, I might write about the best spots, where the river is deep and quiet and trout congregate to feed, to cast my fishing pole. As a biologist, I could write about the ecosystem: the black bear, cougar, bighorn sheep, elk, and other animals, and the piñon, juniper, cottonwoods, willows, and other plants that thrive at different levels among the rocks. As a bird watcher, I might list the types I've witnessed: raptors, piñon jays, hummingbirds, and ravens. As an archeologist, I would certainly write about the petroglyphs in the surrounding area, a sign of possible prehistoric dwelling sites. Through the perspective of each of these working disciplines, the writing would yield different textures and information.

I might also consider the gorge through different literary genres, again in order to yield new language and perspective. When I braved the white-water rapids for the first time on a recent birthday, so as to busy myself from being scared right out of my skull, I invented little fictions for the other people—total strangers, mind you—who shared our raft: (1) a middle-aged woman, beginning to feel time cascading, the white-water rush of years, wanting to get to this activity on her life-wish list while her body could still accomplish it (OK, that's personal narrative—my own!); (2) a divorced father with his little boy and girl, taking them on the most exciting ride of their lives, pointing out ancient petroglyphs, possibly spotting a mountain lion behind a rock, hoping this fun trip would help them remember him after they went back to live with their mother; and (3) two best friends, males in their mid-twenties, always competing, angrily blaming each other for taking the mid-level rapids instead of the ones advertised as "not for the faint-of-heart."

When I wrote a poem about the gorge, it became a metaphor for long-married love: if you stand and gaze across the desert, you almost can't see the gorge at all; it looks like a dark shadow on the land, a wrinkle in the earth. Yet when you walk up to its rim, you are stunned at its enormity; you could never paint or photograph it to get it all in. If you fly above it, or climb down into it, if you let go and float along the sweet, quiet parts of the river, you begin to comprehend how wide, long, deep, and grand it all is, made so by eons of time and the attentions of wind and water. You feel dwarfed by its immensity and moved by its ancient beauty.

Now, if I were to explore the Rio Grande Gorge as an essayist, I would consider taking in any and *all* of those voices and ways of looking. The tone would lean toward exposition, but I would not want to lose my questioning stance or any pertinent narrative anecdotes or poetic imagery. I would *essay* about it, try this and that, and ultimately find myself having some big ideas, perhaps something about its geologic history, its flora and fauna, and its place in the natural and social worlds. I might write from a critical perspective and wonder about the politics of having it named, finally, in 2013 a national monument by President Barack Obama, or the politics of water in northern New Mexico, or the politics of land grants and ownership. Or I might explore the scary possibility of this mighty river drying up forever, a reality many scientists say is inevitable at our current rate of population growth and water use.

Consider demonstrating how to think about a topic you love deeply through different genres and disciplines, then let your students work with a partner to practice doing the same. Together, they can choose a topic—anything at all, a superhero, an insect, a video game, a sport—and talk about how a poet would write about it, or a biologist, a sportscaster, a medical doctor, or a person making a how-to manual (any experts they can imagine). Finally, partners can try pulling this thinking together and writing about the topic as essayists. These try-its almost certainly won't be masterful and there is no need to evaluate them. This should be a joyful exercise. The point is to help students understand the richly textured voice of essay as they collect around their ideas.

Play with Voice

Writers develop their signature voice over years of practice and through intense revision. We can help our young writers begin to find their voices by showing them how to try voices on like different styles of hats. E. B. White says that the essayist can "pull on any sort of shirt, be any sort of person, according to his mood or his subject matter—philosopher, scold, jester, raconteur, confidant, pundit, devil's advocate, enthusiast" (2006, xi). It helps to label voice with adjectives (*somber, flippant, patriotic, slapdash, lyrical, sensitive, stingy,* and so on), and certainly to demonstrate what each sounds like with a sentence or two from your notebook or from a published essay.

We can also help students gain more control over word choice and tone by finding a voice that feels most appropriate for their topics and ideas. Students might try writing about their ideas in different voices to see where they lead, ultimately deciding which fits their ideas best. Here are a few of my favorite kinds of writing voice, but any sort of voice you or your students might imagine could be worth a try.

Cranky, curmudgeonly, cantankerous

Many famous essays became so because they took something considered sacrosanct, obvious, or status quo, and they wrote in cantankerous opposition to it, or at least offered a radically different perspective, allowing readers to see these topics in a new light: "On the Pleasures of Hating" (William Hazlitt); "Against Nature" (Joyce Carol Oates); "Against Exercise" (Mark Greif); "Against Love: A Polemic" (Laura Kipnis); "Against *joie de vivre*" (Philip Lopate).

This is the voice our mothers warned us not to use because we might seem ill-tempered, angry, a bit smart-alecky, but in essay, it can feel powerful, even delightful. Students can try this voice by taking the opposite point of view on an idea accepted by most as obviously good or obviously bad, or simply the way it is, no questions asked. If everyone *loves* pumpkin spice latte, for instance, write about how cloyingly sweet it is, and how it has nothing whatsoever to do with the vegetable flavor of real pumpkin.

Skeptical

Skepticism is a time-honored intellectual point of view, at least as old as the ancient Greeks. It's not mean-spirited or angry, exactly, just . . . skeptical. Doubtful. It questions the validity of things, particularly any kind of truism or cultural convention. Here's an example from a ridiculously well-written essay by a thirteen-year-old: "I do know that there are a lot of things thrown at teenage girls these days. Like the media. They tell us we have to be a size zero, and what do even the prettiest of women promise us we can look forward to? Plastic surgery!" (Cox 2007, 230).

As students work to develop more content about their ideas, they might try on a skeptic's voice, using language like "Most people think *X*, but I am not so sure. In fact, I doubt it. I will need to be convinced." For instance, I might write, "Popular opinion has it that too much screen time ruins kids' minds. I doubt that. What is the evidence of that? Young people read and write more now (because of their digital devices) than ever in history."

Certain, like a trumpet blast

Although I've stressed the questioning, tentative aspect of essay, writers sometimes use a more authoritarian voice. Essayists can make grand claims and propose extravagant theories as long as they flesh them out with their observations, relevant experiences, and the voices of others. Essays that do this well often linger in readers' thinking for years.

What would a grand claim sound like? One of my favorite examples comes not from an essay but a movie. "Love means never having to say you're sorry," from that tearjerker 1970 movie *Love Story*, may be the most iconic grand claim ever made. I have laughed riotously with family and friends over the absurdity of that proclamation, at its utter opposition to the truth, and yet . . . it comes back to me once in a while, usually on a long road trip, when I'm bored and fidgety in my seat, and I start to think, "What the heck does that even mean? Might it be true, in some instances?"

A grand claim, voiced with certainty, like a trumpet blast, has the potential to unravel all kinds of thinking. Students might try, in a playful way, to state grand claims related to their topics and then write about them with a voice of certainty, a voice that presumes to speak for everyone else. So a student writing about her passion for music, for example, would try framing her thinking as if it were true for all young people, not only her: "Teenagers learn how to live and love from the music they listen to. Music teaches lessons in life, and kids obviously learn better from listening to their favorite bands than they do from their parents."

Humorous

Depending on which examples your students have read, they might mistakenly think that all essays, regardless of topic, strike a serious tone. This isn't true, of course.

Plenty of writers explore issues, even grim ones, using humor. David Sedaris has several collections of riotously funny essays. Ellen DeGeneres cracks me up in her collection of essays *The Funny Thing Is . . .*, where she proposes absurdities and exaggerates to outrageous proportions. Other writers throw in witty observations of popular culture or play with language in ways that amuse.

Some students will be better at this than others, and some topics will lend themselves more to humor than others, but consider asking students to write about their topics in a comedian's voice. This may not be the voice they eventually use in their final essays, but trying it out might reveal all sorts of truths they hadn't considered. After all, that's what humorists do best: they tell uncomfortable truths and help us see things in new ways.

If you want a great example of what a humorous voice sounds like while essaying an idea, do an online search for "Louis C. K. hates cell phones," and it should take you directly to an improvised bit by this superb comedian. It's my favorite kind of humor, that which comes from deep ethical truths. I won't ruin it for you by telling you all about it, but after ranting a while about how we use cell phones to fill "the forever empty" inside us, Louis ends with this humorous, yet poignant summary: "You never feel completely sad or completely happy, you just feel kinda satisfied with your products, and then you die." It's a brilliant example of an oral essay in a humorous voice. Louis C. K. takes us from humor to pathos and back to humor again in a matter of minutes; it is breathtaking to witness.

Read, Watch, and Listen

All types of texts—books, movies, art, music, Ted Talks—provide inspiration as well as actual content for elaborating essays. Students can look to any other texts for ideas and images that connect to their topics in powerful ways. For example, for an essay I'm writing about stroke and aphasia, I borrowed an image from the opening credits of a television miniseries called "Olive Kittredge" of a person lying on the ground, staring up at the sky and drifting clouds.

Sometimes writers use connections to popular culture to powerful effect in their essays. Students might weave in references to popular culture phenomena from books like Harry Potter, by J. K. Rowling, or the popular Percy Jackson and the Olympians series, by Rick Riordan, from Suzanne Collins' Hunger Games trilogy, or *The Fault in Our Stars*, by John Green; from games like Minecraft; from manga or anime; from television shows like *Dancing with the Stars*, *The Big Bang Theory*, or *The Simpsons*; from films like Disney's *Frozen*, or a nostalgic nod to *Home Alone*; or from songs like "Happy" or "All About That Bass" or the song that spawned mob dancing, "Macarena."

The purpose for weaving in cultural references like these is to engage the reader, to flesh out an idea, to lean on the context of the familiar book, TV show, film, or song to act as metaphor or even as a kind of echo chamber for the writer's idea. If you point out just a few cultural references in essays (ones you feel certain your students will recognize), this is probably all it will take to get them collecting their own. Encourage students to keep their notebooks always with them and collect these connections wherever they find them.

Quote from Powerful, Related Voices

Essayists frequently weave in quotations from their reading or from conversations to agree with, argue against, and add texture to their own thinking. For an essay about grackles, I borrowed a gorgeous quote from Aristotle about nature that I heard on National Public Radio. Considering someone else's words helps writers sound wise, and as we write or type them into drafts, our minds burst with new energy. The voices of others enliven essays, add weight and depth, and create an effect similar to jazz music, where multiple voices create exciting aural rhythms and texture.

We can invite students to do what essayists do, which is to read things as they are working on a project and collect quotes from books, songs (many kids already do that on their own), movies, commercials, and blogs that specifically speak to them and that "talk back" to their essay topics and ideas. They might organize a special section of their writer's notebooks just for quotations. As a quick try-it, students can put one or two quotes on a notebook page and write—responding, questioning, forming new ideas from the inspiring words of another person—and decide later if this brief dialogue with an invisible other fits into their essay material.

Write Short Bios

Students whose essays are about another person or a relationship might collect biographical information to see how that data helps them think about the person.

The final essays will not be biographies (a different genre entirely), but by including pertinent facts or a time line, essayists can help readers understand a larger idea developing in the essay. A student writing about a grandfather's narrow worldview, for example, might decide that knowing when and where the grandfather grew up helps her understand that his views emerged inside a certain social or cultural context. At the very least, a few carefully chosen dates, place names, and events about the person can add texture to the essay.

If students don't know or can't find biographical information, they can speculate and write to think in their notebooks, imagining the details: "I wonder . . . ," "Maybe . . . ," "Perhaps . . ." Speculation is a hallmark of essay writing, and it can be put to good use here to help students think critically about how humans are influenced by social contexts. Here, from a powerful essay about two people affected, for different reasons, by the Vietnam War, is an example of using biographical details to elaborate a larger idea. The author does not know the facts, or is too afraid to ask, so he *imagines* the biography of the other person, seeking their shared humanity and finding compassion for another human being.

> I wondered about Lily. What village or city had she come from— Chu Chi or Danang, Saigon or Hue? What was her story? Did she still hear the war during sleepless nights? Maybe she had had an American boyfriend, maybe she was in love with a Vietnamese once, a student, and they had intimate moments beside the Perfume River as boats with green and red lanterns passed at dusk. (Komunyakaa 2001, 136)

Interview Experts

Depending on their topics, students might interview experts who can add valuable information and insight to their ideas. An expert doesn't have to be a professional. An expert can be anyone with experience related to the student's topic. For instance, imagine how helpful it would be for a student writing about the fear of moving out of his home to interview a college freshman.

Interviewing someone is a more immediate and intimate kind of research than reading a book or surfing the web, and it can accomplish so much more. During face-to-face (or over-the-phone or over-the-computer) interviews, students might be intrigued by a certain fact or idea, and they can ask follow-up questions or go more deeply into one line of inquiry. An interview can also humanize information because people can't help but convey information with their affect and tone of voice.

While essays may not require expertise, depending on the topic and how far outside the self a writer wants to venture, reaching out to others often helps a writer elaborate the content of an essay.

Imagine Other Perspectives

A powerful exercise for writers is imagining what different people might say about their ideas. For this activity, encourage students to pull out important ideas they're exploring and then use speculative language (see italics in the examples) to explore how others might perceive those ideas:

> If I asked her about dating in middle school, my mom would *probably* say she thinks . . .

> I *imagine* if he knew about it, Marco might think I was being rash in my decision to shave my head because he knows how proud I've always been about my long hair.

> *I wish I could go back in time* to meet Pocahontas and ask her what her life was truly like. She would *probably* laugh (or cry) if she saw her Disney movie self, since her name was actually Matoaka, and the story of saving John Smith's life (she would have been only ten or eleven years old) is probably not true, according to several websites I've read.

As long as they're imagining, students can choose people living or long gone to "respond" to their thinking and may potentially find new insights from this writing. These imaginary responses can easily find their way into an essay draft as long as the writer makes it clear this is what she *imagines* a person might say or think, using language to signal speculation: "We can't ask Abraham Lincoln what the truth was, but *I suspect he might say* . . ." or "Sometimes *I dream about* my father finally saying the words 'I love you.' That's it. That's all I would need to hear."

Connect with Older Notebook Entries

As she heavily revises her poems, Maxine Kumin notices that "the insight hidden there" often stems from a connection between completely dissimilar things, such as the King Tut exhibit at a museum and Pearl Harbor Day. Kumin calls that connection the "*fulcrum* of the poem" (in Graves and Stuart 1985, 81). I love the word *fulcrum* to describe the central idea of a poem (or essay)—the point on which the lever rests, the sort of main activity around which everything else revolves. And I absolutely agree with Kumin that connecting disparate objects, memories, even languages is a way to find electric insights that create that central idea or fulcrum.

Students can reread old notebook entries, looking for anything to bump up against their current essay topics: words, sentences, lists, quotes, whole entries. It's the connection between two seemingly unrelated ideas that surprises, and it gives writing energy and originality and makes readers think, "Oh! I never thought of it that way before!"

Roxanne Gay makes a surprising connection like this in an essay about the Hunger Games trilogy, "What We Hunger For" (2014c). In the middle of the essay, Gay suddenly takes an abrupt and horrific detour from the books themselves and writes about her own middle school years, when she was gang-raped. I can imagine that she has written about this horrific memory in other places before, but in this essay she connects the event to her thinking about the Hunger Games trilogy. When her writing returns to the novels, she talks about appreciating the darkness in them because tragedies do happen to young people, as her connection illustrates, and comfort and salvation can come when we find our ourselves in a book, or when a character overcomes some kind of evil and gives us courage to do the same.

While powerful connections like this may suddenly occur to writers as they draft, that doesn't always happen. Teaching students to mine their notebooks for unexpected connections gives them this tool and may lead to some of the richest essay content they will uncover.

Research

Adult essayists do varying amounts of research to validate and elaborate their ideas. Essays that lean toward investigative journalism published in newspapers, journals, and magazines involve extensive, exhaustive research. But for students new to essay writing, I suggest research be kept to a minimum. In general, we want students to write out of their own knowledge and experience so they learn how to write to think and craft engaging prose.

On the other hand, a bit of time traveling down the delightful rabbit holes afforded by the Internet might help students elaborate. For example, when Randy Bomer was writing his essay "There Is a Hercules of Everything" (on page 176), he found the actual cartoon he was writing about (*The Mighty Hercules*), now over fifty years old, available on YouTube. Watching it, lo these many years later, sent him on a related search of sword-and-sandals dramas, offered a few surprises, and helped him enrich his memories.

For informal research, we are lucky to live in an era where "good enough" answers can be had at the touch of a button. Also, students might need to look up a few details for clarity or texture, things like the population of a city, the height of that tallest building in the center of town, or the name of that mountain pass they drove through in a blizzard (and of course, titles, authors' names, and publication dates for quoted text).

Make a Mind Map

In Chapter 4, I wrote about mind maps as a tool for generating essay ideas. Students can return to this visual thinking tool at the elaboration stage, especially if they feel overwhelmed by their content or have lost focus, or need to step outside of the pages of prose and make a visual outline of sorts. Students can put their chosen topic or idea in the center of a web and draw circles out from there with people, places, names of things, and questions that connect to the central topic. They can push on each one of those circles, too, making miniwebs out from each new connection.

Figure 5.1 is an example from Thea Williamson, a doctoral student at the University of Texas at Austin. Thea was writing about Chinese food, and what she was able to pull out from connecting one thing to another to another filled an entire page.

Notice how Thea began with an initial idea for her essay about Chinese food (1):

From there, she pushed her thinking to name some subcategories, like people, dishes, and flavors, which already reminded her of textures and taste sensations (2).

The third time she looked at her mind map, she allowed the categories to truly overflow with associations (3). Her only task now was to decide where she wanted to place her focus for the essay. She certainly had plenty of content to choose from!

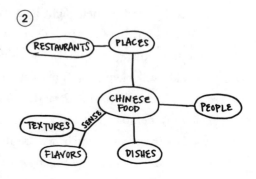

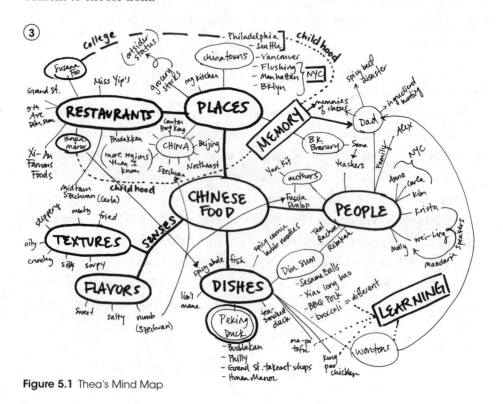

Figure 5.1 Thea's Mind Map

Ask Twenty Questions

You might also remember this activity from Chapter 4 for generating essay ideas. Students can use it again with their selected topics and ideas. Asking questions is a way to step to the side of a topic, removed from endless pages of prose, to imagine what else a reader wants to know, and to open the floodgates to thinking, by making a new list of questions that are now focused on one specific topic or idea.

Lift a Line

Finally, I offer a strategy for elaboration that I learned from my brilliant friend Donna Santman, author of *Shades of Meaning*, a book about interpretation in reading. Students can reread an entry or several entries, looking for a line of text they know has more potential. They can rewrite that line on a clean notebook page and write for five or ten minutes about what's inside that line of text.

I've used this trick for years with writers of every age, and it never fails to yield sometimes pages of additional, elaborated text. A variation I've used with older students and adult writers calls for them to reread to find a place in their writing where they know they are skirting or avoiding the truth. I ask them to rewrite that sentence on top of a fresh notebook page and dig in. It helps students to know that when they write more to tell a truer truth, it need not appear in the essay draft. What happens, however, is that students realize the writing they do when they are not hiding from truth is full of voice and electricity, and they usually decide to fold it into their final draft.

A Few More Elaboration Strategies for Essay

- Argue with yourself on the page. Take whatever bold idea you are exploring and write about why it is "wrong." See what new material comes from doing that.
- Choose the heart or the important place in your thinking so far, put a sentence about that on the top of a clean notebook page, and squeeze more out of it.
- At the top of a notebook page, write, "Why is my topic or idea important?" Write to answer that.
- Swing over to a next-door topic. If you're writing about how ants aerate soil and clean up nature, for instance, write for a bit about spiders and what they are good (or bad) for as a contrast.

6

DRAFTING
THE ESSAY

The easiest way for me to lose interest is to know too much of what I want to say before I begin.

—William Matthews

And it was sometimes hilarious and sometimes sad, like life, like good essays . . . they take off through the woods their own damned selves to go wherever they are going and the author, if he is not a complete dolt, follows after, interested to find out what it is he has to say.

—Brian Doyle, on "Being Brians"

At this point in the journey toward an essay, most of your students have selected a topic and grown ideas about that topic in their notebook. Now your writers are ready to gather that material into a first draft and write toward a shape that best matches and communicates what they want to say. If we believe thousands of authors who have revealed their processes to the public, we know that this moment of moving into a draft requires a leap of faith. Writers must give up control of form for now, give over to the material they have gathered in their notebook, and trust that whatever they put down on the paper will lead them where it needs to go. It's an exciting moment, don't you think?

 ## The Move to Drafts Might Get Messy!

In truth, this moment of moving from thinking, collecting, and layering inside the pages of the notebook to a draft can feel overwhelming. "But how do I start?" is a question I hear from writers young and not so young, when I have pulled the rug out from under them by refusing to assign a prompt and not requiring an outline or graphic organizer or calculated formula for what sentence to put where. Thinking on the page in the writer's notebook can indeed produce a bit of a mess, literally and figuratively, and we honestly worry about that. Do we even have time in school these days to produce messes? Well, I think we need to make the time. We need to make time for kids to reread, as often as they have stamina for, their pages of thinking and collecting. We need to make time for them to talk to us in conferences and to their peers in writing partnerships and groups, and to continually refine their thinking, with the help of conversation—trying on possible structures that make sense for their topics and ideas.

The writing process is not linear. It is recursive, and yes, it can get messy. Practiced writers know this process well, and they have strategies to help them work through it: colored markers, various types of paper, digital production tools, different writing locations, mentor and diversion texts for reading, sticky notes, butcher paper taped to walls, recording devices, enormous mugs of coffee (OK, that's what I need). But many writers also revel in the mess. I call it cognitive dissonance. I respect it and maybe even invite it, the way the ancients wrote about courting the muse because that is where magic and inspiration appeared.

Brian Cambourne, literacy researcher and educator, refers to moments of frustration in reading or learning as the "privilege of struggling" (1988, 4). Wait. Struggling—a privilege? Yes, and Cambourne goes on to assert that there is a "pleasure derived from the struggle . . . perhaps this 'struggle/pleasure' relationship has something to do with the brain's apparent *need* to be continually constructing meaning, to be continually imposing sense and order on chaos" (5).

In schools, it seems that we rush to fill those moments of confusion students sometimes experience, or we insist that kids, especially the ones who "struggle" with writing, need *more* structure and scaffolds to prop them up. You know what? If there were a machine that monitored how often I myself struggle while writing, and how much I have to revise my work, I would probably be given accommodations and assistance all day long! I think we must help young people learn how to sit with difficulty, offering guidance occasionally, providing time, space, an empathetic ear, and colored markers, but letting them work through to the other side and then helping them to name and celebrate precisely what they did to work it out.

Practical Suggestions for Beginning Essay Drafts

OK, so the writing process can be messy and a bit overwhelming. You might reasonably ask, "Yes, so wouldn't now be a great time to teach kids how to outline their essay structure?" My answer: Sure, why not! Offering guidance and suggestions, especially if they come from what *you* do as a writer, or from what you've read about in interviews with working writers, is importantly different from assigning every student to fill out the same graphic organizer all at once. Humans do find comfort in knowing where we are going. We love maps and to-do lists because they give us a sense of order and control over the chaos that is life. So it's worth asking our students whether they also would like some kind of map to find their way out of the notebook to the draft.

Sometimes, I begin writing projects by making lists and webs of possibilities (like Thea's mind maps in Chapter 5) in my notebook, and I count these as outlines. They help me get my thoughts and ideas in front of me so I can work with them, cross some out, add, and switch things around. Then, in the middle of the project, I flat out reject those lists and webs because they no longer describe the text that is unfolding on my computer screen. So I create brand-new lists (some writers call this "backward outlining") based on what I have *already written*, not what I assume I *will* write. Sometimes I sketch different shapes my text might take. Sometimes I hang chart paper on the wall to map out a structure. I would never consider any list or diagram of mine as final and complete; I continue to revise all my writing heavily, and I make brand-new outlines until I am finished.

Contrast these informal and ongoing uses of lists and organizing tools with that nightmare from our pasts, the confusing, formal, and formulaic Roman numeral outline that we despised and made up only *after* writing our school essays. Sound familiar? If, instead, we are showing kids how to plan for writing in informal and diverse ways, then I agree they can be useful. Let's think about how to help the kind of writer who feels more comfortable sketching a rough map for what might come first, next, and so on for a moment, and then I'll describe a fun way for everyone to dive straight into a draft, not worrying about the order of the parts just yet, trusting that we will find an essay structure as the draft evolves.

Make an informal outline

For those who do want a little road map for their first draft, we can introduce several informal outlines in a minilesson, giving everyone in the class these options. More often, however, I quickly demonstrate a few outlines on my clipboard while conferring with individuals or small groups of students when they need extra support. The important thing is for each writer to find what works for him or her because the main goal of our instruction should be to help individuals find writing processes that work for them, now and in the future.

- Storyboard Outline: The storyboard outline is similar to a storyboard used by creators of film, television shows, and commercials. Some kids might sketch the main parts of their essay draft into a series of boxes, especially if their essay leans toward narrative. Search online for "storyboard" for templates to use.

- Time Line: Writers can use a time line for content that contains a strong memoir or narrative bent. Students can draw a horizontal or vertical time line and label important points or highlights within the chronology.

- Graphic Outline: A graphic outline is simply any kind of graphic sketch that makes sense to an individual student as a conceivable essay draft structure: a web; a tree with a trunk, branches, and leaves; floating balloons of thoughts; a superhighway; an apartment building with different apartments, and rooms inside those apartments; a neighborhood with stores, houses, a park, and a temple.

- Talking Outline: Some kids might want to talk their way through the structure of their first draft into a voice memo app on a phone, or into a tablet, or computer, or another recording device.

- Numerical Outline: For a numerical outline, students simply write down the numbers one, two, and so on. Students list, in phrases or sentences, what seem to be the large chunks of the essay draft.

Jump into a draft

In my brief stint as a journalism major in college, I learned the phrase *quick and dirty* for getting a basic news article written in a matter of minutes. (Kids love hearing that term.) That's what this first attempt is, a quick-and-dirty draft. I call my own first stab at a piece of writing a "drafty-draft," and that also seems funny to a lot of kids. Some people call it a flash draft. Call it what you will, the idea is to metaphorically close your eyes, plug your nose, and dive into the deep end, the icy water (again, choose your metaphor), and get it over with. Whether your students do or do not make an outline beforehand, the main idea to teach about this first drafty-draft is that it will change. Don't even say it might change; state with certainty that it *will* change. The road to a finished essay is paved with multiple revisions, and the point here is simply to put a hefty chunk of workable text on the page.

Jumping into a draft might seem overwhelming, for writers and teachers, but it has become one of my favorite moments to teach in the process of writing. I use this playful strategy in my own work, and I know that it works well for most students, though I warn you there might be some whining involved until your students trust that this process can work. Ask students to follow these steps:

1. Reread everything you have been collecting in your writer's notebooks toward your essay. Use a colored pen to star, circle, or otherwise mark passages you particularly like, to make comments or ask questions in the margins, and so on. This process should take only about ten minutes. (Those who chose to create informal outlines—storyboards, time lines, trees, webs—can spend these few minutes looking over your outlines.)

2. Put your notebook and outlines away. [Teachers, you may decide to collect your students' notebooks at this point, only to ensure they are out of sight.]

3. On a piece of draft paper (or a new file on the computer or tablet), for fifteen to twenty minutes, go ahead and write your first draft. Do not worry about your beginning because you will definitely revise it several times. Do not worry about what the structure should be because the material will dictate the final shape as you write and revise later. Do not

worry about proper paragraphing, spelling, and grammar; again, all will be revised and edited. The point here is to write in a rush; get it all out; and trust that the prep work, the collecting and layering you've done in the writer's notebook, has filled you up, and you need to get it down in a first draft.

The fabulous by-product of this process? Because students are hiding (for now) their notebooks, they can't copy the content word for word, so this is automatically a revision of the material. Those who needed to make informal outlines might realize they have invented a brand-new structure that works even better than the one on their storyboard, superhighway, or numerical list. Your students now have a working draft, and good news—they can have their notebooks back as they revise to fold in all that lush material they've collected.

 ## Revision Begins with Listening

Now that your students have a working draft of an essay, the entire process of writing shifts as they will begin purposefully crafting with an audience in mind. You could easily give from a minimum of three days to a week of class time to this part of the process, and you can also ask students to continue with some revision try-its at home each night. During this week you will teach students how to experiment with their drafts (see Chapter 7) and invite them to have fun making their writing better.

In my own writing process, after I move from my writer's notebook to a typed draft, I begin to listen to the words on the page as much as or more than to my own mind. It's as if I am giving birth to a piece of writing, and everyone knows that after babies are born, they have lives and minds of their own!

During revision, I feel I am listening to the *music* of language, and I learn from musicians about how they listen as they compose. Will Holshouser, composer of a beautiful French musette for accordion called *Chanson Pop*, says, "Sometimes following a piece of music through to completion is not about *making* it do something, but about listening to where it is going to go. So I wrote this very melodic first section, and then for the second section it kind of led me on a harmonic adventure. I wanted to throw some dirt in there and mix it up a little bit, but . . . I followed the melody where it went and struck some chords underneath it and that's how it wound up the way it did" (2014).

It sounds as if Holshouser is not in control of his own composing process, but in truth, he has learned to trust the music to go where it must. Writing, like music, has a melody of its own, and writers learn to give in, to listen to "where it is going to go," and follow along with what their ear tells them.

Another proponent of the importance of listening to the text, advertising genius James Webb Young, suggests that when searching for an idea, we do not look at our collection of facts directly or take them at face value. He says it is "almost like *listening* for the meaning instead of *looking* for it" (1940, 18). We have to learn to let go of trying to control the form and give over to the meaning that is emerging in the draft.

Teach Students to Listen to Their Writing

As teachers of writing, if we do agree to abandon the "thug and bully thesis" (Ballenger 2013), and to forestall the use of clever formulas and predictable structures, then we must internalize an extremely difficult first lesson, one that pertains to all of writing: we must learn to trust. Trust the process. Trust the words and sentences to lead students to the full flowering of their voices. And finally, trust that students will be able to look back at their drafts fifty times, alone, in conference with you, and in collaboration with peers, to revise and shape the material so that it makes sense for readers. For now, rather than trying to fit material and ideas into prefabricated pyramids, students can let their material speak to them. What does it want to do? Where does it want to go? What does it want to say?

In "Listening to Writing," Donald Murray (2009b) also encourages listening to the writing in order to know how to structure it. He argues that texts are almost out of our hands, so to speak, once they have reached draft form, so that "neither published writers nor beginning writers have much control over what a piece of writing says as it is talking its way towards meaning. Both must listen to the piece of writing to hear where it is going with the same anticipation and excitement we feel when a master storyteller spins out a tale" (69).

Oh, how I love the image of writing talking its way toward meaning, and we merely have to sit back and listen, as if to a magical storyteller! Well, maybe we can do more than sit back. Our students can lean forward to ask for help from their writing partners or groups, or from us in a conference, to answer a few of the questions Murray suggests writers ask of their drafts:

- What form, order, structure is evolving?

- What more does the writer—and eventually the reader—want to hear from the piece of writing?

- What questions have to be answered by the piece of writing? (64)

All this talk about listening to writing may strike some as a bit mystical and magical, unless you have experienced it. Learning to hear voice in writing begins with reading voraciously, internalizing the sound of craft. Then we must write—a lot and over many years—and receive feedback from multiple living, breathing readers, people who edit our writing and who respond with applause, laughter and tears, fan letters, and comments on social media. Over time as we internalize our readers' responses, sure enough, our writing begins to talk back to us.

The good news for our student writers is that we can give them that feedback by conferring with them throughout the process of writing, responding as readers who are interested in their meaning and not merely detectors of errors in the final product (K. Bomer 2010). We can also teach our students how to be great writing friends for each other, and we can provide class time, perhaps five or ten minutes several times a week, for students to share their writing and give constructive response to each other.

We can teach students how to plan for the work they will do with their partners and how to use their brief meeting time most productively. In a way, when students get feedback from their friends and teachers, they are borrowing their ears, and this is how they'll develop the ability to listen to their own writing. Here is a little guide to writing partner work.

A Guide to Productive Writing Partnerships

1. Before you meet with your partner or writing group, quickly reread your draft, and then choose one place in your writing where you need some help.

2. With your partner/group, decide who will go first or who will be the focus for today's discussion.

3. If it is your turn, tell your partner/group what you want them to listen for or what help you need.

4. Read your one problem section out loud. This is key. You will hear the text differently when your physical voice speaks your written words into the air in front of an audience.

5. Partner(s), listen carefully to your friend's writing, especially to the issues that she/he has identified.

6. Partner(s), give kind and honest feedback. First, say what you heard that is going well. What are the strengths? What is beautiful? Then, ask questions, and collaborate with the writer about some possible solutions to her/his issue.

Ultimately, writers find themselves alone with their drafts, and then they must become their own best listeners. Most writers talk about reading their writing out loud in the privacy of their studios and offices, in order to literally give voice to the words on the page. We can teach students to do that also. In my classrooms, I always created a cozy, private corner of the room where my students could go to read their pieces out loud as they were revising or to practice for our upcoming publishing celebration, where they would read in front of an audience of family members, students, and teachers from other classrooms.

Helping Students Revise with Reflective Writing

Published writers continually ask themselves questions as they read and reread their drafts, but students might use their writer's notebooks to respond to some of the questions practiced writers ask automatically. Reflective writing has the effect of metaphorically taking a deep breath in the midst of high-octane draft writing, quieting the mind for a few minutes so writers can listen to that voice that arises from the text and make decisions about what and how to revise.

Here are a few more questions from Murray's article "Listening to Writing" (2009b) that I particularly like for this purpose:

- What did you hear in the draft which surprised you?

- What did you hear that was most interesting?

- What sounds so right it can be developed further?

- What does the draft ask you to include in it?

- What is the draft telling you about the subject that you didn't know before? (68)

Notice that these questions treat the draft writing almost as if it has a human voice speaking to the writer, and they propose reading the draft through appreciative lenses, noticing what sounds good that can be extended and also what's surprising. Surprise in the act of writing is something most practiced writers recognize, delight in, and learn to court. In fact, the pleasure of surprise is a main reason writers write.

How different this way of looking at early drafts is from what most people have experienced in school settings, where we were taught to look for misspellings, incorrect punctuation, and, in the case of school essays, the proper placement of our thesis statement and topic sentences. In fact, I do not recall a single lesson about revision from my own K–12 English language arts instruction. Instead, what most of us learned was how to edit our papers and make them legible. Because of this, generations of people believe that revision equals finding spelling, grammar, and punctuation errors and correcting them. Before word processing, that process usually also meant the drudgery of recopying (or retyping on a typewriter with a broken ribbon and a dried-up bottle of correction liquid) the text, which often resulted in additional, unforeseen errors.

I always make a distinction for my students between what the publishing world calls copyediting—that crucial close reading for surface errors that get in the way of the meaning—and revision, the reworking of major chunks of text to *find* that meaning. Later, as we near the finished essay, a few days before publishing, we will definitely turn our attention to editing for grammar and spelling. For now, however, we can teach our students that revision is the lifeblood of writers. It is our saving grace, so to speak. In my book *Writing a Life*, I went so far as to say that "revision is hope" and, a few paragraphs later, "revision is forgiveness" (2005, 160). Poet and novelist James Dickey claims, "For every word I keep, I throw away one hundred. . . . I work like a gold-miner refining low-grade ore: a lot of muck and dirt with very little gold in it" (quoted in Graves and Stuart 1985, 85).

And so, if revision is hope, forgiveness, and a mining through the muck for bits of gold, then let us turn our hopeful eyes and hands to the work of revising essay drafts. Our students may now assume that the structure of their essay has been determined by the fact that it exists as a draft on the page, only needing some commas and proper spellings. I want to disrupt that assumption with several minilessons about revising, particularly shapes and structures. A shapely essay will invite readers to stay on the journey from beginning to end and help make the author's meaning and intentions clear.

7

SHAPING AND FINE-TUNING THE ESSAY

The hero of the essay is the author in the act of thinking things out, feeling and finding a way; it is the mind in the marvels and miseries of its makings, in the work of the imagination, the search for form.

—William Gass, "Emerson and the Essay"

love shapes. And I love finding the shapes and structures inside of things, like paintings, music, and film. Architecture mesmerizes me, especially when it pushes the envelope for what buildings look like and how they function. Frank Gehry's Guggenheim Museum in Bilbao, for instance, or Frank Lloyd Wright's Fallingwater house in Pennsylvania. When I look at buildings of all kinds, I love to contemplate whether they adhere to Louis Sullivan's tenet of modern architecture: "form ever follows function." This means that every detail of a building, including the final ornamental or aesthetic touches—clay tile roof or slate—exists in service to what that building will be used for. But sometimes an architect pushes against the idea of functionality to design something admired as a work of art, not merely for its coherent usefulness. Gaudi's shocking basilica, the Sagrada Familia, in Barcelona, Spain, for instance, uses biblical stories and symbols and tries to mirror trees and branches, and other mystical and natural allusions. To me it looks like an enormous, beautiful, asymmetrical cake with melting candles.

In their book *The Emotional House*, about home interior design, Kathryn L. Robyn and Dawn Ritchie claim that when we decorate our rooms, we need to keep in mind that "shape equals function," or put another way, "the form of something determines its task" (2005, 47). So, for instance, they say that if you do not care for entertaining guests, you might signal that by filling your living and dining areas with pointy, straight-backed chairs or delicate antique chairs that look too fragile to sit on. If, instead, you love having company and want them to stay as long as possible, your chairs and couches should be overstuffed and covered with a soft, casual fabric that is easy to clean. Robyn and Ritchie believe that you determine what can happen in your home and in your life by applying appropriate shapes and designs to invite what you want.

Of course, writing has an architecture as well, and authors also consider both aesthetics and function when they shape and arrange their texts. The structure of some writing is fairly stable, determined by function and social purposes, like legal briefs, recipes, and police reports. But contemporary novelists, essayists, poets, and playwrights bend the boundaries of genre so that what we think of as a classic narrative structure becomes difficult to discern when novelists play with time, for instance. Or poets write things that look like blobby paragraphs, called prose poems. Perhaps many expository and informational texts have more reliable, functional structures. But for the essay, everything depends on the purpose or stance of the text, the audience, and what the writer wants to invite to happen inside the piece.

By this point in the book, you can probably predict what I will say about the imaginable shapes and structures of essay. You are right: it depends. Skim a collection of essays, and you will notice that some begin with a personal anecdote, and perhaps end with that same story, in a circular structure. Others cleave to facts and other kinds of support, sounding more like a feature article or journalistic reportage. Still others take us on wild rides through history and memory and end with a big, unanswerable question. No matter what, the shape of a great essay feels inevitable. It just works.

If an essay leans toward memoir or narrative, it might have a chronological structure, and weave ideas in and out, or build up to a big idea near the end. If largely expository, an essay might begin with a grand proclamation and slowly zoom down to end with the tiniest, quiet detail. Or the opposite: it might begin with a tiny detail (like Brian Doyle's hummingbird heart) and zoom out to encompass the largest whale heart, and then to human joys and sorrows to explore the beauty and fragility of all hearts. There is no formula, no particular placement of the big ideas in the true essay. Essay finds its shape from its *content* and meaning.

Donald Murray reminds us that writers must have "faith that there can be order in the world, and the form which evolves in the process of writing in itself stands as meaning" (1982, 6). In other words, a form begins to emerge through the act of writing, determined by what the writer wants to say. Then, synergistically, the structure begins to create meaning in the piece. It is an exciting process, but once again, it demands a level of trust on the writer's (and teacher's) part that all will turn out well in the end.

Finding the Shape of the Essay

At last, we arrive at the question I'm sure has been lurking in the backs of most readers' minds: how are we going to teach students to organize their writing? If the essay does not follow a formula, then how will it find shape and structure and, ultimately, its meaning? To help your students find the organic forms inside their drafts, I offer some ways to play with the content to find what shape fits best. The following tools for revision should not be viewed as a checklist that your students must soldier through, dutifully completing each one. A revision of shape that makes sense for Esther's essay may not work for Julian's draft. Instead, you might present several of these in minilessons with demonstrations from your own drafting and revision process, from excerpts of mentor texts, or from student writers whose revision work can model the before and after.

Nonfiction writer Susan Orlean believes that since essay follows the path of an author's thinking, and that the author should be "powerfully present" in the writing, whether in first or third person, then "the best kind of structure should be organic, revealing only the very natural way a smart person's mind works through a topic, making connections and forming conclusions as they occur" (2005, xvii). Let's use Orlean's claim that an essay's structure should mimic our natural way of thinking as our first possible tool for shaping the essay.

Make Thinking Visible: Expository

Students who are writing an obviously idea-based, expository type of essay might revise to make their thinking visible as it unfolds in the draft. In Chapter 3, I provided some examples from published essays that name the act of thinking directly in the prose, and students can turn to these examples or ones from other mentor texts to borrow phrases that narrate an author's thought processes. Here, in addition, are a few examples from the mentor essays in the back of this book, with the thinking language in italics:

> *And there is another thing, while I'm at it.*
> —KATIE WOOD RAY, "YOU ARE WHAT YOU EAT"

> *Perhaps* at seven I'd made up the feeling that parents, even foster parents, should know what you wanted.
> —ISOKE NIA, "THE LIST"

> *Even now I'm not quite sure why* I was willing to risk my mother's wrath . . .
> —VICKI VINTON, "THE THING ABOUT CATS"

Narrating the twists and turns of one's thinking creates an intimacy, a shared space between writer and reader, as if you are sitting together, enjoying a delicious meal and conversation, or taking a walk through a park and talking. The conversation partner is missing from the page, so the writer has to pretend one is there, responding to her thoughts, and using the language of thinking and changing of mind.

With this revision tool, students can actually narrate their thinking as if it is happening in the moment, using present tense:

As I type these words, it occurs to me . . .

Now I'm beginning to suspect . . .

Reading over what I just wrote, I see that I have not been completely honest. The truth is that . . .

Or, students can decide to tell the story of their thinking as it happened across time:

At first, I thought . . . , but then . . .

My old thinking was that . . . , but then something happened that changed my mind.

All my life, I've believed that . . . , and now I find out how horribly wrong I was.

Make Thinking Visible: Narrative

Many contemporary essays are structured—in part or in whole—as chronological narratives: this happened, then that happened. How this kind of essay differs from the genre of memoir or personal narrative is a reasonable question, but when we read pieces that simply narrate a story next to those that attempt to abstract an *idea* from a story, we can see and hear a difference: this is what I wonder, this is what I think about what happened. The writer weaves reflections or big ideas in and out throughout the chronology, like the warp and weft on a loom. Or they might appear as a resounding ending:

After everything that happened, I think . . .

That event made me question everything I knew, and now I think . . .

If students are writing essays that read more like stories, you will definitely want to help them revise toward reflection and an abstracted idea that arises from the narrative. In writing conferences, or with partners or small groups, show students how to reread their drafts and look for places to insert the language of thinking (see examples above). You can also refer them to mentor texts that clearly develop reflection and ideas around narrative, whether personal or about someone else. Actually highlighting the language of reflection in these essays will help students see it more clearly and understand better how to revise with reflection in mind.

Several of the essays at the end of this book tell stories of events or memories, then extract ideas from the narratives. For instance, in "What I Want to Be," Randy

Bomer begins with a humorous narrative scene, a dialogue between his three-year-old self and his mother about what he wants to be. He moves from that moment to a description of a photograph of himself dressed as a cowboy when he was two years old. He remembers feeling, in that outfit, that he was *being* a cowboy. From these bits of narration, Randy grows a big idea about identity: everyone wants to be recognized as *being* a specific something or someone, and not just doing a job.

Imitate the Shape of a Favorite Essay

Students who clearly love a particular mentor essay might want to study its shape and try to imitate it with their own writing. Of course, for this to be a helpful revision tool, students must be able to see an essay's shape. In Chapters 1 and 3, I wrote about the shape of "Joyas Voladoras," and in Chapter 3, I listed a variety of structural features with excerpts from adult essays. To help you develop a practiced eye for seeing structure in any essay (so you can help your students), let's put on a pair of surgical loupes, those magnification glasses with head lamps for seeing important details up close, and focus on the shapes of a few of the mentor essays included at the end of this book.

1. Randy Bomer's "There Is a Hercules of Everything" begins in memoir. He narrates the moment as a tiny three-year-old when he realized there was something in the world that operates like an abstracted big idea. From a television cartoon version of Hercules, little Randy develops a theory that the meaning of Hercules as "strongest of anyone" can apply across other contexts. If Hercules is the strongest person in the world, and black is the strongest of colors, and hot the strongest water temperature, then perhaps there is, indeed, "a Hercules of everything." So most of this essay follows a fairly standard narrative chronology of Randy watching the cartoon, then thinking about it later while coloring and again while playing with water in the bathtub, weaving in this growing idea about one thing being stronger, having more power than another thing. Then, in the final fourth of the essay, his theory fully blossoms into his current and ongoing thinking about power in our world and how some groups of people use power over more vulnerable groups.

2. "The Thing About Cats," by Vicki Vinton, begins with the story of Vicki trying to lure her neighbor's cat into her bedroom when she was seven, knowing that she would get in trouble if her mom found out because she was allergic to cats. Vicki then reflects on her desire to own that cat, and then follows this reflection with a fantastic list of true facts about cats from history and stories from literature that point to cats being magic. This part of the essay leans toward information writing, as many adult essays do, and in Vicki's deft hands, the list is never dull; it functions as a kind of thinking through why cats are so alluring, and why she wanted so much to bring one into her room, against her mother's wishes. She ends with an open-ended wondering, a proposition for why cats might be so special—precisely because they are elusive, and if they decide to sit on your lap, you feel chosen and loved.

3. Gianna Cassetta originally wrote "Ice Girls" as an op-ed piece, so its tone purposely leans toward argument. The lens is critical, noting facts about the continued violence and inequality women experience in the United States. Gianna embeds the argument in narrative, briefly telling the story of going to an NHL hockey game with her two young sons. When she saw the scantily clad women sweeping the ice, she was troubled enough to begin researching to see if anyone had been protesting this absurdly sexist practice. What she found out made her even more furious, and then come paragraphs of facts and statistics about gender inequalities that persist today. Gianna makes an emotional plea at the end, hoping that her sons will not have to grow up in a world where women are treated unequally.

4. Deb Kelt's "Tattoos: Marked for Life" might be described as having a collage or mosaic shape. There is an overarching subject (tattoos) and a central idea (why she doesn't have one). But her thinking is structured like multicolored tiles in a mosaic or photos in a collage: body image, skin, age, music, son Charlie, time, and impermanence. "Tattoos" also takes readers on a journey of changing thinking as it peels back layers of truth: at first, she thought *this* was the reason; but no, *this* reason is more honest; but then tragedy arrived and made *this* the reason; but no, finally, it is *this*.

5. In "You Didn't Know Me Then," by Lester Laminack, there are several meaningful structures at work. Time moves in a strict chronology through Lester's life, from four years old to middle adult, but the scenes he recounts also become more intense, clear, and frightening as the essay moves forward. The repetition of the phrases such as "You didn't know me then," "I knew you," and "I was with you" directly amplify and expand the crucial moment, the epiphany, if you will, at the end of the essay. Weary of denying the truth and edging so close to taking his own life, in a powerful closing image, Lester looks into the mirror and finally meets himself.

Fine-Tuning the Craft of the Essay

Revision is my favorite part of writing because every time I look back at my work, I see things to add, delete, and make better. With all my hard thinking and generating work finished, revision feels like play! If I had my way, I would revise to the end of time, but since I have publishing deadlines, I work at a fevered pace and then, reluctantly, turn the thing in.

After revising for shape and structure, students can spend several days fine-tuning the craft of their essays. Your minilessons on these days will highlight the features of strong essay writing, many of which will be detailed on the charts you made as you studied mentor essays during reading immersion. Not every feature makes sense for every student's essay, so be sure to offer revision tools as a menu of possibilities. You might demonstrate them in minilessons using your own writing, mentor texts, or student work. You will also find these tools useful for working with individuals in writing conferences. Here are a few of the features of essay I find myself turning to again and again when teaching revision, with examples from the collection of essays at the end of the book.

Patterns, Repetitions, Echoes

In Chapters 1 and 3, I wrote that many essays have lyrical, poetic features, one of which is patterns of words, phrases, and images. Repetition, when used purposely and skillfully, creates emphasis, rhythm, music, and meaning. Repeated words and images can act as clues or stepping-stones to a turning point or as a way of gathering momentum toward an intense emotion or revelation, and they can actually pull the reader toward that climax and help with understanding. The key is to use repetition intentionally, saving it for significant elements.

For example, in "Ice Girls," Gianna Cassetta echoes a famous quote by Arthur Schopenhaur, about how truth has to pass through three phases, the second of which is to be "fiercely and violently opposed," in her sentence "I must complain." She then repeats "I must complain" in sentence after sentence, creating a kind of angry rant that we can rally behind and hope will lead to Schopenhaur's third phase, which is that the truth of gender inequity in our country "becomes self-evident."

One simple shirt with rainbow-colored hearts on it both opens and closes Olugbemisola Rhuday-Perkovich's essay, "They Don't Tell You About That," so that the end echoes the beginning. We can see that object in the opening paragraph, and we learn that her mother wore it often right before she died, and by the end of the essay, the shirt becomes precious, as we understand how unbearable is Olugbemisola's loss. Olugbemisola also repeats, with variations on the wording, the idea that years have passed since her mother's death, and yet she has not stopped grieving for her, arguing against the cliché that time heals. At odd moments, she says, "the wound suddenly rips open, and all of the jagged edges hurt so much that I can't breathe." Anyone who has lost a beloved knows the truth of this.

As your students look over the drafts of their own essays, ask them to notice if certain words or phrases repeat or if there is an emerging pattern of some sort. If not, they can consider whether a pattern or echoing makes sense to their particular idea and structure and layer it in during revision.

Extended Images and Metaphors

In exploring the central idea of an essay, a writer may call forth a visual image or metaphor, then flesh it out and extend it across pages. Isoke Nia does this in "The List," where she describes a literal, paper list with the names of things each person in her family most wishes to receive for birthday and Kwanzaa gifts. But the list also works metaphorically; when money is scarce, the list itself becomes the gift that reminds her family of "shiny" times. And finally, the list becomes a metaphor for being a good human being and parent, when Isoke instructs those who take in foster children to *put this on their list*: the way to treat your child is to get to know who she is and what she likes, to truly *see* her, for that is what love is.

Georgia Heard's essay, "Querencia," revolves around the metaphorical word *querencia*, which in Spanish can mean want and desire but can also describe a safe place, a sense of home. Georgia first misses her home when she moves from New York City to Florida, but then, over time, finds her *querencia* again when she realizes that home is not so much a physical location for her, but the metaphorical feeling that comes from her life's work as a writer.

Students can study their drafts and search for images that might be extended across pages. They can also use partner talk or notebook work to imagine metaphors that aren't yet in their drafts. Explaining the big idea of an essay and then following the explanation with "It's kind of like . . ." can lead to metaphorical thinking. A powerful image or metaphor can be added to a draft during revision, and even woven in and out if it makes sense to the meaning as a whole.

Turning Points

In *Writing a Life: Teaching Memoir to Sharpen Insight, Shape Meaning, and Triumph over Tests* (2005), I describe turning points (moments the earth shook and nothing was ever the same) as fertile ground for memoir writing. Some essays revolve around one or more turning points or pivots as well. If the essay leans on narrative, the turning point might function similarly to the way it would in fiction or memoir, as a climactic moment from which an idea or interpretation emerges.

In "Drop-Off Cats," Amy Ludwig VanDerwater tells the story of the stray cat Mini Monster showing up at her house. The essay begins with exposition, explaining that when you live in the country, stray cats are abundant; they appear in "kitteny heaps" (oh, how I love that language and image) on your road and you have to deal with them.

Then, using language like "lurking along the edges of our fields for weeks," and the classic signal of a turning point in stories, "One day . . . ," Amy writes a microstory about this poor little guy, and we are hooked.

Often, when students narrate events and experiences in their essays, the narration falls flat because it lacks the tension that good story structure achieves. If so, they might step away from their draft to create a time line or storyboard for the narration, which can help them know where to slow down and layer in thicker description, including what they were thinking or feeling at that moment, in order to build tension.

Titles

Some essays have titles as bland as toast; they simply name what the content is about, like "Dogs" or "Flowers That Grow by the Ocean." But many other essays blossom beneath lyrical titles that carry extra weight and meaning. In John Nichols' collection of essays named, poetically, *Dancing on the Stones* (2000), his titles are so interesting and lovely, I'm almost content to hang out in his table of contents: "I Never Met a Cloud I Didn't Like," "A Butterfly Bomb in Taos," "Rafting? Schmafting! *I Want My River Back!*," "Danger in the Dining Room," and my favorite, "The Holiness of Water."

Revise Essay by Cutting

My favorite writing tool is the Delete button, or a fat marker to strike through words, sentences, whole paragraphs. It's never easy to let go of content, but there is something deeply satisfying about eliminating—like tightening loose screws on a table leg.

Young people struggle to cut their writing, and the essay genre, with its seemingly casual, meandering quality, can invite wandering too far off course. When students need to find their way back to the path, teach them to ask questions like these:

- What is the heart of my essay? (Cut whatever does not feed into that heart.)
- What am I trying to say in this essay? (Cut whatever clouds that.)
- Do I see accidental repetitions? (Cut anything that's redundant rather than artful.)

You can ask your students to pore over their pile of mentor texts to find titles they might imitate. In their writer's notebook, they might record five favorites and dash a quick sentence or two about why—it's mysterious; it's funny; I like this metaphor; it reminds me of a song I love; and so on.

When I teach poetry, I demonstrate how poets often find a title by picking a word or phrase from the body of the poem that echoes and elevates the poem. The same idea can apply to essay. Ask your students to scan their drafts for important words or phrases and try them out as titles. The writer's notebook is the perfect place to do this trying-out work. Also in their notebook, students can try out five to ten other possible titles for their essay and choose which one they like best.

Beginnings

In the first few sentences, essayists invite us to join them as they think about the most interesting ideas, emotions, and stories on earth. They open the door quickly, with wit, passion, inventiveness, and luscious language.

Olugbemisola Rhuday-Perkovich hands the reader an amazing, nearly sarcastic, and justifiably angry metaphor to begin her difficult essay "They Don't Tell You About That": "When my mom was in a rehabilitation hospital, we had to label all of her clothes, her name in black Sharpie as though she were off at camp."

Katie Wood Ray's opening to "You Are What You Eat" entertains with her droll, gently sarcastic wit. After the first two sentences, you can almost hear that "buh-dump-bump" drumbeat that comics sometimes mimic after telling a joke: "I was eating in a restaurant a while back—alone, as usual when I'm traveling—when the waitress came by to ask me if my steak was cooked to my liking. 'It's fine,' I told her, 'but could you take these three green beans back and have another go at them?'"

In "The List," Isoke Nia goes straight for the jugular, honestly, and without self-pity, in her first sentence: "You don't really expect the Macy's saleslady to take you back to that place in your life that marks you as a foster child."

Young writers often choose a beginning early on and it takes some heavy lifting to get them to rethink that first idea. To help students consider whether their beginnings need revision, first review your mentor essays and look closely at how each one opens, naming the different possibilities you see. After this, you can model thinking through several beginnings to your own essay, talking with your students about why one works better than another. Then, ask students to try three to five new beginnings in their writer's notebooks and choose which one they prefer. They can also ask for the votes of their partners or small groups. A warning here: when the beginning of an essay changes, writers usually have to rearrange the content that follows, so be sure to alert your students to this fact and have them carefully read through and revise from their new openings.

Endings

The writer Cheryl Strayed says that "the invisible, unwritten last line of every essay should be *and nothing was ever the same again*. By which I mean the reader should feel the ground shift, if even only a bit, when he or she comes to the end of the essay" (2013, xv).

In school, most of us learned that the final paragraph should basically repeat the thesis statement, perhaps with a hope and a prayer we would have the linguistic dexterity to rephrase, muscle up the verbs, and tie it all up in a bow, without precisely repeating ourselves. But the endings of essays have more in common with those of poems or great fiction than with the formula we learned in school. They can leave us with new questions. They can resonate long after we close the book or turn off the computer.

The ending of Deb Kelt's "Tattoos: Marked for Life" includes a string of stunning adjectives expressing who her baby Charlie is and will always be, unable to be represented by any mark on her body, and yet permanently a part of her.

Georgia Heard's ending has a familiar trumpet-blast quality, like an aphorism, or a banner above a doorway, "No matter where I am, my writing is my querencia, and I'm home."

Amy Ludwig VanDerwater's ending rips my heart out when I think of that filthy, sick kitten she took in and made whole. In what could sound like a thesis statement in less talented hands, as well as a moral imperative, Amy states with authority that "drop-off cats love like dogs" because they are grateful for the kindness of humans.

Young writers often rush the endings of their own essays, so you'll need to devote some time in class to focus on endings. As you did with beginnings, you can study the endings of several mentor essays, naming and charting the specific craft moves you notice. You might teach students to pick up a word, phrase, or image from somewhere inside the essay and let it make a strong or beautiful echo in the ending. Or students can try creating several different endings to their essay and then reading them out loud to a partner or small group if they need help with deciding which one sounds best. As with revised beginnings, if your students change their ending, they will need to reread the entire essay again to make sure everything fits the new ending.

 ## Speaking of Endings . . .

Thus ends the "how to write an essay" portion of this book. My hope is that you and your students are able to imagine your way into brilliant and beautiful essays from the

More Activities for Revising Essay

- To help you consider organization, divide your draft into chunks and number them or give them little sub-titles. The subtitles can help you find the importance or essence of each chunk. (If it's hard to title a certain chunk, you may not need that part.) You might even discover you like numbered or titled sections as a way to shape and structure your essay.
- Experiment with different structures by moving the chunks around and redesigning the order. Begin with what you had as an ending, or vice versa.
- Write a six-word essay (variation on the *Smith Magazine* Six-Word Memoir Project: www.smithmag.net) that captures the essence of your essay. For example, Brian Doyle's "Joyas Voladoras" could become *Hearts: fragile body-and-soul engines.* Evaluate the essay in light of this essence and revise accordingly.
- Make a visual representation of your essay, perhaps a collage or mosaic. What images speak to the meaning and tone of your essay? What colors best represent your ideas? When you finish, notice if your visual has colors or images you might introduce into your draft to add texture.
- Make a word cloud of your essay with Wordle (www.wordle.net) or other word cloud generator. What words did you use the most often (those would be the largest in the Wordle cloud). Are those the words you *want* to use the most? If not, find those words in your draft and replace them.
- Reread your draft with one focus—voice, tone, humor, image—and revise to build up that one feature.
- Try different tools and materials to give you energy and help you resee your essay: sticky notes; note cards; chart or butcher paper to make a new outline; software revision tools; PowerPoint or Prezi slides.

try-its, activities, and sample texts found in Chapters 4 through 7. The next chapter will explore how the features of essay and writing-to-think can inform academic writing across disciplines.

But here, to demonstrate a perfect, trumpet-blast type of ending to this chapter and all the chapters that have come so far, and to show how writers can appropriate (or "steal," as Austin Kleon [2012] encourages) others' voices to echo their own ideas and arguments, I'll end this chapter with the voice of the radiant essayist Annie Dillard:

> *The essay is, and has been, all over the map. There's nothing you cannot do with it; no subject matter is forbidden, no structure is proscribed. You get to make up your own structure every time, a structure that arises from the materials and best contains them. The material is the world itself, which, so far, keeps on keeping on.* (1988, xxii)

8

STUDYING ESSAY CAN IMPROVE ACADEMIC WRITING

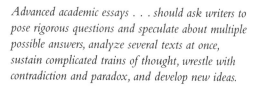

Advanced academic essays . . . should ask writers to pose rigorous questions and speculate about multiple possible answers, analyze several texts at once, sustain complicated trains of thought, wrestle with contradiction and paradox, and develop new ideas.

—Kristin Dombek and Scott Herndon, *Critical Passages*

met Deborah Cromer, president of the Wisconsin State Reading Association, when I was presenting a session at the WSRA Conference titled "Essay, Argument, and Academic Writing." Deborah came up afterward to introduce herself and to hand me this lovely haiku poem that perfectly captured the essence of my talk.

> *Preparing to write*
> *you knew what you thought until*
> *writing changed your mind*
>
> —DEBORAH V. CROMER

I had been talking about how writers need time and a place to *write to think* before they can develop rich, reasoned arguments, and I mentioned that often, writers do not know everything they are thinking until they discover it in the act of writing itself. Deborah, a wonderful poet and essayist herself, told me the story of her teen-aged son, Robin, who, in the middle of writing the essay portion of the ACT exam, completely changed his mind from his original outline. Now, this news might cause any reasonable parent or teacher to clutch his or her heart for a moment, worrying about Robin's performance on this timed, high-stakes test. But Deborah knew her son to be a strong writer, a bright and creative intellect, and she trusted that all would be well in the end. (It was.) To me, Robin was simply doing what all writers do, writing to discover what he truly meant and wanted to say. Continual practice of writing-to-think can help students become confident and fluent writers of all kinds of texts, including high-stakes test responses.

In this chapter I argue that spending time writing to think in true essays will translate in important ways to whatever forms your students are required to write in middle school, high school, college, and career. Before I delve into that territory, however, I offer my personal experience as a student and in my former career as a professional writer because it illustrates how academic and career writing has never meant one specific *kind* of writing, and that the best answer to what works to get young people ready for college and career is *It depends*.

Reflecting on a Lifetime of Academic and Career Writing

As a college undergraduate, though I was already earning money and identifying as a writer, I struggled to figure out how to "play school" with college-level writing requirements, for I was underprepared to tackle the diversity of expectations for writing in my college courses. It seemed that the term papers I had to write in high school bore little resemblance to what my college professors required in history, philosophy, political science, or literature classes. College-level writing, it turned out, was protean. It took alarming twists and turns depending on (1) the preferences and prejudices of each professor and (2) the discourse boundaries that belonged to each discipline.

In my first (and last) semester as a journalism major, for instance, I practiced (to death) putting the important facts, names, dates, and events in the first paragraph, preferably in the first sentence, if I could fit it all in. Pressure loomed to save column space, so the last comma in a series of items before a final coordinating conjunction (the Oxford comma) was dropped. Paragraphs were never more than three sentences, and sometimes only one. And the last few paragraphs of any article needed to be expendable in case the editor needed more space for breaking news or, more frequently, paid ads.

Lab reports for science classes followed a strict format: introduction, materials, methods, results, and hypothesis. My fifteen-page philosophy paper required endless explanations, like the peeling of an onion, of concepts I was exploring. I couldn't merely write, "The death penalty robs human beings of their rights"; I had to define what I meant by the terms *death*, *life*, and *human rights*. Later, in a master's program in rhetoric and composition, I learned that argument, unlike any formula I had previously memorized, has deep roots in ancient drama and oratory, and that it is dialogic in nature (thank you, Mikhail Bakhtin), taking on different voices and perspectives that align or diverge. And finally, during a brief stint as a student at Oxford University in England, I received a message from my don (professor) on the top of my final paper for Twentieth-Century British Drama. Apparently, while my ideas were "stellar," they were "horrendously organized" (he was not longing for a five-paragraph formula, either). "Don't take that personally," he said as he handed my paper to me: "No American can write worth a damn."

Well, OK then!

When I tell these stories to groups of teachers in workshops, I see heads nodding. Many of us faced similar experiences with challenging college writing. Dombeck and Herndon write of helping young people transition from typical high school to complex college writing: "Students are met on arrival by professors who expect different kinds of essays than those they were trained to write in high school. To complicate matters, expectations vary from discipline to discipline, and from class to class" (2004, 1).

Giltrow's research reveals that college instructors use wildly divergent language to express an expectation for student writing, including argument, thesis, claim; evidence (what does or does not count?); inclusion of outside commentary or staying close inside a single text; critical thinking; and even what "audience" means (2000, 137). These "moving targets" can leave students baffled by the "inscrutability of hard-to-please professors' remarks about student writing" (137).

I paid my way through college by tutoring in writing centers at three different universities, where I witnessed daily the confusion students felt when writing across disciplines. Ironically, one of the challenges for students who came to the writing centers was that professors were frustrated with their stilted, "formulaic" writing. Students would bring assigned writing from different courses, with words scrawled in the top margin to the effect of "I cannot discern your thinking in this paper" and my favorite comment: "I [course professor] wrote this book, so I already know what *I* think; I want to know what *you* think." The formulaic thesis–support essay usually fails as a venue for higher-level academic work, yet the formula dies hard. In K–12 education, we continue to promote the five-paragraph "essay" formula (though we mean analysis or argument) as if it were the monolithic form for all academic writing. It is not.

When I finally crawled out of university life after gleefully experimenting with one master's program after another and entered (kicking and screaming) adulthood and a nine-to-five workday, I became a technical writer for an engineering company. In this work I discovered the challenges and occasionally the real dangers of translating scientific, mechanical, and technical terms into something a layperson could read. Next, I wrote public relations and employee resource materials for a large bank and learned how to write with enthusiasm! About the most mundane things! After that I became a grant writer in two different nonprofit development offices, where I learned to use writing to seduce enormously wealthy donors (by telling the story of an organization's mission, pulling at heartstrings, and promising a named building).

Nowhere in my college courses or professional writing career did I use anything resembling what Richard Andrews calls the "ritualized form with little expression and thought" (1995, 168) of the thesis–support, five-paragraph format. Writing for college and my career required—more than anything—an ability to read and learn from model texts, a flexibility with language and form, attendance to the needs of varied audiences, and skillful adaptations to the idiosyncratic expectations of professors and bosses.

Fast-forward to today, and as a college instructor, the spouse of a college professor, and the friend of a few dozen more professors who sometimes have conversations about their teaching experiences at parties, I like to think of myself as somewhat knowledgeable about what is necessary for young people to be "college ready." It turns out that what we all wish our students could bring to college is fluency and flexibility in writing and thinking that will carry them through the learning of any subject in any discipline. Being able to articulate thinking, solve problems, and respond to and analyze course concepts and texts goes a long way toward helping students do well in college-level coursework. And yes, strong sentences, spelling, grammar, and punctuation matter also. There is no way around that, though to be honest, it's not as if the students who still have trouble with conventions have not spent the past twelve years trying to learn and get better at the mechanical aspects of language—it just continues to feel abstract and complicated for them for various reasons, much as every single aspect of algebra continues to elude me.

A Five-Paragraph Formula

Touted Benefits	Disadvantages
Teaches the rules before you can break them.	These rules are found only in K–12 schools and don't apply anywhere else.
Introduces a structure; guides; scaffolds.	Often shuts down thinking about meaning and can paralyze writers. The scaffold becomes more important than the content.
Many K–12 teachers are familiar and comfortable with this formula.	Doesn't allow for differentiation for all learners. Doesn't challenge. Negates individual voice.
State standards, college admissions, and freshman composition courses require this form. It's a disservice to kids not to prepare them for this.	Most assessment rubrics do *not* require five paragraphs or even a thesis statement. College admission offices are looking for strong, creative, unique writing voices.
Helps assessors looking for a checklist of features.	Narrows the assessment. Breaking out of the formula often receives higher scores on standardized writing tests.

STUDYING ESSAY CAN IMPROVE ACADEMIC WRITING

Essaying and Academic Writing

I am a fan of great writing in any form imaginable (even fortune cookies!), and that includes strong analytical and argument writing. Writing is a tool for learning, and when students' prose shows a wrestling with ideas, a fluency and facility with language, and a deep understanding of concepts and ideas, rather than a regurgitation of a teacher's lessons or a barely disguised, repurposed "essay" purchased from an "Essays R Us" site on the Internet, I rejoice! I believe the essay elicits more of the first scenario, and formulas drive students to the Internet searching for answers to the second.

With the dominance of argument in the current Common Core State Standards and other state writing curriculums, we need to build understandings of the deep nature and processes of argument and analysis rather than reaching for packaged formulas. Formulas close down thinking, causing writers to make decisions in advance and then go cherry-picking for evidence to plug in. As Newkirk notes, the tone of these pieces often sounds more like a lawyer than a reader (1986a, 148). And Heilker points out, "The thesis/support form, it seems, is inherently paradoxical: it begins with where it has already ended; it introduces the topic with its conclusion; it opens with airtight closure" (1996, 4). Indeed, when I have watched students of all ages at work on formulaic templates for writing about reading, it sometimes reminds me of a group of folks endlessly panning for gold in a piddling stream, searching for page numbers and quotes to prove their one halfhearted thesis statement.

Instead of formulas, we need to teach students strategies, such as those in Chapters 4 through 7 of this book. Suppose we invited students, for a unit of study lasting from four to five weeks, to take on the essay. Paul Heilker, who teaches college composition, suggests that "the essay shakes students awake, forces them out of their somnambulant approach to composition classes. Students can't crank out an effective essay the way they can a serviceable piece of exposition" (2006, 202). What might students learn from an essay unit of study—about writing to explore and discover what they think and know, or what they feel passionately enough to argue about, finding a strong voice, elaborating their central topics and ideas, discovering an organic shape and structure—and how might those lessons transfer to more formal academic pieces? Let's think about which moves from a unit of study in essay would translate well to any type of academic writing.

Writing to Think About Concepts and Texts

The act of thinking is not linear. No one—not even, especially not even, Einstein—begins at point A and arrives at point B in a straightforward trajectory. Instead, thinking stops and starts, loops, overlaps, reveals, and revises. This whirligig of thinking can feel overwhelming for young people without tools to help them visualize their thought journeys.

The act of writing provides such a visual tool, one of the most powerful humans have for aiding the process of thinking. Writing allows us to watch words appear before our eyes, and then reread them, sometimes before we have completed the sentence, granting us a tiny burst of thought energy, or a moment to change our minds. Not much else grants us these permissions.

Before young people know what their argument might be, how they might compare the brave female characters in dystopian novels with Shakespeare's female characters, or how geography impacted the southeastern United States in the 1850s, for instance, they need to have time (hours, not minutes) and a place (notebook, journal, tablet, computer file) to write to think, sound off, make absurd claims, explore different angles, practice tones of voice. As I explained in Chapter 4, that practice writing looks like pages of prose, lists, sketches, circles and arrows, notes in margins, and then some more pages of prose, some of which will not make it to the final draft, and none of which gets graded.

Simply filling out a graphic organizer—Roman numeral outline, pyramid, hamburger, or any other required prewriting tool—will not suffice as a way to help students find out what they think. Writing, at least in the early stages of a project, is not an equation a writer can simply plug words into that will add up to a final paper. Only students developing their *own* thinking tools, then freewriting for a period of time, and then looking back at what they have written, stimulating new thoughts about it, will do that successfully.

Talking with Partners or Groups

With academic projects, when students are given time to share their ideas and early notebook entries with their peers, they benefit from the support and genuine questions of multiple readers. Beyond the initial stage of generating ideas, students also need time to talk as they are collecting, layering, and drafting, to test out their early drafts with a partner or small writing group, and then to go back to their writing with new thinking and ideas for revision. We can give writing partners some guidance for what to consider when they respond to each other's developing drafts:

- Is the point (thesis statement) clear?

- Which evidence is strongest?

- Are there places you are not convinced?

- Does the order flow well?

- Are there sentences you stumble over when you read them out loud?

Studying Models of What's Expected

Numerous students and adults have told me that they felt clueless in high school and college about how to write their lab reports, history papers, and literary analyses because they did not have a vision for what those texts looked and sounded like. We can help our students develop a vision for academic writing by sharing models of what we expect. We can use examples written by former students that exhibit what we hope students can accomplish, and we can model powerfully by composing our own arguments or science reports, step-by-step, right alongside our students.

We can also study essays that lean toward argument, reportage, or analysis. The 2007 edition of *The Best American Essays*, edited by David Foster Wallace, contains numerous academic-leaning essays. Wallace writes in the introduction to this volume that he purposely selected (because he got to do the "decidering") essays that he admired for their clarity of thought and style, but more importantly, ones that he believed needed to be published in response to a state of emergency in our world at the time. He thought he might name these pieces "service essays," and he cites one called "Iraq: The War of the Imagination," by Mark Danner, as a prime example of writing that is able to compress into a few pages "an immense quantity of fact, opinion, confirmation, testimony, and on-site experience in order to offer an explanation of the Iraq debacle that is clear without being simplistic, comprehensive without being overwhelming, and critical without being shrill" (2007, xxiii).

Quite a few essays in the 2007 collection feel closer to journalism, academic writing, and argument than the more open-ended structures I have championed in this book, though still, not one of them fits a formula. I love Wallace's choices in this volume and, even though they are challenging, if I were teaching high school English, history, or journalism, I would have this volume at the ready for models of powerful academic writing. Another fantastic source for nonformulaic academic writing can be found in the Best American Science and Nature Writing series.

How Essay Writing Supports Academic and Test Writing

It might be useful, as a department or with grade-level colleagues, to lay your specific standards and requirements for writing next to the features and practices of a unit of study in essay to see where they overlap. For example:

What a Study in Essay Includes	Benefits for Academic Texts and Test Writing
Observing, wondering, responding to texts and the world	Performing close textual reading and analysis
Writing to think	Crafting original ideas and arguments
Discovering one's voice as a writer	Writing with self-confidence; feeling less temptation to plagiarize
Playing with different kinds of voice suited to each subject or idea	Achieving fluency with tone and voice suited to a specific task or purpose
Having something to say to the world	Finding a strong thesis or argument
Incorporating the voices of others	Including external resources to support thesis; analyzing text; blending in quotations from primary and secondary sources
Collecting and layering from a vast array of objects, places, people, ideas	Including evidence from books, experiments, theories, research
Revising multiple drafts	Building a habit of rereading for what needs to be added, deleted, rearranged; editing
Finding logical, organic shapes and structures to fit content, purpose, audience	Understanding that different organizational principles apply to different genres, content, purpose, and audience

Composing Multiple, Revised Drafts

Science projects and history papers need to go through the same writing process as a short story or a memoir, and that includes making multiple drafts of a project. Academic writing requires revision considerations similar to those of any essay, including logical organization (though not formulaic); a clear, engaging, and consistent voice; a powerful beginning and ending; and a middle portion richly elaborated with whatever counts as evidence: facts, quotes, statistics, results of experiments. Students can share their draft with peers and then revise and create a new draft based on readers' responses before turning in the final paper.

 ## Reimagining What Counts as Writing About Reading

And now, in the second part of this chapter, I invite you to dream big, to imagine how the kind of essay I describe in this book is the perfect vehicle for thinking about a subject or for demonstrating understanding of a subject. I will focus here on reimagining essaying about literature, for that practice can apply to multiple disciplines, particularly history, philosophy, and political science.

I want kids to love to read, and I believe too much school-centered writing—book reports, analytical or literary essays, literary criticism—kills the love of reading. Formal literary criticism exists only in academic settings, so unless all of our students grow up to be literary scholars and university professors, knowing how to do this kind of writing has nothing much to do with being career ready or ready to read for the rest of their lives.

Reading, we know from the transformative work of Louise Rosenblatt, is a transaction between the text and the reader (1938). We bring to texts our experiences with the wide world—culture, relationships, other texts we've read, memories, and emotions—in order to understand and interpret what we are reading. Why must we lose this wealth and diversity to one lifeless thesis statement, when instead, we might open up to countless, valid, meaningful, and vibrant interpretations by *essaying* about our reading? Students often fall in love with reading (and writing) when we create daily opportunities for informal writing-to-think about reading. We can ask students to take notes, sketch, and diagram in the midst of their reading so they can bring rich content to their partner, small-group, and whole-class discussions. (For brilliant and comprehensive instructions for writing-to-think about reading and to prepare for discussions, see Randy Bomer's *Time for Meaning* [1995] and *Building Adolescent Literacy in Today's English Classroom* [2011]).

Around the world, and across time, writers (including Montaigne, of course) have composed essays about the texts they are reading. Sometimes, these essays appear in places like the *New York Review of Books* or the *Los Angeles Review of Books*, where authors have the luxury of thinking long in essays, weaving in personal, global, and textual connections, rather than the thumbs-up/thumbs-down, short-form book reviews in magazines and newspapers, or in the comments section of websites about books. Essayists sometimes write to applaud and share beloved texts with others, sometimes to criticize, and mostly, I think, to talk back into the silence that follows reading.

Let me return to an example of essaying about reading I mentioned in Chapter 5, Roxane Gay's stunning and brutally sad essay called "What We Hunger For" (2014c), where she brings a world of funny, tragic, and deeply intelligent aspects of her own experience and thinking to the book trilogy The Hunger Games, by Suzanne Collins. Near the beginning, Gay lures us in with a smart-alecky and delightful voice, as she quickly dispatches the competition between the two boys in Katniss' life, offering her vote for "Team Peeta." "Gale?" she writes. "I can barely acknowledge him. Peeta, on the other hand, is everything. He frosts things and bakes bread and is unconditional and unwavering in his love, and also he is very, very strong. He can throw a sack of flour, is what I am saying . . . and he is a good kisser" (138).

Gay explores Katniss as a survivor, broken in places, yet able to endure and persevere as she faces the darkest realities imaginable. Some people, Gay admits, consider these novels too dark for adolescents, but she pulls out all the stops in her response to that notion. Gay relates that as a girl in eighth grade, she was invited by her boyfriend to meet him in a cottage in the woods, where he and a group of his friends gang-raped her. Gay argues that young people experience deeply tragic events, as she did, and they need stories that help them know they are not alone in their grief, and especially, they need stories of characters surviving their traumas, perhaps becoming stronger than ever. "More than that," Gay writes, "*The Hunger Games* moved me. . . . I particularly appreciated what the book got right about strength and endurance, suffering and survival" (139).

Roxane Gay's essay about the Hunger Games books takes us on an adventure of her thinking about the texts, and she presents a strong though not at all formulaic argument for what the texts represent and the power they have for readers young and older. If Gay presented this essay in an English literature class of mine, I would be more than pleased with her deep and thoughtful reading and ability to pull out large themes and support those ideas with references to her life and to the texts. Isn't this what we hope for in the best academic writing?

Consider inviting your students to make some noise about the things they read—novels, science articles, poems, songs, graphic novels, fan fiction—in essays. They might, like Roxane Gay does in many of her essays, write honestly about how contemporary literature and film continue to portray African Americans in demeaning ways. Or they might connect personally with a topic, as Briallen Hopper (2014) does in her moving essay about helping her friend who has cancer. Hopper compares her experience with John Green's rendering in *The Fault in Our Stars* and claims Green's is the best novel about cancer out there, "rewriting the story of our own lives," for someone with this disease and the friends trying to help him or her. Or middle school students might find great mentors for writing about reading in the marvelous collections of essays from multiple young adult authors about Rick Riordan's Percy Jackson series: *Demigods and Monsters* (Riordan 2013); the Hunger Games series: *The Girl Who Was on Fire* (Wilson 2011); the Divergent series: *Divergent Thinking* (Wilson 2014); or even the essays authored by psychologists about the Twilight series: *The Psychology of Twilight* (Klonsky and Black 2011).

Writing essays like these, students discover who they are, not only as composers of essay, but as readers and thinkers. I believe this counts as academic writing—that essaying provides a powerful and accepted way of interacting with texts; in fact, it is the most authentic form of writing about texts in the world. We can post students' essays about texts online, and soon enough, they will amass a following of people who also want to "talk" about what they are reading.

Activities for Essaying About Texts

Evocative texts will invariably lead to different interpretations, so students can also *essay* as a way to interpret texts and open their thinking. When these essays are shared in class, students might be utterly stunned by someone else's understanding, and they will learn that their own thinking can grow and change from hearing multiple perspectives.

Microessaying

I adapted this activity from Tom Newkirk's process of writing narrative accounts of reading (1986a 149), and I deigned to name it *microessaying*. I've used it with kids as young as nine and with adults in workshops, and I think it brilliantly mimics thinking in the midst of reading. If people write honestly about what they are thinking, visualizing, anticipating, and connecting with in texts, the result will look and sound like a tiny essay. This type of interpretive response might contain more questions than answers; it most likely will change its mind at least once about what is happening in the text, about characters' personalities, and about the large themes at play.

This activity can be done with any kind of short text—poems, preferably unrhymed ones, work extremely well for this exercise, as do fiction excerpts and essays—so that the whole class can experience writing-to-think about a text together. I always look for evocative, mysterious pieces that are not easily defined or categorized. The whole activity can take as few as ten minutes and should not take more than twenty.

1. Begin by reading, and then showing, the title of the piece. Ask students to write about the thoughts, images, connections, and anticipations the words of the title bring up.

2. Read and then show the first stanza of a poem or first paragraph or two of a prose piece. Ask students to write what new thoughts, connections, or images are occurring. What questions or confusions arise?

3. Proceed with another stanza or several paragraphs. Ask students to write how their thinking is changing. Repeat all the way to the end.

4. Finally, ask students to quickly reread their writing. Where and why did their thinking change?

What students will have at the end of this process is a story of their thinking, a microessay, complete with questions and fluctuating interpretations. This writing-to-think work becomes a powerful jump-start to partner, group, or whole-class discussion.

Inkshedding

Russell Hunt, an English professor at St. Thomas University, invented *inkshedding*, a powerful adaptation of freewriting, with his colleague Jim Reither. Hunt and Reither wanted their university students to think about the texts they were reading and to have unfettered written conversations with their peers rather than compose for professor evaluation (for more information, see www.stthomasu.ca/~hunt /dialogic/inkshed.htm).

I've modified their procedures and demonstrated inkshedding with students in grades 5 to 12, in science, history, English, even math classes. For this activity, it's important that students are sitting in groups (four to five works well) and have read the same text. When introducing the activity, I usually write the steps one at a time (on the board or project them in some way) as students move through each activity, and I time each step to move the class along whether students feel finished or not:

1. Write for five minutes in response to this question: What do you think is the *essence* of this author's argument? [You can substitute any reflective frame here: *most important word or sentence; turning point; most outrageous claim; least convincing evidence.*]

2. Pass your paper to the person on your right. Read the paper that was passed to you and write a response: question, agree, disagree, and explain why. You have two minutes to do this.

3. Keep passing the papers until everyone at your table has read and responded to all of them. [Each additional pass takes a few extra minutes.]

4. Hand the paper back to its original author. Read what everyone wrote in response to your original thinking.

5. Now, have a grand conversation!

Again, the writing-to-think that students do for this activity mimics draft essay writing and it literally includes multiple voices.

Lifting an essential word, phrase, or sentence

The strategy of lifting a concise essential piece of a text works similarly to the Lift a Line method of elaborating writing from Chapter 5. This time, students can search for an important word, phrase, or sentence from any text they are reading. They can put the lifted words (with quotation marks) on the top of a page in their notebook and write what they are thinking or wondering about them, what connections they are making between those words and the rest of the text so far.

Tweaking the formula

Several middle school teachers who work with Mary Ehrenworth, deputy director of the Teachers College Reading and Writing Project, have begun to explore, with Mary's brilliant guidance, writing about reading in a more playful way. These teachers invite students to think through some ideas about the book first, and then let those ideas build to a claim or thesis statement in the last few sentences. In other words, kids write about what they think about a book *before* (or instead of) fitting their writing into the forms and requirements of academic papers. Sometimes they come to a ringing conclusion about the book, but sometimes they arrive at an even deeper question.

Teri Bussler, a teacher in Marshall, Michigan, asked some of her eighth graders who were struggling with the standard formula to write their heart and soul out in a single powerful sentence at the top of the page. She told them to forget the introduction because it was throwing them off—they were getting lost trying to hook the reader and were focused on audience before they knew what was in their mind. Instead, she advised them to just state something loud and proud and then write their way forward to explain it.

Time for Practice

Bottom line: to improve academic writing, kids need to practice *writing*. Period. They need to practice writing for multiple readers, not only the teacher. And they especially need to practice writing for themselves, to find out what they think and feel about things. We need to offer students more time and space for writing that does not fit inside a box, follow a standard outline, or fulfill the items on any checklist of standards. As National Council of Teachers of English president-elect Doug Hesse writes, "We should promote school and career skills as but one aspect of literacy. We should value not only workers but also citizens, not only students passing tests but also social beings making connections, not only information processors but also idea creators" (2014).

Two final thoughts from two powerful thinkers. Peter Johnston (2012) reminds us of the power of children believing that they may not have precise knowledge or skill or answers to questions *yet*. Essaying educates for *yet*, for growth and process rather than benchmarks, tests, and evaluation. And Kim Stafford (2003) reminds us of the power of writing what we almost know, a passion he follows in his own notebook writing and in his teaching. He promises that "this anxious feeling is the growing place" (6). What we almost know. That feels like freedom to me.

Resources for Thinking About Academic Writing

PERSUASIVE WRITING

Caine, Karen. 2008. *Writing to Persuade: Minilessons to Help Students Plan, Draft, and Revise.* Portsmouth, NH: Heinemann.

Calkins, Lucy, et al. Units of Study in Opinion, Information, and Narrative Writing, Grades K–5. Portsmouth, NH: Heinemann.

ARGUMENT

Andrews, Richard, and Sally Mitchell, eds. 2000. *Learning to Argue in Higher Education.* Portsmouth, NH: Boynton/Cook.

Calkins, Lucy, et al. Units of Study in Argument, Information, and Narrative Writing, Grades 6–8. Portsmouth, NH: Heinemann.

Hillocks, George Jr. 2011. *Teaching Argument Writing, Grades 6–12: Supporting Claims with Relevant Evidence and Clear Reasoning.* Portsmouth, NH: Heinemann.

Smith, Michael, and Jeffrey Wilhelm. 2012. *Oh, Yeah?! Putting Argument to Work Both in School and Out.* Portsmouth, NH: Heinemann.

WRITING ACROSS THE DISCIPLINES

Dawkins, Richard. 2008. *The Oxford Book of Modern Science Writing*. Oxford, UK: Oxford University Press.

Fleischer, Cathy, Ethan Konett, and Kelly Victor-Burke. 2015. "Discussing Disciplinary Literacies." NCTE on Air. August 17. www.youtube.com/watch?utm_source=Inbox+Issue +-+2015-08-18&utm_medium=Email&utm_campaign=Inbox&v=RGFb4-HvdoE.

Folger, Tim, ed. 2002–2016. Best American Science and Nature Writing series. New York: Mariner Books.

RETHINKING COLLEGE COMPOSITION

Dombeck, Kristin, and Scott Herndon. 2004. *Critical Passages: Teaching the Transition to College Composition*. New York: Teachers College Press.

9

ASSESSING ESSAY

Soon after I began reading the essays, I became embarrassed by my reductionist need to quantify the depth and range of my students' freewheeling thinking, to measure in millimeters human feats of imagination and synthesis. I'd asked the students to surprise, delight, and inform. That they had.

—Tom Romano, *Clearing the Way*

n every moment of the writing process, practiced, published writers are assessing both their process and their drafts—tweaking here, crowbarring there—and the more they read and write over time, the more critical their lenses become on their own work.

In classrooms, effective assessment helps students name and celebrate what is working in their writing and also see what needs revision. Assessment allows students to step back from their work, examine their processes, and move on to new projects with the learning that comes from experience. And of course, careful assessment of students' needs as writers helps teachers know what to teach. The key is, when we as teachers view assessment as something writers do throughout their lives, we can embrace it and believe in its value to help young people become more confident and powerful writers.

In complete and utter contrast, evaluation—assigning a numerical or letter-grade *value* to writing—erodes young people's confidence as writers. If I ruled the world, grades and numbers would not exist, especially in writing instruction. Instead, teachers would talk with students in conferences or in written comments about what works beautifully and brilliantly in their writing processes and texts and explain how to build on those foundations to strengthen all their writing work. In this chapter, we'll explore how to assess the kind of essay that cannot be fed into a computer for scoring, the kind of essay that requires a human to read it from beginning to end and to notice and delight in the thinking adventure the student has crafted.

In my book *Hidden Gems: Naming and Teaching from the Brilliance in Every Student's Writing* (2010), I describe how teachers can find phenomenal craft in the most tentative piece of student writing (in any genre), name that craft like an artist, and help the writer craft that way again in the text—building on strengths rather than searching for errors with a red pen. The book includes a chapter on assessment and evaluation because I know teachers struggle with the idea of grading when they are also attempting a more holistic approach to writing instruction. I mention the book as a reference for more in-depth study of writing assessment.

Assessing What Students Already Know and Feel

It can be eye-opening to begin a study of essay by asking students what they already know, think, and feel about essay. This is an important assessment; it helps to hear what students have experienced and what their attitudes are toward this genre, especially if they have internalized a definition that insists upon five paragraphs or a bun and some meat, lettuce, and tomatoes. Students have responded to those questions, sometimes with near-panic. When Allyson Smith, a stunning writing teacher in Blue Springs, Missouri, asked her fourth graders, "What do you know or wonder about essay?" they responded with comments such as "It's something hard you do in high school," "It gets turned in to the teacher," "Will I have enough time?" and "It makes my hand tired." Allyson knew she would need to do a lot of reading immersion and writing-to-think in notebooks to change the perceptions of her students.

Some teachers have students write a quick pre-unit essay to establish what they already know and can do that might help focus their teaching for the following weeks. Students' first attempts will reveal if they are accustomed to writing to a formula because the predictable structures will be evident. What we can't discern solely from written essay samples are students' attitudes toward essay. Do they find it easy to craft an expository piece that reflects their honest ideas and observations, or have they already, as most middle and high school students I've met, decided that essays are boring? Do they struggle to find voice when they write in response to prompts inside prescribed formulas?

Asking for verbal or written responses will help us get closer to what our students know and feel about essay before we begin our unit of study. We might ask students to write for ten minutes in their notebooks in response to the question *What is an essay?* We can invite students to explain what they know about essay so far from their own reading and from their experiences in school. When I've done this exercise with students, I've found strengths to build on and also plenty that I would need to dismantle and redirect.

 ## Assessing What We Teach

When I earmark four to five weeks out of a school year to teach a certain genre of writing, I am confident there is something in that study, a set of concrete, essential features, that will benefit my students. This set of features determines most of my minilessons and writing conferences, and it appears in quick verbal and written reflections that help me know if my students understand and can apply those features to their work in progress. If, like most teachers, I must assign grades to my students' writing, then their good-faith attempts to learn and apply those particular features can become criteria, along with signs they are clearly engaged with the writing process (for instance, keeping a notebook, revising drafts).

Essay, of course, has multiple benefits for young people, many of which can't be measured. But if you are required to assign grades for writing, my first and best suggestion for creating a list of expectations for essay is to do that work with your students. In a minilesson or two, you can craft a reasonable list of essential features for essay, including descriptors for a rubric that will surpass anything I could offer in this chapter. You can put up the "What Is an Essay?" charts you made at the beginning of the unit with the list of features your students noticed from reading a mountain of mentor texts. No doubt that list has some features that are hard to quantify with points or a letter grade, such as "Makes you cry." Instead, focus on specific aspects of essay—action items, if you will—that students can more or less accomplish, such as "Explains an idea about an event, object, person, or place."

In the following sections, I list six essential features I hope every student carries away from a deep study of essay and five process and revision strategies that are critical to essay writing. This list repeats many of the features and habits of writing described in previous chapters, now collated into a handy menu of items. The features are not numbered, lest anyone think there is a hierarchy, but honestly, the first three would always be my top three goals for teaching essay. The rest of the features are more flexible. I can revise them (add, delete) depending on my classroom community, the time of year for this study, and what genres we have studied previously that school year.

You might decide to use this list as a place to begin thinking with your students and colleagues about what matters in the study of essay. Most likely, you will want to add features of essay or habits of writing that come from the content knowledge you and your students have acquired around essay and from your site-specific expectations and requirements.

Salient Craft Features of Essay to Assess

Demonstrates writing-to-think

In a writer's notebook and in essay drafts, the student demonstrates writing-to-think, a tentativeness and openness to changing course, a desire to explore and inquire, and then names that thinking with language such as the following:

- I think . . .

- Could it be possible that . . . ?

- It occurs to me now . . .

- I used to think . . . , but reading this book changed my mind.

Explains, develops, and circles around a big idea

The student extrapolates a big idea(s) to explore from the topics, observations, memories, and passions that appear in the essay, and understands that the driving feature of essay is exposition rather than storytelling or a regurgitation of facts and information. For example:

- Grown-ups forget what it feels like to be fourteen.
- The experience of time shifts depending on what you are doing, where you are, and whom you're with.
- Music helps people remember things.

Finds a shape and structure from the content

The student finds a logical, clear, and efficient structure that makes sense for the content of the essay. Some possibilities for structure include the following:

- general idea leading to specific detail
- specific detail leading to a general, extrapolated meaning or idea
- exposition, with small chunks of narrative woven in to elaborate
- narrative, with exposition woven in to elaborate
- ending that echoes or circles back to beginning
- numbered or lettered sections
- sections with subheadings.

Weaves in, seamlessly, the voices of others

The student finds quotations from reading, sources on the Internet, song lyrics, overheard conversations, or family sayings to push against, agree with, or flesh out thinking. For example:

- "[Stephen Colbert's] genius term *truthiness*, the state of something coming true because you find it to be so, became my mantra" (Schelde 2007, 211).
- I have a friend who tells me to "buck up" whenever I'm sad, but I don't have a clue what she means or how to do that.

- I see little girls (and grown-up women too!) belting out "Let It Go" (from the movie *Frozen*), and I can't help but wonder, "When will they finally get what that song is really about?" It's not about getting rid of stress or a bad boyfriend or whatever; it's about unleashing your true self, your true power into the world. It's a feminist song, a song about coming out, a song about celebrating difference!

Weaves in, seamlessly, facts, references, and events from history

The student finds things in the world that connect to the topic and idea of the essay. These bits of information do not require extensive research, but rather come from living wide-awake to the world and keeping a writer's notebook full of observations, facts, and quotes, which can become a resource for a layered and textured essay.

Finds a strong, consistent voice

The student finds a strong voice (e.g., bombastic, humorous, sarcastic) to best communicate the intended meaning. The voice is consistent throughout the essay and is appropriate for the occasion and the intended audience.

Process and Revision Strategies to Assess

Tries out different strategies to collect and layer

In the writer's notebook, the student tries at least three elaboration strategies, working to extend and expand upon the topic and idea of the essay. Some of those elaboration strategies may lead to new ideas and new thinking, which may also get layered into the essay draft.

Tries out different orders of parts

The student experiments with at least two different ways to order the parts of the essay, considers what would have to change with each arrangement, and decides on a structure and order that helps the ideas and writing flow and make sense for readers.

Writes at least three different beginnings

In the process of composing drafts and revising, the student finds different ways to begin the essay, chooses one, and demonstrates changes inside the body of the text for tone and cohesion. The beginning is the entry to a journey.

Writes at least three different endings

In the process of composing drafts and revising, the student finds different ways to end the essay, chooses one, and demonstrates rereading the entire text and making changes in light of the new ending for tone and cohesion. The ending brings the journey home.

Finds language that communicates meaning and engages readers

The student revises at the word level, engaging the reader with robust verbs and language that paints pictures, repeating important words and phrases, and, most importantly, writing honestly from the mind and heart.

Creating a Rubric from Criteria Lists

From your final menu of essay features and habits of writing, I suggest that you, your students, and your colleagues select only four or five that you think pertain most specifically to your students, or that align with standards, testing, and administrative expectations. You can then place these four or five features and habits into a rubric and think together about how to describe what an A or a 4 would look like for each one. In addition, you and your colleagues might decide on two or three general qualities of good writing (including grammar and conventions) to teach in this unit that you can also then assess. Thankfully, missing commas are, as we know, easy to mark.

Or, instead of looking for the same four or five features and habits in every student's work, you might decide to assess much more broadly and be on the lookout for a wider range of qualities from your study. When you come at assessment from this angle, you can allow student work to demonstrate the footprints of four or five habits and features for an A, three for a B, and so on. You might assign additional points for features not even on your list, as a way to acknowledge that a particular writer has found inventive ways to essay.

A Powerful Alternative to a Rubric

Alternatively, a more holistic and appreciative approach to assessing your students' work would be to look at the entire process—generating topics and ideas, collecting and layering around one topic and idea, drafting, revising, and editing—and simply note as many positive attributes as you can see. In this way, you can name specifically and particularly what each student has actually accomplished rather than fitting the assessment into the prescribed categories of a rubric. After all, even the most inclusive rubric fails to describe the fresh, beautiful writing that many students do, surpassing our own vision for what is possible. If we read a student's work first with a beginner's mind, open to what is *there*, we can read to be *surprised*, to come away with a list of ten things the student has done well!

Incorporating Peer Assessment and Self-Assessment

Because I believe so strongly in the power and efficacy of peer assessment, I teach students how to give positive and constructive advice to each other in any study. This arrangement creates the ideal learning situation: when students write for authentic, meaningful response, they learn quickly and lastingly what works best for readers. The work with peers is constant and ongoing; writers can talk to each other informally every day, and in more formal meetings two or three times a week, for ten minutes at the beginning or the end of a period of writing.

As embedded assessment, all along the process of composing essay, students should learn to ask reflective questions as they read and talk about each other's work. On sticky notes or note cards, students can write a sentence or two in response to questions (similar to the partner questions I described in Chapter 8) and then give those notes to the person who shared that day. Also, near the end of the essay unit, but before publication (when it would be too late), students might use a list of craft features and read their peers' essays through those lenses. This peer assessment can be shared either verbally or on note cards, and then writers can use the feedback as they make final revisions and edits to their essays.

Self-assessment, of course, is the assessment that matters most because ultimately students must be able to review and critique as practiced writers do—throughout the entire process of writing. Students must able to step outside of their own compositions and look at them critically, asking themselves where the writing is strong, where it sings, and also where it needs work. To help them accomplish this, we can ask students to use the list of craft features we've developed to assess their own writing, or to respond to reflective questions like those I list in the next section. The bottom line is, without this skill of self-reflection, there is probably less transfer of the content knowledge of essay.

When we ask students to respond to reflective questions, we can embed our teaching expectations directly inside the wording of the questions. But rather than assigning our (always subjective) judgments for how a student performed each one, we turn that work over to the student, asking for an honest self-appraisal on the work of the unit. We should not look for "correct" answers to these questions, but instead be interested in the language a student uses to express her understanding of the essay genre, her articulation of the thinking and working through the process, and her feelings and attitudes toward this genre and writing in general. When we read our students' self-reflections, we usually learn more about them as writers than we do from any other assessment.

Sample Reflective Questions for Self-Assessment

Notebook work

- What material keeps bubbling up in your notebook?

- What try-its or strategies for thinking and writing help you get a lot of writing work done, and why?

- What strategies do not feel useful, and why?

- How do you know you have found your best topic choice?

- What collecting and layering work do you know you still have to do?

Early drafting

- What is helping you move from your notebook to the draft?

- How are you using your notebook alongside your essay draft?

- What revision work do you know you still need to do?

Final drafting

- How do you know your essay is finished?

- If you had another week to work on it, what would you write or revise?

Post-essay study

- What new thing(s) did you learn about essay?

- What are you most proud of trying in this essay?

- What did you learn from writing essay that you can transfer to writing you will do in the future?

Being Brave and Pushing Back on Evaluating Writing

In Chapter 2, when I postulated that one reason the five-paragraph essay formula remains popular is that it is easy to grade, I wrote that statement with tremendous humility. School systems now seem to operate largely on evaluation and account-ability, and many teachers feel their ability to make decisions in the classroom has been taken away. But increased evaluation means that now more than ever, I want my work in the world to push back on the whole notion of assigning a letter or number grade to student writing, as I believe grades destroy potential writers, people who could otherwise feel confident at manipulating words to help them achieve their life dreams and goals.

To be honest, given the open, multifaceted, variously structured, and often personal nature of essay, I find it nearly impossible to imagine creating a rubric from the features in my list. I can't bear to put inside little boxes what would be an A idea or structure versus a C idea or structure. Would it be possible, I would continually ask my administrators when I was a classroom teacher, *not* to grade writing? I'm happy to report that many schools around the country where I now work as a pro-fessional developer are entertaining this possibility.

Or if I must grade, may I give a pass or fail, so that if I required five habits of writing or features of essay I wanted my students to definitely incorporate in their texts, and a student used only one, that could be considered a fail?

Or if there must be a rubric, might I put into the boxes certain attitudes and behaviors of writing—*writes one notebook page each night; tries three revision strategies; listens and gives positive feedback to classmates in writing groups*—rather than judging the quality of the words themselves? And if there must be a rubric, can I compose what goes in those boxes with my students, after they have spent several weeks reading and writing essays, so that my students are co-constructing their knowledge and understanding of this genre and developing their own criteria for what gets the highest value?

In this slender chapter, I hope I've given a running start to those who must grade, and I hope you and your colleagues enjoy good and productive conversations as you decide how to tackle assessing your students' essays in positive, appreciative ways.

Let Them Be Heroes

That they [essays] continue to be written and read is enduring proof that, all indications to the contrary, our voices matter to each other; that we do wonder what goes on inside each other's head; that we want to know each other, and we want to be known. Nothing is more meaningful—more human, really— than our efforts to tell each other the story of ourselves, of what it's like to be who we are, to think the things we think, to live the lives we live.

—Susan Orlean, *The Best American Essays 2005*

As I stated in my introduction, the essay is an exquisite genre of writing that should be taught in schools because it helps students develop their own topics and ideas, discover their own writing voices, and structure prose organically, according to the content. In conclusion, it will help students write well in all academic areas in college and help them succeed in their careers.

No, seriously. What final words can I offer to persuade for a study of essay in every writing classroom? Let me try.

In 2014, an extraordinary podcast aired, a spin-off of *This American Life* called *Serial*. The premise was a single story, narrated weekly over the course of twelve episodes. The premiere season of *Serial* involved a murder mystery so intriguing, so infuriatingly complex and unsolvable, despite intense efforts by teams of people to solve it, that it made a huge splash in popular culture. People argued about the suspect's innocence or guilt at work and online. The podcast won a Peabody Award in 2015; it even got a brilliant parody treatment on *Saturday Night Live*.

What works about the format of *Serial* is that it happens in real time. It is the opposite of the standard-fare murder mysteries on television, where the problem is set up, the murderer found, and sometimes the suspect is even tried and convicted, all within a single show. True, single-episode formulas can satisfy, like a fast-food burger. But in *Serial*, besides the fact that the story is real, and still, as of this writing, not satisfactorily solved, the truly addictive feature is that we hear the host of the show, investigative journalist Sarah Koenig, actively thinking through the case, investigating and finding new clues each week. Koenig wavers in her belief in the innocence or guilt of the convicted suspect, whom she comes to know fairly intimately, and she never reaches a definitive answer. She makes a decision by the last episode (I won't tell you what she decides, in case you have been otherwise disposed by family and work and haven't heard about the conclusion of *Serial*), but she does not have an answer.

Serial is like an essay that way.

There are times in life that can only contain "On the one hand . . ." and "On the other hand . . ." Times that you simply cannot take a position of authority, though you may long to. And oh, the questions—the ultimate moral and ethical questions that we'd best be honest about not having all the answers for, lest we find ourselves sounding like fools. Thoughtful people meditate on big ideas like guilt and innocence, spirituality, social justice, and human rights, and perhaps they find themselves thinking a certain way about that big idea one day, and the next day they question that thinking. Things are complicated. We face competing desires daily: for instance, though I try to live in a way that helps sustain our jewel of a planet, the disturbing fact remains that I have to drive across a large city (in a hybrid car, but still!), and I simply cannot do without air-conditioning for too many months in my scorching Austin, Texas, home. This is a conundrum I have not solved yet, though I worry over it a lot.

We have to learn how to be mature thinkers, how to deal with uncertainty, how to contain competing desires and agendas in our decisions. That is life. We can't come down too quickly on one side—we have to circle around an idea, see it from another perspective.

I believe that reading and writing essay can teach young people how to explore multiple possibilities, to test out competing propositions, and how to live with uncertainty in their lives. This essay business is decidedly *not* a wishy-washy curriculum! On the contrary—essay is a rigorous intellectual undertaking. It takes strength not to rush to form an impenetrable thesis statement. It takes courage not to reach cognitive closure on everything.

As I work with young people on this more open-ended, ambiguous, and exploratory type of writing, I find that kids who sometimes have difficulty filling out worksheets or coming up with answers to every question can experience excellence with essay. Essays can give young people a belief in their own voice, show them they have a center that speaks, a "me" inside them that has something to say and a way to say it. Essays ask writers to set sail on unchartered waters, with their hearts and minds as compasses. For these reasons, I will continue to fight for essay's meaning—*to try*.

Dagoberto Gilb titled a collection of his essays *Gritos*, which, he explains, means the particular cries, not sung notes, but more like wails or shouts of joy and extreme laughter, interjected into Mexican songs and celebrations. It can also name the cries of coyotes in the distance, and the rallying cry that reportedly signaled the start of the Mexican War for Independence in 1810 and that continues in celebrations every September 16.

Essays feel like *gritos* to me: soulful, aching cries in the wilderness of surprise, joy, anger, grief, freedom, and celebration. I want children to be able to put their particular cries, their *gritos*, into the world and for the world to read them and respond. Why would we deny our students the ability to be soulful and beautiful?

Also, I want young people to experience the pleasure of thinking deeply about something, circling ideas, naming possibilities. When Sarah Walker, a teacher in Austin, Texas, asked her seventh graders what they learned from spending time writing essay, Avery wrote:

> So what did I learn about this? Maybe that I can go really, really deep into writing and stay there under the water of words in the deep end of the essay pool. I like that. The water/peer pressure pushes down and yet an amazing piece of writing is churned out. It floats to the top waiting for a someone to read it. Someone does. Meaning, I can go deep and even under pressure I can write.

Our children do not always have to be answering some trumped-up charge of what they will need for that distant, mythical college or career. Often, what we call writing instruction merely teaches how to conform, how to obey. True writing composes meaning for the writer, first, and then for the (usually) invisible other, the reader. Writing should not conform to prescribed, standardized formulas that live only inside school walls and do not help young people face life with purpose and significance. Kids yearn to feel that someone in the world *needs* their words and thoughts and actions.

Carole Edelsky and Karen Smith have asked educators, "Is that writing—or are those marks just a figment of your curriculum?" (1984, 24). Perhaps there are occasions when we need kids to make marks to satisfy curricular mandates, but there must be many more times when young people are writing for themselves, tuning in to their own thoughts, feelings, and purposes. How has schooling taken such a dramatic turn away from the life of scholars like Montaigne—rich with reading, writing to think, creating art—to a system of product delivery and accountability, judgment and evaluation?

If the "hero of the essay is the author," as William Gass suggests, then young people must have as many chances as possible to be heroes. And if the essay is a journey, then young people must be able to take a hero's journey to find out what they think and who they are. Writing to discover what we care about is brave and also pleasurable. It makes an external record of a most beautiful human endeavor, which is to think and question; to change our minds; to be surprised at how much we didn't know we knew; to taste ourselves and to find what we are hungry for.

Drop-Off Cats

Amy Ludwig VanDerwater

When you live in the country, cats just appear. Dropped off in newspaper-lined bins, left in kitteny heaps in a ditch on your road, thrown out of moving cars, crawling up your porch. They arrive nameless refugees without passports or luggage, from another world, another life, and you find them homes or take them in.

Our latest is Mini Monster, named for another older, bigger cat—Monster. Lurking along the edges of our field for weeks last summer, he'd make brief eye contact only to disappear again. One day, he made it to the porch. Long fluffy tail. Dark stripes. One eye. Like a weary pirate, patchless and hungry, he joined the ranks of our barn cats and found food.

Animals trust children. Patiently, with soft voices and fingers full of salmon treats, Hope, Georgia, and Henry waited. Reaching gently, touching his back, his tail, his head, they lured this frightened and mangy beast into friendship. Long dark fur hung off of him in mats, tiny creatures crawled his head, and his left eye wept green goo. One day I got close enough to stuff Mini into a cat box and whisk him to the vet. A few hundred dollars later, neutered, dewormed, deloused, demited, and diagnosed with Hohner syndrome for his eye, he became a pet again.

Sometimes I ask Mini about his past life. "Did you live with an old lady who fed you tuna?" "Are you a father?" "Do you miss it there?" He doesn't answer, just presses his head into the crook of my arm and vibrates. I watch him nuzzle our dog and feel he must have had a dog in that other place. I clip a mat from behind his ear and wonder if he remembers being groomed; he's so still. These musings are sort of like wondering about your boyfriend's past. You long to know but you will never know and maybe it's better that way. Mini is between five and fifteen years old; our vet made up a birthday for him.

So why? Why pay money we need for a working car to heal a broken cat?

We help the cat because we can, because we are here, and because we were asked. We heal the cat because he needs us. He is a symbol for the world, a world that sometimes does show up on the porch and ask for help. By feeding Mini, petting him, and loving him, we make the world a tiny bit kinder.

The cats don't all live inside, but Mini does. A circle of fur on Cali's dog bed, a stretched-out baby in Georgia's arms, a curled-up comma on our couch. He's become a home-soundtrack, a loud in-and-out breathing purr that sounds like a growling "Thank you thank you" when anyone even walks in a room or pours water into the steel bowl.

I grew up a dog person. As children, we were told, "There's a difference between dog people and cat people; and we're dog people." I understand that difference; dogs love you and cats love what you do for them. But drop-off cats love like dogs. They know what humans are capable of. And we know too.

Amy Ludwig VanDerwater is the author of books for children including *Forest Has a Song*, *Every Day Birds*, and the forthcoming *Read! Read! Read!* She blogs poetry at *The Poem Farm* and notebooks at *Sharing Our Notebooks*, and you can find her online at www.amyludwigvander water.com or in real life in Holland, New York, surrounded by cats and dogs.

You Are What You Eat

Katie Wood Ray

was eating in a restaurant a while back—alone, as usual when I'm traveling—when the waitress came by to ask me if my steak was cooked to my liking. "It's fine," I told her, "but could you take these three green beans back and have another go at them?"

What is it with fine restaurants and their carefully rationed, barely cooked green beans? My emerging theory is that the more expensive my meal, the less the beans will be cooked and the fewer I will find on my plate. I've tested this theory out in many places and it always holds: If the meal is under fifteen dollars (think Cracker Barrel), the beans will be cooked, seasoned, and heaped on my plate. More than fifteen dollars, forget about it.

I come from a long line of women who start their green beans early in the morning and let them simmer on the stove all day just so they'll get fatter and fall apart when you serve them. And boy do we serve them, generously.

One of my fondest memories from childhood is sneaking a few green beans from the pot on my grandmother's old wood cooking stove. They were there all day, along with a few leftover biscuits, and they were never too hot, just warm and simmery and, well, cooked.

My friend Mary says the beans I'm getting in fine restaurants are cooked *al dente*. She says it with a bit of an accent. She says she likes them that way. I think the term is meant to mask a culinary travesty, as if by calling it something fancy they can make people think they're supposed to like it. Sort of like *double latte* or *au jus*. And the more French it sounds, the more you feel like a dolt for not wanting it that way.

And there is another thing, while I'm at it. Where I come from, we don't really want green beans when we say we want green beans. Actual green beans (or *haricot verts*, as the French like to say) are pathetically thin, rubbery imitations of real beans. They look like they've been picked weeks before they're ready. What we want are Greasy Backs. Pole beans. Half runners. Something with a little heft to it and bursting at its bean seams.

The *coup de grâce* (doesn't that make it sound fancy) of cooking these beans, however, are the thick pieces of fatback we add to them for seasoning. After an hour or so, the water the beans are cooking in should have that familiar fatty sheen to it, telling you you've got them on their way to just right.

For years at family gatherings I've carefully removed each piece of this delicious meat from my beans before my vegetarian sister-in-law has arrived for dinner. It works. She loves my beans. Can't get enough of them. "They don't cook them this way in DC," she says.

Well, duh.

My mother cans, or more precisely, she *jars*, a few dozen quarts of these little gems every summer. It's a weeklong affair. She goes to the same little vegetable stand out on Six Mile Highway and buys baskets of them just at the height of the picking season. "I always wait for the half runners," she says.

She and my dad sit on the porch with newspapers in their laps and string every one of those beans by hand. She then cooks them once, good and long, knowing full well we'll all cook them again, good and long, before we serve them, and then carefully jars and seals them.

She brings me a few quarts each season, jars wrapped in dish towels nesting in a worn old wicker basket. What gifts they are. I always think of her as I unhinge the lids and hear that familiar little *pop.*

Just the other day, I watched as my two-year-old nephew practically inhaled a bowl of warm green beans my mom had been simmering all morning. They'd cooked so long they fell apart as he dug into them with his chubby little hands, but he didn't seem bothered by the mess of it all. He loved those beans, and he's never known them any other way.

It occurred to me in that moment, watching him smiling and eating: we really *are* what we eat. AJ and I share a love of this food, fixed just this way, because we share a love for the person who fed us—my mama, his nana. And just as her DNA courses through both our veins, so too our belief in the *rightness* of this food for our souls.

Katie Wood Ray is a teacher, a writer, and most recently, an editor. She works with really smart teachers from all over to bring good practice to life in professional books. She's the mother of five big dogs who all like green beans (as long as they're cooked).

What I Want to Be . . .

Randy Bomer

When I was very little—maybe three years old—I only wanted to be . . . married to Denise, the little girl who lived next door. I told my mother I was moving out.

"Where will you live?" she asked, with a note of curious surprise.

"Here," I said.

"How will you get money to buy food?"

"I'll get a working business, like Daddy."

"A working business! Like what?"

"I can work at a filling station." This really didn't even strike me as a hard question.

"What do you know how to do at a filling station?"

"Wash windshields." Clearly, I had already thought about how easy that looked.

"Well, Randy, you can't even reach the windshields."

"I'll climb up on the cars."

That's my earliest memory of knowing what I wanted to be when I grew up. I wanted to be Denise's husband. And I wanted to climb up on cars to wash windshields. I was ready to begin right away. I didn't even think I needed to grow up to be what I wanted to be when I grew up.

I think, all through my childhood, I had an idea, on any given day, what I wanted to be. I'd think about it lying in bed, not sleeping, which was a good part of every night.

I have this early photo of myself, dressed up like a cowboy. No, not just dressed up, *being* a cowboy. I'm only two years old, but I have the wide-legged stance, the boots placed delicately on the ground, a hat perched on my head, and six-guns at forty-five-degree angles to my shoulders.

When people say, "what I want to be when I grow up," they are talking about a life they want, a kind of person they're becoming. They want to live like a cowboy, look like a cowboy, be seen by others as a cowboy. It's what they want to be known for—how they want to be recognized, not just a job they want. A cowboy gets to wear a certain kind of hat and footwear, hold particular tools. Other people recognize him as a cowboy when he goes by. It's not just his work that makes him a cowboy.

That's one difference between the me in the cowboy picture and the me as a gas station guy. The cowboy picture had not one bit of practicality to it. I was not, of course, trying to figure out how to buy food. (If you'd asked me, I'd have said I'd just kill my food.) I wasn't thinking about doing a cowboy's duties. I was just *being* a cowboy—the whole deal. In the gas station story, I was not hoping to look like a gas station guy or have others recognize me as one. That was about a jobby-job.

For a while, I thought I would be a doctor on weekdays, a professional football player on Saturdays, and a preacher on Sundays. Why should I choose, when there were so many days in a week? If I became only a doctor, how would I get to have fun playing football? And what would God do without me? It seemed unfair to have to grow up and lose parts of myself that I had right now. I could not accept growing up if it meant being just one thing.

My father used to say to me, "I don't care what you are when you grow up. I don't care if you dig ditches. But just make sure, if you do, that you're the best dadgum ditch digger you can be." I never wanted to be a ditch digger. I had never even seen anyone doing that job, but it sounded pretty hard.

This talk with my dad always seemed like a conversation about jobs, but now I think we were really talking about becoming a sort of person when I grew up. And that's a whole different way of thinking about what I want to be. "What I want to be" is not just a question about a job or who I want to work for, because a job isn't all a person is. The guy who washes the windows at the gas station (if such a person still existed) might also be passionate about beautiful colors and care about the environment.

I can imagine some kids still thinking, "Well, I'm going to be an astronaut." But maybe those kids should ask themselves what's so great about astronauts. If they love outer space, maybe they know that all their lives, they want to study and learn about one thing, deeply. If they like the uniforms astronauts wear, then maybe they know that they want to wear clothes that make them feel powerful, or that have everything you need right in your pockets. Maybe they are wishing to become some kind of person, and not just for a particular job.

When my dad used to talk to me about what I would be when I grew up, it wasn't really about something in the future. It was something that had happened that day that made him want to talk to me about it, something I was trying to do in drama, or in sports, or music, or school. I think the real point was that I was becoming someone I was going to be *today*. It wasn't really about the future; it was about the present.

Maybe, whenever we think about what we're going to be when we grow up, we're thinking about ourselves right now as someone who can become something different. When we say the words "what I want to be . . . ," we are crawling into a chrysalis.

Randy Bomer *teaches at the University of Texas at Austin. He loves art and music, and for lunch, he loves chili. He is lucky to be married to the lady who wrote this whole book.*

There Is a Hercules of Everything

Randy Bomer

This is the first time I got a big idea, when I was three years old. I don't know where the idea of a big idea came from, but I do know where this particular big idea came from. The idea was this: there is a Hercules of everything. Whatever kind of thing you are thinking about, there is one of those that will overpower all the others.

On some afternoons, there was a cartoon on TV called "The Mighty Hercules." It wasn't that I was crazy about Hercules or about this particular show, but in those days, you just had to watch what was on. Just today, I found a few of these cartoons on YouTube, and they are terrible, but my standards were lower when I was three.

Because of the cartoon, Hercules was on my mind back then. Whenever my mom did something strong, like pick up something pretty big, she would look at me, make a muscle, and sing "Hercules!" just like the song from the cartoon. It became part of the comedy show of our family.

It was pretty easy to think about the strongest man who ever lived. Even though there were other strong men in the movies, I had the idea that Hercules was the strongest of them all. I think my sense of order just needed one of them to be stronger; I wanted these things to be clear.

Around this same time, I was doing a lot of coloring. There were several years in there that were definitely the most productive of my life, coloring-wise. Often, I'd color alone, but I also remember other kids coloring beside me, mostly my cousins. We focused on our own page, not looking at each other, talking about what we were doing, how we were trying to get some effect with the colors—like experiments.

We tried colors on top of each other, just to see what it looked like. I don't think we knew anything about mixing two colors to get a new one. We were just seeing whether, if you colored over red with green, you could still see the red. And yes, you could. The waxy crayons didn't really make solid streams of color—more like a series of very close wax bumps of color—unless you really mashed down on the crayon, which was exhausting. Mostly, you ended up with red *and* green bumps there. You could still see them both. But black was different. If you took a black crayon and colored over any color with even moderate pressure, what you had at the end was black—that's it. Black was the only color that could cover any other. This, to me and my cousins, was a major scientific discovery.

Here comes the moment when I got the big idea.

I had been sitting in the bathtub for a while, and the water was getting cold. A few times recently, my mom had fixed this situation by just running more hot water, and the hot water had turned the cold water hot again. So even though maybe I wasn't supposed to do this myself, I turned on the hot water and traced with my hand the path through the water of the rising temperature. Hot water, I thought, is like black. It can turn the cold water into hot; it can just cover up the cold. Black is the Hercules of colors; hot is the Hercules of water. There is a Hercules of everything.

I told my mother this after my bath, and she just said, "Hmm," like she wasn't totally sold on my idea. That worried me a little, but it also meant that this idea was just mine. I saw that I'd have to work on my own, figuring out the Hercules of each type of thing. Maybe the Hercules of animals was lions. I'd have to think about it. The Hercules of toys: maybe army guys. I didn't know; it was going to need some work. But I was excited to have a *theory* to work on.

In a way, I have kept working on that theory. I still like to think hard about power. Out of respect for my three-year-old self, I'm going to try out some new thoughts based on those old ones.

I've heard parents say that when little kids are interested in superheroes, strength, and even dinosaurs, what they're really working on is an understanding of power—who has it, how it works, how you can get it. The idea of power does seem useful in the bigger idea I had. The way I saw it, Hercules, black, and hot water each had power over the other things—bad guys on the show, other colors, and cold water.

Sometimes, people unfairly use power to get what they want, and one way to try to stop them from doing that is to call what they are doing "using power." That way, it doesn't seem like what is happening is just right and natural; it helps everyone to see that this is a matter of trying to cover up someone else's colors. If we want the world to be fair for everyone, we have to be able to think about power.

The examples in my three-year-old idea—Hercules, black, and hot water—might even represent three different kinds of power. Hercules used his strength either against people (to stop them from doing something wrong) or for people (to help them if they were trapped by something). But everyone isn't like Hercules, and people's use of power isn't always as cheerful and good as his was. People use power over each other all the time, sometimes to help others, sometimes to push them down and keep them down, to get ahead.

The power of the black crayon, the Hercules of Colors, was to cover over other colors, to make them invisible, even while they were still there. Are there ways that people do that to each other? I think so—when some people can demand so much attention or respect, or when they think only their own experience is what counts, that they make other people's voices, other people's colors, disappear.

What's interesting to me about hot, the Hercules of Water, is that I was mostly wrong about it. What I was noticing was correct at that moment, of course—when I added more hot water, it made the overall temperature change. But the same thing would have happened if I had added cold water. I just didn't want to do that! Hot water and cold water affect each other; it's not really a matter of one having power over the other. The power of hot and the power of cold can go back and forth; it's more like taking turns. Maybe that's the kind of power we should try to have among people. Maybe no one needs to be the Hercules of everything.

Randy Bomer teaches at the University of Texas at Austin. He loves art and music, and for lunch, he loves chili. He is lucky to be married to the lady who wrote this whole book.

The Thing About Cats

Vicki Vinton

When I was seven I fell in love with my neighbor's cat. Her name was Smokey and she had long, soft fur the color of slate and eyes that blazed like topaz. I was welcome to play with her at my neighbor's house, which I often did. But what I loved more were those times when Smokey scooted beneath my neighbor's fence and wandered into my backyard—or better still, when I was able to lure her into the house and upstairs to my room where I could pretend she was my very own.

Of course, getting her from the yard to my bedroom wasn't exactly easy. She wouldn't come when I called, so I'd make a trail of kibbles from the fence to the back door or pull a long piece of twine through the grass that she'd try to catch. But more often than not something would distract her—a butterfly, a leaf, an acorn falling from a tree. Then she'd freeze, cock her ears and crouch down to pounce, and completely forget about me. And even if I regained her attention and got her through the door, I'd have to sneak her past my mother, who expressly forbade me to bring a cat into the house because I was allergic to them.

Even now I'm not quite sure why I was willing to risk my mother's wrath and Smokey's indifference, if not downright rejection, just to get her into my room. A dog would have been far less trouble, as most of the neighborhood dogs I knew obeyed commands like *come* and *sit*. In fact, with their tails thumping or wagging and their paws ever ready to shake hands, dogs were far more eager to please than cats, which, to me, might have been their problem. Pet a dog, a saying goes, and it will think you're a king. Pet a cat and it thinks it's a king. Perhaps even at the age of seven, I preferred the idea of playing with royalty rather than an obedient sidekick.

And in that I wasn't alone.

Across the globe, over six hundred million cats live among people, making them the most popular pet in the world. And cats have had a hold on people's imaginations for centuries. The ancient Egyptians, for instance, believed cats were demigods (half-animal and half-god) who captured the glow of the setting sun in their eyes and kept it safe until dawn. In fact, cats were so revered in ancient Egypt that, during the reign of certain pharaohs, killing a cat was punishable by death—even if it was an accident.

Not everyone, however, has looked on cats so fondly. In the Middle Ages, for instance, thousands of cats were stuffed into sacks and tossed into fires to burn after a pope declared them evil. And cats have been associated with bad luck and witches for hundreds and hundreds of years, whether it's the old Russian witch Baba Yaga, whose house, perched atop giant chicken legs that moved, was guarded by a black cat, or Harry Potter's friend Hermione and her ginger cat Crookshanks, who more than once helped thwart the plans of Harry's archenemy Voldemort.

Of course, Hermione is a good witch and Crookshanks a good cat, using his intelligence to help his owner, as dogs in books and movies often do. Think of Dorothy and Toto, Opal and Winn-Dixie, even Shaggy and Scooby-Doo, who, while not exactly intelligent, is certainly one of the gang. All these dogs are loyal companions, offering their services when their owners are in need. Cats, however, are portrayed differently. They're often depicted as tricky or sneaky, with mysterious powers and agendas of their own—like the Cat in the Hat, who, in the name of fun, almost gets poor Sally and her brother into serious trouble, or the Cheshire Cat from *Alice in Wonderland*, who speaks in riddles and tends to fade away, leaving behind only his grin, whenever Alice most needs him.

This may be because cats do, in fact, seem to have mysterious, magical powers. They're able to land on their feet from falls that might easily kill other animals, and they can squeeze out of tight spots and spaces without getting injured or trapped. And while scientists can now explain how they do this through a mix of anatomy and physics, to this day, they don't exactly know why or how cats purr.

They also disagree about when, where, and how cats became domesticated. Cats seem to have started living with us about ten thousand years ago, after we left hunting and gathering behind and started growing crops. They were drawn by the rodents, who also appeared to steal and eat the grain, but whether we actually tamed them is open to debate. It seems just as likely that they tamed us—to pet them, to feed them, to let them into our houses where it was cozy and warm—just as an old Chinese legends says. According to the legend, cats were put in charge of the world and could speak back then. And they used that power to delegate jobs so that they could lounge around and play while humans did all the work. Eventually they lost the power to speak, but it didn't matter at that point, because by then you could say they had us wrapped around their little paws.

Certainly Smokey seemed to own me, more than I owned her. And now that I've outgrown my allergies and have two cats of my own, I feel that even more. Oh, the cats come to me when I open the door—and open a can of food—but nothing in their faces or behavior suggests they're excited to see me. But when one decides to jump into my lap, curls up there and starts to purr, I think I feel more special and chosen than I ever would with a dog. And maybe that's the thing about cats. They please us not by fetching our slippers or rolling over when we command, but by pleasing themselves—and being unknowable.

Vicki Vinton is the author of the Heinemann books *What Readers Really Do* and *The Power of Grammar*. When she's not at her desk writing (with, if she's lucky, a cat in her lap), you'll find her in classrooms, helping teachers and students learn more about reading and writing. And here's a little secret about her and cats: when she was little, she thought all cats were girls and all dogs were boys and they married each other!

Querencia

Georgia Heard

S everal years ago, I moved to Florida from my New York City home of twenty-five years. On the first day in my new house I went outside to get the mail, and stopped to pick out a piece of trash stuck in the flowering *Plumbago* plant. When I plucked it out I realized it was a torn piece of someone's stationery with one word, *querencia*, printed on it, and part of a hand-written phone number.

Not your everyday kind of word that ends up in the bushes in your front yard. *Querencia*. That's *my* word. I've told the story to friends dozens of times about when I first learned about querencia. It's when I witnessed my first, and last, bullfight in Spain and watched the wounded bull, pierced repeatedly with the matador's sword, retreat to the side of the ring. Someone said, "He's finding his querencia. A place where he feels safe, and will be more dangerous to the matador."

Querencia comes from the Spanish verb *querer*, which means to desire, to want, and it also means home. Above my apartment door in New York City, I displayed a wooden sign with *querencia* printed on it. My home.

What was I to make of this piece of paper appearing in the bush in my new yard with my word on it?

I felt disoriented when I first moved to Florida. Not because it isn't beautiful, and the weather nice, but because it seemed too beautiful: gated neighborhoods with sparkling lakes surrounded by emerald green golf courses, cerulean skies stretching as far as you could see, and no one walking down the sidewalks. Where was everyone?

I missed my car-honking, traffic-snarled street on the Upper West Side, where a roaring garbage truck woke me up early every other morning. I missed the guys at the corner deli who stacked oranges and apples in neat rows, and waved every afternoon as I passed by. Missed the scrawny maple tree outside my window sprouting early spring buds in February, reminding me that winter was finally over. I couldn't just meet my friends around the corner at Bennie's Burritos on Broadway, and order the best burritos in the world, bursting with black beans, salsa, and guacamole.

I taped the little slip of paper with the word *querencia* on it to my wall near my writing desk, and after several months it seemed like a fortune cookie with a message for me. It reminded me of some lines from one of my favorite poems by William Stafford, about having something like a *thread* that stays with you no matter what else changes in your life.

Now, I'm getting used to the magnificent white clouds rolling across my window, the balmy air, and not being woken up early by the roar of garbage trucks. That torn piece of paper that drifted into my yard helps me remember my thread, my querencia. No matter where I am, my writing is my querencia, and I'm home.

Georgia Heard is a poet and a teacher. In books like *Writing Toward Home, Awakening the Heart*, and her latest, *The Woman in This Poem*, she explores the beautiful idea of querencia in all its many forms.

The List

Isoke Titilayo Nia

Y ou don't really expect the Macy's saleslady to take you back to that place in your life that marks you as a foster child. It was the list. The simple Kwanzaa wish list I pulled out of my bag at a counter in New York's largest department store, Macy's. The saleswoman thought it was awful. Thought it showed a remarkable degree of greed and presumption. Thought it lacked the spirit of the season. She voiced all of that in a single sentence: "THEY'RE WRITING LISTS NOW— WELL, I NEVER!"

For a split second I felt bad, but it was the holiday season. It was the time for gifts and clearly I was there to purchase one for someone I love. So I smiled, boldly accepted her disdain, and informed her that yes, *they* are writing lists now and that in fact *lists* were a tradition in my family. I emphasized the words *tradition* and *family* because, having been a foster child, those words are not words I got to say often.

I grew up in a foster home, and I was the only child I knew who was a foster child. *Foster* was a crazy word and I didn't understand it and neither did any of my friends. I grow quiet when I remember. Compared with some who faced constant beatings and lack of food and less than warm clothing, I fared well. I was not that foster child. But there were things missing from my childhood, things so different and so hard to explain, most times I keep my story to myself.

My foster mother just didn't get it. She didn't get that there is a kind of knowing that makes a foster child *your* child. There is a kind of attention given to this child that transfuses her into your family. It mixes her blood with your blood and from the outside, from the many windows into a family, people can't see *foster* anymore. They just see *your* kid. That's what was missing from my foster care. And it seemed to magnify itself during the holiday season. Maybe because in December, especially in America, everything is magnified. All the shiny parts of life are more shiny and all the dull, sad parts, more sad and more dull.

My foster mother thought if the tree was full and if she spent a certain amount of money, she'd made Christmas. But even at seven I knew that Christmas was made from love. I knew gifts were special and that brown paper wrapping and one special gift would make Christmas, if that gift showed you knew something, one thing, *anything* about the child you were raising. I believed the perfect gift could erase just a little bit of the word *foster*.

Perhaps at seven I'd made up the feeling that parents, even foster parents, should know what you wanted. I'd listen to kids at school and we always seemed to know exactly what we wanted. We'd point and name and list, and when we returned to school my classmates always seemed to have gotten at least one thing they wanted. Those first few days back after the holidays were torture for me. I wore that sign FOSTER on my forehead and I listened and nodded and did not share.

I used to imagine my foster mother went into a store at Christmas and said to the salespeople, "What do you have for nine-year-olds?"

And they, smarter than she, would say, "What does your child like?"

And she'd say, "My foster child, she's nine."

Nine is not a description. Nor is seven, eleven, or eight. Nine is a number. It's actually a rather common number. In fact, before becoming adults, all people get to be nine.

So the salespeople, wanting to sell things, did just that. My foster mother felt good with her purchases. She had them wrapped, brought them home, and put them under the tree. On Christmas morning, I woke with anticipation and opened all the strangers who were my gifts, displaying them in a huge circle around me. I'd try to focus on one thing that would be my story gift (the one I'd brag about at school), and when none became my friend, I left the strangers, *my gifts*, and the tree and tinsel and paper and went back to the room I shared with the person who didn't know me.

Gifts are supposed to bring joy and show children how much they are loved and really just make them know that you recognize them as individuals. And for a foster child, they are another way of saying you're ours. We belong to each other.

So in my family, we make lists. We make lists for birthdays and Kwanzaa and anniversaries. We make lists because I was a foster child and I know the feeling of getting gifts for an entire childhood and not remembering a single one. I know the feeling of wanting just once to join my classmates in the ritual of gift storytelling. So we make lists.

In my family we treasure gifts and I just can't get enough of that look that comes on the face of all of those I love when they get a gift, any gift, one gift, they really want. A gift that makes them tell a story. I love that their gifts are not strangers. I love the yells and the running in a circle and all the shiny of every holiday.

I know that this practice might make us sound a little greedy, a little self-absorbed, maybe even a little materialistic, but it's not. It's about love and knowledge and even though it was a tradition born from a lack of attention, it has become a marvelous way to build stories around the shiny times in our lives. In our leanest years, the years when we could not purchase or make gifts, the lists were the gifts. We'd just sit and talk about what was important and there were no packages—just shiny faces and laughter.

To be a good foster parent you have to spend the 364 days that are not Christmas learning something about the child you brought home. You have to be able to answer the question, *What does she like?* Most of all, you have to make sure that when you bring a child into your home, *foster* is not part of her description. You just want her to be your kid.

Put this on your list.

Isoke Titilayo Nia works with teachers around the country to help them implement writing workshops in their classrooms. A longtime resident of Brooklyn, New York, Isoke celebrates her birthday for an entire month and makes her wish list well in advance. She especially likes gifts wrapped in purple, her favorite color.

Ice Girls

Gianna Cassetta

Truth passes through three phases:
First, it is ridiculed.
Second, it is fiercely and violently opposed.
Third, it becomes self-evident.

—Arthur Schopenhauer

recently treated my family to behind-the-glass seats for an NHL hockey game. For us, watching hockey together is a time of joy when we feel a genuine and uncomplicated connection. As a lifelong hockey fan, I found it every bit as magical as I imagined it would be. That is, until six young women skated onto the ice wearing midriff-bearing stretch shirts with cleavage peepholes and micro-miniskirts with thigh slits. As they began sweeping the snow with their shovels, my seven-year-old turned to me and asked, "Mom, why are those girls wearing bikinis? They must be really cold."

Months later, my son's question still troubled me. I took to googling "NHL Ice Girls" and "Do the Rangers have ice girls?" and "Is anyone protesting about ice girls???" I discovered that fifteen NHL teams (and counting) have some version of ice girls, but that after a sexual harassment lawsuit in 2007, the New York Rangers dismantled their ice girls and opted for fully clothed ice *people*. I also discovered a "Say No to San Jose Sharks Ice Girls" Facebook page with close to two thousand likes.

Interestingly enough, I also found a chorus of voices—sportswriters, reporters, bloggers—unabashedly ridiculing anyone who finds fault with the presence of ice girls at hockey games. Just listen:

> "Oh yeah, there are cheerleaders in the NHL. Only they don't just get to stand around looking pretty. To earn their keep, these women clean all the snow off the ice during TV time-outs."

"Go look on the [Say No to San Jose Sharks Ice Girls] page. 90% are over-weight and not the least bit attractive, so it is my opinion that is why they are protesting."

"In a country filled with major political and economic issues that are drag-ging us to the brink of destruction, there are still those people who have time and energy to complain about bare midriffs?"

Without a doubt, I've seen and experienced sexism firsthand, but I've always believed no one was going to box me in, hold me down, or shut me up, despite their sexist views. You see, I always thought about sexism as it related to *me*. I'm embar-rassed that the thing that made me feel angry and sad and defeated, the thing that forced me to think beyond myself and see sexism through the eyes of two little boys, was the NHL ice girls.

Almost one hundred years after the passage of the Nineteenth Amendment to the United States Constitution, and forty years after the Equal Rights Amendment, we still straddle Schopenhauer's phase one of truth when it comes to equity for women in the United States. Gender equity is still a joking matter. I don't think I had ever really gotten that before.

Right here in the United States, women still make about seventy-six cents to a man's dollar. Employers can deny women access to birth control when their own religious beliefs are "substantially burdened." One in four women will experi-ence domestic abuse, and yet a well-known newscaster feels righteous enough to go on national TV and wonder what a battered NFL player's wife did to provoke the abuse. Campus rapes are rampant, and a woman is sexually assaulted every two minutes in the United States.

I think I agree with the indignant sports blogger. With such profound injustice happening under our noses, how could I have the time and energy to complain about a bare midriff on a girl who is earning her keep by providing the NHL with the invaluable, regulation-required service of sweeping the snow off the ice?

Because I must. Because I cannot look away. The snow sweeper with the bare midriff, the cleavage peephole, the micro-mini, and the thigh split is one more manifestation of the objectification of women. Her presence may be entertaining. It may be as American as apple pie. But every time an oversexualized woman *is the entertainment*, that woman becomes less of a person in someone's eyes. When someone is less of a person, it is all the easier to abuse, neglect, ignore, or mock her.

And so I cannot look away. Men in our culture, especially white men, enjoy unearned privileges—the privilege to decide which issues deserve serious consideration or ridicule, the privilege to control what is or is not entertainment, the privilege to enjoy the presence of an oversexualized woman at a sporting event.

Someday, my sons will be men. So with everything I have, I must find the energy to complain, to oppose our society's unrelenting, disdainful objectification of women.

I can't take back the moment my sons watched women sweep ice from the rink in bikinis. But I can complain about it. Loudly and repeatedly. I want my sons to look at women not as objects but as equals—and not just their mothers and wives and daughters, but also the women they work with, the women who sit next to them in classrooms, the women on the phone, on the bus, at the checkout. I must complain because I could not bear it if my sons treated someone with less respect merely because she was a woman. I must complain because there is no humor to be found in inequity. And I cannot look away.

Gianna Cassetta is a former teacher and principal who now coaches teachers and principals as well as writes books for them. She loves the New York Rangers and her favorite season is hockey season.

They Don't Tell You About That

Olugbemisola Rhuday-Perkovich

When my mom was in a rehabilitation hospital, we had to label all of her clothes, her name in black Sharpie as though she were off at camp. I have one of her tops from those days, worn white cotton, short-sleeved, determinedly cheerful hearts in every color of the rainbow dotted all over. She wore that one a lot; sometimes her skin was so sensitive that even the lightest fabrics hurt. That shirt has been in every one of my closets, packed and unpacked with each move, laundered and folded carefully and pushed to a back corner.

It's been years since my mom died.

The other day, I was thinking about organizing a memorial service, a tasteful celebration of her life, getting her gang back together. I'm good at coordinating. In the year after she died, I held many gatherings of friends and family at home, at the park, at the beach. I hugged everyone back. When I was in high school, I planned a surprise birthday party for her. It was an unqualified success, at least it seemed so; she appeared happy and surprised, and we all enjoyed the birthday rap performed by my classmates with perhaps more enthusiasm than talent. I could do a memorial. *It's time,* I thought. *I've lost touch with so many of our friends from that life. I'll see them again, we'll reminisce, exchange contact information. They'll hug me, and tell me how proud she'd be. I'll wear something muted and tasteful and they'll tell me I look pretty even though we'll all know better.* It could be nice. *Appropriate,* I thought.

And then I cried.

Some days, years become minutes, like I'm shoved through a nightmare tesseract and in an instant I'm back in the hospital lounge, sitting cross-legged on a vinyl chair that's supposed to be comforting. But my mom just died and I'll never be comforted again. I don't want to be mature, or tasteful, or make anyone proud. It's been years and still I am shocked frozen. I want to crawl back to bed, pull the covers over my head, and cry—real, ugly sobbing that doesn't care if it makes you uncomfortable.

They tell you that time helps, and heals. That you are blessed to have precious memories, that she loved you so much, and that they know how you feel. I'll probably say the same thing to someone one day. But sometimes those stupid, empty, meaningless words make me want to slap and scream because nothing helps, *my mom is dead, do you understand?*, and even after all this time I will pick up a book or trip on the sidewalk and that "healed" wound suddenly rips open, and all of the jagged edges hurt so much that I can't breathe. I don't even want to.

They don't tell you about that.

After my mom died, I signed up for a writing course at the university where she taught. It was a class in creative nonfiction. Or maybe journalism. I don't remember. I wrote listless, lackluster assignments and rarely spoke in class. My final assignment was titled "I Don't Want to Write About My Mom." It was probably terrible too; I don't remember. I do remember my professor catching up to me, eyes brimming with concern, after I'd turned it in. I remember his glasses, his beard. Maybe he said he was sorry for my loss. I was angry, at myself, at him, at writing, for not being able to help like it was supposed to.

Right after, at least three people gave me a book: *Motherless Daughters*. It was probably a good book. I never opened it.

I've stopped waiting for that moment when I'm going to breathe deeply, and see my mom and my life with her through a constant, rosy glow. I know that some days I will be able to talk about the time my mom and I couldn't stop giggling about the priest's BO. Or how she'd told me about the first time she'd tasted white sugar, on the plane from Jamaica to New York, and I'd make her tell me again and again. Some days I will go to the store and buy a banana, and thoroughly enjoy it because the last thing my mom told me was to eat bananas. And then I read her some corny jokes and we smiled.

And some days I won't be able to get out of bed. And I will not have bananas in my house.

A few years (or minutes) after my mom died, I wrote about some of the unbearable moments during her illness, of the heaviness that threatened to crush me completely. In those moments, I'd be lifted by an invisible Presence, by something that felt alive and able to carry me through, out of the wilderness of despair and back into Love. It was a contemplative, spiritual essay.

Some days I can't bring myself to pray.

Last month, as I dressed for bed, I reached for that shirt. I put it on for the first time; it was so soft. I remembered the time we had Christmas dinner in that hospital, and how Mom came to every one of my band concerts, and let us have ice cream for dinner sometimes, and I reminded myself to call one of those old friends. Then I went to sleep.

Maybe one day I'll organize that memorial, welcome everyone back into the old days and we'll laugh and we'll cry, and maybe some of us won't show up because we couldn't get out of bed. And maybe I'll tell a story about my mom; probably I'll listen to some. Maybe I'll wear the soft white shirt with the hearts and everyone will tell me that it looks pretty even though we'll all know better. Maybe I'll do that. But whatever I do to honor my mom, it won't be pretty.

It will be beautiful.

Olugbemisola Rhuday-Perkovich is the author of *8th Grade Superzero* and the forthcoming *Two Naomis*, with Audrey Vernick. She believes in the power of a good book, a long walk, and a nice cup of tea (snacks optional but strongly recommended). Olugbemisola lives in New York City, where she loves to write, teach, and make things, and needs to get more sleep. Find her online at http://olugbemisolabooks.com.

Tattoos: Marked for Life

Deb Kelt

am a nontattooed person.

I don't have inspirational quotations running down my arm; there are no angel wings on my back. Not a single wreathy vine on either of my ankles. No flowers, no butterflies, no crosses.

Ink-free, I am—but probably not for the reasons you think. Maybe you're predicting this will turn into a rant, but I don't have judgment for people who have tattoos. Whatever you want to do—or not do—with your body is OK with me.

All I'm saying is: I don't have any tattoos.

Oh, I have been tempted by the ink of others. One guy I knew had a gigantic *Virgen de Guadalupe* tattooed across his entire back. It was gorgeous, intricate. "Why did you want this?" I asked him one day.

"I told *la Virgen* that if I made it across the desert—if she protected me and brought me to this country alive—I would do this for her. So as soon as I got here, I got this tattoo." I fought back tears and yearned for that kind of faith.

Then there is my dear friend Song. She has more tattoos than anyone I know. Up and down her arms, across her chest, down her legs. She has tattoos dedicated to her man, tattoos she got with best friend Naomi, snakes, oranges, flowers, ice-cream cones, hearts, hula girls, stars, roses. And they are stunning on her. Like a Renaissance tapestry: each tat a beautiful stitch on the intricate cloth that is her skin.

But Song is tiny—a delicate bird. The tattoos are almost ironic on her small frame, both ladylike and tough. Like salted caramel. A little sweet, a little tart.

I talked to Song about getting a tattoo. But the more I studied her, the more I knew it wouldn't be the same. For me—a total endomorph who has never been called petite—I realized I couldn't pull this off. I would look too husky, like a female Popeye. I realize the feminist in me should embrace my tough side, my brawny side. But since you've come this far with me, I'll be totally honest: I struggle with body image, and I have the Weight Watchers membership card(s) to prove it. Though I can look at my mother, my grandmother, and my great-grandmother and see only beauty in their hips, I've never had those gentle eyes toward myself. In my mind, tattoos would emphasize the parts of my body that I have never really liked—the big parts, the unwieldy parts, the parts that flop when I want them to be still, the parts that don't look so good in sleeveless shirts.

No need to highlight that shit permanently. You know?

(And since we're talking about superficial stuff, I should also add that I have battled my skin for most of my life, too. I've always wanted clear, porcelain skin. Like an English schoolgirl. It never happened. Not that I was ever going to tattoo my face, but the thought of intentionally marking up my skin after trying to clear it for so long seemed wrong to me.)

A lot of people get tattoos because of the music they like. My brother, for instance, got a music tattoo when he was eighteen.

It's from Pink Floyd, *Dark Side of the Moon*.

I can hear some of you reading this and muttering, "Who the heck is that?"

My response: "Exactly."

That's the thing with musical tattoos. Who's to say the band you love now will last for a lifetime?

Mostly I'm too much of a dilettante to get a music tattoo. I love the Jam and the Replacements and Miles Davis. But I'm not one of those walking music encyclopedias. I like their songs. A lot. But don't ask me to recount B sides or obscure facts. My interest in music has been wide but never deep, and if you're going to get that needle stuck in your arm with the ink pulsing through, I think it needs to be deep.

The closest I ever came to getting a tattoo was when my son Charlie died. He lived for three days. It was the most wrenching, difficult thing I had ever been through, and even thinking about it now, the grief kicks me still.

During the hazy, tear-soaked months following his short life, tattoos were on my mind. The pain of it seemed welcome—a physical way to make sense of the searing despair I woke up to every morning. The thing about losing a small baby is that you have to grieve someone you never really knew. You have to make sense of losing what could have been, an unseen future—like hope exploding. Many people turn to tattoos during this kind of loss, to mark the ephemeral grief.

But as the grief grew less intense, the pull of tattoos faded. Mostly I couldn't decide on an image, and finally it just overwhelmed me. I let the whole thing go.

Last week I remembered my tattoo quest, when I saw fog off the freeway. It was so low to the ground, just hovering. Thick and wild. The top of the fog was diffuse and feathery; so was the bottom. I tried to get a sense of how tall the fog was, and I realized there was no way to measure it. The edges were blurry. No stops and no starts.

Tattoos aren't like that. They have definite stops and starts. (Unless you get a really crappy one that bleeds all over the place.) And thinking about all this now, I'd say that's the real reason I never got a tattoo. When you have a son who lives for only three days, stops and starts get complicated. The hours he lived were small, yet the emotions were infinite. It made little sense. For my Charlie, time was a lousy measure.

Albert Einstein once said, "The most beautiful thing we can experience is the mysterious." I'm pretty sure he didn't have any tattoos.

To me, little Charlie will always be like the fog—mystical, ineffable, beautiful, unstill. Unquantifiable and impossible to mark. And yet indelible. Across my very soul.

Deb Kelt taught reading and writing to high school students for twenty years. When she's not thinking about teaching, Deb enjoys rocking out in the living room with her little boy Isaac, jamming to the Beatles or Rolling Stones. (Neither mother nor son has these as tattoos.)

You Didn't Know Me Then

Lester Laminack

You didn't know me then, but I knew you. I was there when you were hiding under the bed holding your baby tight with tears blurring your vision. I saw them giggle and wink at each other, and I heard them talking about boys and baby dolls. I heard them threaten to take your baby and give it to a girl. You were only four and you believed them.

I wanted to hug you and your baby and tell you none of it was true. You did not know me then, but I knew you.

I was with you when you stood on the porch watching your brother and uncles, your father and grandfather, each with a shotgun balanced in the crook of an arm, walk down the road and into the fields with three bird dogs. I felt your angst as the longing to belong battled with the comfort of staying at the house with your mother and grandmother, the aunts and a cousin who was still just a baby.

I was there when you leaned against the house your great-grandfather built. Four generations of boys who knew how to hunt and fish and mend fences had romped about there. I tasted the salt in those silent tears as you watched real men disappear and the yelping of dogs became an echo of memory.

I was there, but I could not tell you to go inside and be with those your seven-year-old mind understood best. I wanted to promise you it would be OK, but you did not know me yet.

I was with you at the table in fourth grade. You were staring at him, noticing the fullness and curl of his eyelashes, the Gulf-of-Mexico tourmaline color of his eyes, the golden streaks left in his brown hair by the summer sun. I inhaled with you when he turned those eyes directly on yours and spoke through clenched teeth, "Stop staring at me! Are you queer or something?" I heard those words rumble through your mind like far-off thunder.

I wanted to hold you and assure you that he was indeed beautiful and it was normal for you to notice. I wanted to assure you there would be others you'd admire who would also find you beautiful. But, I remained silent, for we had not met.

I was with you when you met him the summer before seventh grade. I felt your fascination with his movements and the cadence of his voice. I delighted in your awareness of the ways in which you two were similar. I was there when you realized there were other boys in this world like you. I was cheering for you as you felt those feelings for the first time. I delighted in the banter and the furtive touches, those first flirts. I wanted to whisper, "Relish these moments." I wanted you to recognize the humanity of a first crush and a hoped-for kiss. But I stayed silent. You could not have heard me.

I was with you when you walked into that bathroom, a cluster of smoking seniors passing a cigarette, the tip glowing red. When you turned to leave, I felt the hand grab your belt and pull you backward. I was there through it all. I heard their words and saw what they did. I was with you when you hid in the stall, squatting with your feet on the black seat of a toilet. I was there. I heard the racing drumbeat in your chest. I saw the movie in your mind play out "what if they find me later" scenes. I was there. I wanted to wash your face and brush your corn-silk hair and restore your twelve-year-old faith in the world. I wanted to clean your glasses and promise you this would not happen again. I wanted to assure you they would never come looking for you. But I could do nothing. I was mute to you.

I was there when you gave in and your lips met his. Your heart raced and you let yourself feel the joy of falling for him. I was there all afternoon with you floating on the bliss. And when night fell I was there as you lay in the darkness wrestling with the guilt your mind conjured from the tangled notions of normal and good. I was there as you struggled, knowing your brother would share school photos of his newest girlfriend and everyone would comment on how pretty she was. You held tight to a pillow trying to remember the feeling of holding and being held, knowing those were feelings you could never share. I wanted to sit on the side of your bed, push the hair out of your eyes, and dry your tears. I wanted to tell you the truth about the world's notions of normal and good. I wanted to tell you that you'd outlive those fears and that love would overcome guilt. I wanted to tell you that living in kindness and truth would leave you with nothing to feel guilty about.

But my words were not spoken because you did not know me.

I was with you across the years through joy and sorrow, excitement and worry, and pleasure and pain. I was always there, waiting. When you boarded that plane with notebooks and work and a container of pills, I heard the thoughts bouncing wildly in your mind. I was there when the man in the seat next to yours noticed what you were reading and began a conversation that revealed his life's journey. His story so closely matched your own. We listened as he told you about the moment he claimed himself as a worthy human being. He called late that night and asked for your story. His words echoed in your mind for two days. I was there the third night in the hotel after dinner. You put your things away and stepped into the bathroom to brush your teeth. I was there, waiting. You put away the toothbrush, rinsed your mouth, and looked into the mirror and finally saw me. We cried. Together we filled the sink with tears. Together we opened the container of pills and poured them into the toilet. Together we flushed the pills and claimed our life as worthy.

Lester Laminack is a writer and consultant who works with schools throughout the country. He is the author of over twenty books for children and teachers and divides his time between Asheville, North Carolina, and Beaufort, South Carolina. When he isn't working and writing, he sets off with his camera in search of breathtaking sunsets, fog kissing the ground, dolphins playing in the marsh, and friends laughing out loud.

Mentor Text Resources

Grades 4–6

Picture books that sound essayistic, beginning with the simplest text to the most complex:

Rotner, Shelley, and Sheila M. Kelly. 2010. *Shades of People*. New York: Holiday House.

Serres, Alain. 2012. *I Have the Right to Be a Child*. London: Phoenix Yard Books.

Ada, Alma Flor. 2005. *In the Barrio*. New York: Scholastic.

Aston, Dianna. 2013. *An Egg Is Quiet*. San Francisco: Chronicle Books.

Blume, Judy. (1974) 2014. *The Pain and the Great One*. New York: Atheneum Books for Young Readers.

Wood, Douglas. 2002. *A Quiet Place*. New York: Simon and Schuster Books for Young Readers.

Schuett, Stacey. 1995. *Somewhere in the World Right Now*. New York: Dragonfly Books/Knopf.

Shoshan, Beth. 2012. *That's When I'm Happy*. Bath, UK: Parragon Books.

Moss, Thylias. 1998. *I Want to Be*. New York: Puffin.

Baylor, Byrd. 1986. *The Way to Start a Day*. New York: Aladdin.

Rylant, Cynthia. 1998. *Appalachia: The Voices of Sleeping Birds*. Orlando: HMH Books for Young Readers.

Dahl, Roald. 2007. *Matilda*. New York: Puffin. [The beginning paragraphs]

Middle School and High School

Coplen, Michaela, ed. 2015. *The Best Teen Writing of 2015*. New York: Scholastic.

The annual Scholastic Art and Writing Awards publication of *The Best Teen Writing* contains phenomenal writing of all genres. The 2015 edition contains sections

labeled "Personal Essay" and "Critical Essay," and every essay in those two sections
would make a great mentor text for middle school and high school students.

Goldwasser, Amy, ed. 2007. *Red: Teenage Girls in America Write on What Fires Up Their Lives Today.* New York: Hudson Street.

Goldwasser's collection has some of the best writing by students (young women, ages thirteen to nineteen) I have read. Many pieces more strictly fit a definition of memoir and personal narrative, but quite a few work beautifully as essay. Topics of several of the submissions are for mature audiences.

Nye, Naomi Shihab. 1996. *Never in a Hurry: Essays on People and Places.* Columbia: University of South Carolina Press.

High School

Atwan, Robert, ed. The Best American Essay series. New York: Mariner Books.

Bresnick, Paul, ed. Da Capo Best Music Writing series. Cambridge, MA: Da Capo.

Epstein, Joseph. 2015. *Masters of the Games: Essays and Stories on Sport.* Lanham, MD: Rowan and Littlefield.

Gutkind, Lee. 2005. *In Fact: The Best of Creative Nonfiction.* New York: W. W. Norton.

Rosen, Michael J., ed. 2000. *Mirth of a Nation: The Best Contemporary Humor.* New York: HarperCollins.

Stout, Glenn. The Best American Sports Writing series. New York: Mariner Books.

Online: High School Students

Canvas: For teens, by teens (www.canvasliteraryjournal.com)

This is a gorgeous online literary journal full of equally beautiful writing by teenagers. Search in the archives for back issues, and click on the category called "Non-fiction." Or just go straight to this page (canvas literaryjournal.com/starstruck) to read one of the most elegant and intelligent essays by a young person I have read.

Teen Ink (www.teenink.com)

This website houses multiple genres of writing by teenagers. You will need to explore a bit in the "Nonfiction" category to find essay-like pieces. There is a subcategory called "College Essays" that has some powerful personal essays.

The Electric Typewriter (http://tetw.org)

The essays on this site, written on a wide variety of topics, including sports, the arts, popular culture, and technology, are for adults; however, many would make phenomenal, appropriate mentor texts for high school students.

Young Writers: Short Stories, Poems, and Essays by Teens (www.youngwriters magazine.com)

This website is still under construction as this book goes to press; however, the site exists, and it already has an available backlog of truly stunning essays by teens.

Youth Radio (https://youthradio.org)

This website contains extraordinary essays, feature articles, journalism, and personal narratives by young adults. Many are produced to include sounds, interviews, or music, which adds rich texture to the words. These would be lovely models for students making online, voiced, and produced essays. Click on "Listen Now" to go straight to a list of pieces by teenagers.

Works Cited

Allison, Dorothy. 2005. "Two or Three Things I Know for Sure." In *Short Takes: Brief Encounters with Contemporary Nonfiction*, edited by Judith Kitchen, 93–96. New York: W. W. Norton.

Ammons, A. R. 1965. *Tape for the Turn of the Year.* New York: W. W. Norton.

Andrews, Richard. 1995. *Teaching and Learning Argument.* London: Cassell.

Andrews, Richard, and Sally Mitchell, eds. 2000. *Learning to Argue in Higher Education.* Portsmouth, NH: Heinemann.

Atwan, Robert, ed. 2007. Foreword to *The Best American Essays, 2007*, viii–xi. New York: Mariner Books.

Atwan, Robert, ed. 1986–2015. The Best American Essays series. New York: Mariner Books.

Bakewell, Sarah. 2011. *How to Live; or, A Life of Montaigne in One Question and Twenty Attempts at an Answer.* New York: Other Press.

Ballenger, Bruce. 2013. "Let's End Thesis Tyranny." *The Conversation* (blog), July 17. *The Chronicle of Higher Education.* http://chronicle.com/blogs/conversation/2013/07/17/lets-end-thesis-tyranny/.

Barnhouse, Dorothy, and Vicki Vinton. 2012. *What Readers Really Do: Teaching the Process of Meaning Making.* Portsmouth, NH: Heinemann.

Baylor, Byrd. 1978. *The Way to Start a Day.* New York: Atheneum.

Bloom, Lynn Z. 2008. *The Seven Deadly Virtues and Other Lively Essays: Coming of Age as a Writer, Teacher, Risk Taker.* Columbia: University of South Carolina Press.

Bomer, Katherine. 2005. *Writing a Life: Teaching Memoir to Sharpen Insight, Shape Meaning, and Triumph over Tests.* Portsmouth, NH: Heinemann.

———. 2010. *Hidden Gems: Naming and Teaching from the Brilliance in Every Student's Writing.* Portsmouth, NH: Heinemann.

Bomer, Randy. 1995. *Time for Meaning: Crafting Literate Lives in Middle and High Schools*. Portsmouth, NH: Heinemann.

———. 2011. *Building Adolescent Literacy in Today's English Classroom*. Portsmouth, NH: Heinemann.

Bomer, Randy, and Katherine Bomer. 2001. *For a Better World: Reading and Writing for Social Action*. Portsmouth, NH: Heinemann.

Bowden, Charles. 2001. "In the Bone Garden of Desire." In *The Best American Essays 2001*, edited by Kathleen Norris and Robert Atwan, 30–45. New York: Mariner Books.

Brande, Dorothea. 1934. *Becoming a Writer*. Los Angeles: J. P. Tarcher.

Cambourne, Brian. 1988. *The Whole Story: Natural Learning and the Acquisition of Literacy in the Classroom*. Auckland, NZ: Ashton Scholastic.

Coates, Ta-Nehisi. 2015. *Between the World and Me*. New York: Spiegel and Grau.

Cox, Dani. 2007. "Ms. President." In *Red: Teenage Girls in America Write on What Fires Up Their Lives Today*, edited by Amy Goldwasser, 229–35. New York: Penguin Random House.

Dahl, Roald. 1988. *Matilda*. New York: Viking Kestrel.

D'Ambrosio, Charles. 2014a. "By Way of a Preface." In *Loitering: New and Collected Essays*, 11–21. Berkeley, CA: Tin House Books.

———. 2014b. "Salinger and Sobs." In *Loitering: New and Collected Essays*, 225–59. Berkeley, CA: Tin House Books.

———. 2014c. "Winning." In *Loitering: New and Collected Essays*, 145–59. Berkeley, CA: Tin House Books.

Dansdill, Timothy. 2005. "Writing to Learn Across the Personal Essay: The Art of Digital Pastiche." In *Direct from the Disciplines: Writing Across the Curriculum*, edited by Mary T. Segall and Robert A. Smart, 103–14. Portsmouth, NH: Boynton/Cook.

Day-Lewis, Cecil. 2013. *The Poetic Image*. Kowloon, HK: Hesperides.

DeGeneres, Ellen. 2004a. "Making Your Life Count (and Other Fun Things to Do with Your Time!)." In *The Funny Thing Is . . .*, 51–57. New York: Simon and Schuster.

———. 2004b. "That's Why Prison Wouldn't Be So Bad." In *The Funny Thing Is . . .*, 15–19. New York: Simon and Schuster.

Didion, Joan. 1980. "Why I Write." In *The Writer on Her Work*, vol. 1, edited by Janet Sternberg, 17–25. New York: W. W. Norton.

———. 1981. "Marrying Absurd." In *Slouching Towards Bethlehem*, 89–93. New York: Washington Square.

Dillard, Annie. 1988. Introduction to *The Best American Essays 1988*, edited by Annie Dillard and Robert Atwan, xiii–xxii. New York: Mariner Books.

Dombek, Kristin. 2014. "Letter from Williamsburg." In *The Best American Essays 2014*, edited by John Jeremiah Sullivan and Robert Atwan, 22–33. New York: Mariner Books.

Dombek, Kristin, and Scott Herndon. 2004. *Critical Passages: Teaching the Transition to College Composition*. New York: Teachers College Press.

Doyle, Brian. 2005a. "Being Brians." In *In Fact: The Best of Creative Nonfiction*, edited by Lee Gutkind, 163–73. New York: W. W. Norton.

———. 2005b. "Joyas Voladoras." In *The Best American Essays 2005*, edited by Susan Orlean and Robert Atwan, 28–30. New York: Mariner Books.

Draaisma, Douwe. 2004. *Why Life Speeds Up as You Get Older: How Memory Shapes Our Past*. New York: Cambridge University Press.

Edelsky, Carole, and Karen Smith. 1984. "Is That Writing—or Are Those Marks Just a Figment of Your Curriculum?" *Language Arts* 61: 24–32.

Elbow, Peter. 1981. *Writing with Power*. New York: Oxford University Press.

———. 2012. *Vernacular Eloquence: What Speech Can Bring to Writing*. New York: Oxford University Press.

Epstein, Joseph. 2012. "Duh, Bor-ing." In *The Best American Essays 2012*, edited by David Brooks and Robert Atwan, 102–10. New York: Mariner Books.

Fink, Sheri. 2014. "Two-Minute Case Against Limits." Cultivating Thought Author Series, edited by Jonathan Safran Foer. http://cultivatingthought.com/author/sheri-fink/.

Gass, William. 1985. "Emerson and the Essay." In *Habitations of the Word*, 9–49. New York: Simon and Schuster.

Gay, Roxane. 2014a. "Bad Feminist: Take Two." In *Bad Feminist: Essays*, 314–18. New York: HarperCollins.

―――. 2014b. "The Solace of Preparing Fried Foods and Other Quaint Remembrances from 1960s Mississippi: Thoughts on *The Help*." In *Bad Feminist: Essays*, 207–17. New York: HarperCollins.

―――. 2014c. "What We Hunger For." In *Bad Feminist: Essays*, 137–46. New York: HarperCollins.

―――. 2014d. "When Less Is More." In *Bad Feminist: Essays*, 250–53. New York: HarperCollins.

Gilb, Dabogerto. 2003a. "Living al Chuco." In *Gritos*, 70–72. New York: Grove.

―――. 2003b. "Pride." In *Gritos*, 243–46. New York: Grove.

Giltrow, Janet. 2000. "'Argument' as a Term in Talk About Student Writing." In *Learning to Argue in Higher Education*, 129–45. Portsmouth, NH: Heinemann.

Graves, Donald, and Virginia Stuart. 1985. *Write from the Start: Tapping Your Child's Natural Ability*. New York: New American Library.

Gutkind, Lee, ed. 2005. *In Fact: The Best of Creative Nonfiction*. New York: W. W. Norton.

Heilker, Paul. 1996. *The Essay: Theory and Pedagogy for an Active Form*. Urbana, IL: National Council of Teachers of English.

―――. 2006. "Twenty Years In: An Essay in Two Parts." *College Composition and Communication* 58 (2): 182–212.

Heller, Zoe. 2004. "Can Writing Be Taught?" *The New York Times Sunday Book Review: Bookends*, August 19: 35.

Hesse, Doug. 2014. "2015 Call for Program Proposals." National Council of Teachers of English. www.ncte.org/annual/call-2015.

Hickey, Dave. 1997. "The Delicacy of Rock-and-Roll." In *Air Guitar: Essays on Art and Democracy*, 96–101. Los Angeles: Art Issues.

Hoagland, Edward. 1988. *Heart's Desire: The Best of Edward Hoagland*. New York: Touchstone/Simon and Schuster.

Holshouser, Will. 2014. "Accordionist Interprets French Waltz Tradition in 'Musette Explosion': An Interview with Terry Gross." *Fresh Air*. National Public Radio. November 10.

Hopper, Briallen. 2014. "Young Adult Cancer." *Los Angeles Review of Books* (July 16).

James, LeBron, and Lee Jenkins. 2014. "I'm Coming Home." As told to Lee
    Jenkins. *Sports Illustrated* (July 11). www.si.com/nba/2014/07/11/lebron-james
    -cleveland-cavaliers.

Johnston, Peter. 2012. *Opening Minds: Using Language to Change Lives*. Portland, ME:
    Stenhouse.

Jordan, June. 2003. "Nobody Mean More to Me than You and the Future Life of
    Willie Jordan." In *Some of Us Did Not Die: New and Selected Essays*, 157–73. New
    York: Basic Civitas Books.

Kerstetter, Jon. 2013. "Triage." In *The Best American Essays 2013*, edited by Cheryl
    Strayed and Robert Atwan, 123–31. New York: Mariner Books.

King, Stephen. 2001. "On Impact." In *The Best American Essays 2001*, edited by
    Kathleen Norris and Robert Atwan, 120–31. New York: Mariner Books.

Kingsolver, Barbara. 2002a. "Letter to a Daughter at Thirteen." *Small Wonder*,
    144–59. New York: HarperCollins.

———. 2002b. "Letter to My Mother." *Small Wonder*, 160–75. New York:
    HarperCollins.

Kitchen, Judith, ed. 2005. *Short Takes: Brief Encounters with Contemporary Nonfiction*.
    New York: W. W. Norton.

Kleon, Austin. 2012. *Steal Like an Artist: 10 Things Nobody Told You About Being Cre-
    ative*. New York: Workman.

Klonsky, E. David, and Alexis Black, eds. 2011. *The Psychology of Twilight*. Dallas:
    Benbella Books.

Kohn, Alfie. 2015. *Schooling Beyond Measure: And Other Unorthodox Essays About
    Education*. Portsmouth, NH: Heinemann.

Komunyakaa, Yusef. 2001. "Blue Machinery of Summer." In *The Best American
    Essays 2001*, edited by Kathleen Norris and Robert Atwan, 132–40. New York:
    Mariner Books.

Levy, Ariel, and Robert Atwan, eds. 2015. *The Best American Essays 2015*. New
    York: Mariner Books.

Loh, Sandra Tsing. 2012. "The Bitch Is Back." In *The Best American Essays 2012*,
    edited by David Brooks and Robert Atwan, 218–30. New York: Mariner Books.

Lopate, Philip, ed. 1994. *The Art of the Personal Essay: An Anthology from the Classical
    Era to the Present*. New York: Anchor Books.

Macrorie, Ken. 1984. *Searching Writing.* Upper Montclair, NJ: Boynton/Cook.

Mathis, Ayana. 2014. "What Will Happen to All That Beauty?" *Guernica: A Magazine of Art and Politics* (December 15). www.guernicamag.com/features/what
-will-happen-to-all-of-that-beauty/.

McConnell, Patricia B. 2009. *Tales of Two Species: Essays About Loving and Living with Dogs.* Wenatchee, WA: Dogwise.

Merkin, Daphne. 2001. "Trouble in the Tribe." In *The Best American Essays 2001,* edited by Kathleen Norris and Robert Atwan, 181–92. New York: Mariner Books.

Miller, Brenda. 2001. "A Braided Heart: Shaping the Lyric Essay." In *Writing Creative Nonfiction,* edited by Carolyn Forché and Philip Gerard, 14–24. Cincinnati, OH: Story Press.

Montaigne, Michel de. 2003. *The Complete Works: Essays, Travel Journal, Letters.* Translated by Donald M. Frame. New York: Everyman's Library.

Murray, Donald M. 1982. *Learning by Teaching: Selected Articles on Writing and Teaching.* Portsmouth, NH: Boynton/Cook.

———. 1989. *Expecting the Unexpected: Teaching Myself and Others to Read and Write.* Portsmouth, NH: Heinemann.

———. 1996. *Crafting a Life in Essay, Story, Poem.* Portsmouth, NH: Boynton/Cook.

———. 2009a. "Internal Revision: A Process of Discovery." In *The Essential Don Murray,* edited by Tom Newkirk and Lisa Miller, 123–45. Portsmouth, NH: Heinemann.

———. 2009b. "Listening to Writing." In *The Essential Don Murray,* edited by Tom Newkirk and Lisa Miller, 55–71. Portsmouth, NH: Heinemann.

Nehring, Cristina. 2003. "Our Essays, Ourselves: In Defense of the Big Idea." *Harper's Magazine* (May): 79–84.

———. 2007. "Christina Nehring on What's Wrong with the American Essay." *Truthdig,* November 29. www.truthdig.com/arts_culture/item/20071129
_cristina_nehring_on_whats_wrong_with_the_american_essay.

Newkirk, Thomas. 1986a. "Looking for Trouble: A Way to Unmask Our Readings." In *To Compose: Teaching Writing in the High School,* 147–59. Portsmouth, NH: Heinemann.

———. 1986b. *To Compose: Teaching Writing in the High School.* Portsmouth, NH: Heinemann.

———. 2005. *The School Essay Manifesto: Reclaiming the Essay for Students and Teachers.* Shoreham, VT: Discover Writing.

———. 2009. *Holding On to Good Ideas in a Time of Bad Ones: Six Principles Worth Fighting For.* Portsmouth, NH: Heinemann.

Newkirk, Thomas, and Lisa C. Miller, eds. 2009. *The Essential Don Murray: Lessons from America's Greatest Writing Teacher.* Portsmouth, NH: Heinemann.

Nichols, John. 2000. *Dancing on the Stones.* Albuquerque: University of New Mexico Press.

Oliver, Mary. 2001. "Dust." In *The Best American Essays 2001*, edited by Kathleen Norris and Robert Atwan, 218–20. New York: Mariner Books.

Orlean, Susan. 2005. Introduction to *The Best American Essays 2005*, edited by Susan Orlean and Robert Atwan, xv–xviii. New York: Mariner Books.

Orozco, Daniel. 2007. "Shakers." In *The Best American Essays 2007*, edited by David Foster Wallace and Robert Atwan, 158–69. New York: Mariner Books.

Pollan, Michael. 1990. "Why Mow? The Case Against Lawns." In *The Best American Essays 1990*, edited by Justin Kaplan and Robert Atwan, 220–30. New York: Mariner Books.

Ray, Katie Wood. 2006. *Study Driven: A Framework for Planning Units of Study in the Writing Workshop.* Portsmouth, NH: Heinemann.

Riordan, Rick, ed. 2013. *Demigods and Monsters: Your Favorite Authors on Rick Riordan's Percy Jackson and the Olympians Series.* Dallas: Benbella Books.

Robinson, Marilynne. 2007. "Onward, Christian Liberals." In *The Best American Essays 2007*, edited by David Foster Wallace and Robert Atwan, 210–220. New York: Mariner Books.

Robyn, Kathryn L., and Dawn Ritchie. 2005. *The Emotional House: How Redesigning Your Home Can Change Your Life.* Oakland, CA: New Harbinger.

Rodriguez, Richard. 2005. "The Brown Study." In *In Fact: The Best of Creative Nonfiction*, edited by Lee Gutkind, 119–32. New York: W. W. Norton.

Romano, Tom. 1987. *Clearing the Way: Working with Teenage Writers.* Portsmouth, NH: Heinemann.

Rosenblatt, Louise. 1938. *Literature as Exploration.* New York: Modern Language Association.

Rushdy, Ashraf. 2001. "Exquisite Corpse." In *The Best American Essays 2001*, edited by Kathleen Norris and Robert Atwan, 261–69. New York: Mariner Books.

Rylant, Cynthia. 1991. *Appalachia: Voices of Sleeping Birds*. New York: Voyager Books.

Sanders, Scott Russell. 1993. "House and Home." In *Staying Put: Making a Home in a Restless World*, 17–36. Boston: Beacon.

Schelde, Sarah. 2007. "What Truthiness Taught Me About Being (Un)Cool." In *Red: Teenage Girls in America Write on What Fires Up Their Lives Today*, edited by Amy Goldwasser, 211–13. New York: Penguin Random House.

Schine, Cathleen. 2005. "Dog Trouble." In *The Best American Essays 2005*, edited by Susan Orlean and Robert Atwan, 181–94. New York: Mariner Books.

Schleiff, Meike. 2007. "The Beautiful Cause of Death That Had Me Dying for a While." In *Red: Teenage Girls in America Write on What Fires Up Their Lives Today*, edited by Amy Goldwasser, 31–36. New York: Penguin Random House.

Segall, Mary T., and Robert A. Smart, eds. 2005. *Direct from the Disciplines: Writing Across the Curriculum*. Portsmouth, NH: Boynton/Cook.

Seltzer, Richard. 1988. "A Mask in the Face of Death." In *The Best American Essays 1988*, edited by Annie Dillard and Robert Atwan, 207–19. New York: Mariner Books.

Serres, Alain. 2012. *I Have a Right to Be a Child*. Toronto: Groundwood Books.

Shubitz, Stacey. 2013. "Instagram Can Help Treat Writer's Block," August 22. *Two Writing Teachers* (blog). https://twowritingteachers.wordpress.com/2013/08/22/wriblk/.

Singer, Peter. 2007. "What Should a Billionaire Give—and What Should You?" In *The Best American Essays 2007*, edited by David Foster Wallace and Robert Atwan, 266–80. New York: Mariner Books.

Stafford, Kim. 2003. *The Muses Among Us: Eloquent Listening and Other Pleasures of the Writer's Craft*. Athens: University of Georgia Press.

Stafford, William. 1986. "A Way of Writing." In *To Compose: Teaching Writing in the High School*, edited by Thomas Newkirk, 25–27. Portsmouth, NH: Heinemann.

Strayed, Cheryl. 2013. Introduction to *The Best American Essays 2013*, edited by Cheryl Strayed and Robert Atwan, xv–xvii. New York: Mariner Books.

Tallent, Elizabeth. 2014. "Little X." In *The Best American Essays 2014*, edited by John Jeremiah Sullivan and Robert Atwan, 152–64. New York: Mariner Books.

Tammet, Daniel. 2012. *Thinking in Numbers: How Maths Illuminates Our Lives*. London: Hodder and Stoughton.

Updike, John. 1992. "The Mystery of Mickey Mouse." In *The Best American Essays 1992*, edited by Susan Sontag and Robert Atwan, 306–13. New York: Mariner Books.

Vergara, Camilo Jose. 2011. "The Looming Towers." *Columbia Magazine* (Fall). http://magazine.columbia.edu/features/fall-2011/looming-towers.

Wallace, David Foster. 2005. "Consider the Lobster." In *The Best American Essays 2005*, edited by Susan Orlean and Robert Atwan, 252–70. New York: Mariner Books.

———. 2007. Introduction to *The Best American Essays 2007*, edited by David Foster Wallace and Robert Atwan, xii–xxiv. New York: Mariner Books.

Wampole, Christy. 2013. "The Essayification of Everything." *Opinionator* (blog), May 26. *New York Times*. http://opinionator.blogs.nytimes.com/2013/05/26/the-essayification-of-everything/?_r=0.

White, E. B. 2006. *Essays of E. B. White*. New York: Harper Perennial Modern Classics.

Wilson, Leah, ed. 2011. *The Girl Who Was on Fire: Your Favorite Authors on Suzanne Collins' Hunger Games Trilogy*. Dallas: Benbella Books.

———. 2014. *Divergent Thinking: YA Authors on Veronica Roth's Divergent Trilogy*. Dallas: Benbella Books.

Wood, Douglas. 2002. *A Quiet Place*. New York: Simon and Schuster.

Wood, James. 2014. "Becoming Them." In *The Best American Essays 2014*, edited by John Jeremiah Sullivan and Robert Atwan, 195–201. New York: Mariner Books.

Woolf, Virginia. 1984a. "The Modern Essay." In *The Common Reader: First Series*, 211–22. New York: Harcourt.

———. 1984b. "Montaigne." In *The Common Reader: First Series*, 58–68. New York: Harcourt.

Yang, Wesley. 2012. "Paper Tigers." In *The Best American Essays 2012*, edited by David Brooks and Robert Atwan, 274–95. New York: Mariner Books.

Young, James Webb. 1940. *A Technique for Producing Ideas*. West Valley City, UT: Walking Lion.